THE WILTSHIRE WOOLLEN INDUSTRY
IN THE
SIXTEENTH AND SEVENTEENTH CENTURIES

THE WILTSHIRE WOOLLEN INDUSTRY

The industrial area c. 1600 is shaded. Roman numerals refer to the hundreds as follows:

I. Bradford
II. Branch and Dole
III. Calne
IV. Chippenham
V. Damerham
VI. Heytesbury
VII. Malmesbury
VIII. Melksham
IX. Potterne and Cannings
X. Swanborough
XI. Underditch
XII. Warminster
XIII. Westbury
XIV. Whorwelsdown

THE WILTSHIRE
WOOLLEN INDUSTRY

IN THE SIXTEENTH AND
SEVENTEENTH CENTURIES

BY

G. D. RAMSAY, M.A.
Fellow and Tutor of St. Edmund Hall

SECOND EDITION

FRANK CASS & CO. LTD.
1965

First published by Oxford University Press
and now reprinted by arrangement with them.

This edition published by Frank Cass & Co. Ltd.,
2 Park Square, Milton Park, Abingdon, Oxon, OX14 4RN

First edition   1943
Second edition 1965

Transferred to Digital Printing 2005

ISBN 0-7146-1355-X (hbk)

PREFACE TO THE FIRST EDITION

THE research work preparatory to the writing of the following study was done mainly in the years 1934 to 1937, and the text as it now stands was all but complete in September 1939 at the outbreak of war, which has deferred its publication.

It is impossible for me to acknowledge by name all who have so kindly helped me. The never failing encouragement of Professor F. M. Powicke was more prized by me than its author perhaps realized. I have received much patient aid from the Principal of St. Hilda's College throughout, and my text has also benefited from criticism by the late Dr. Eileen Power and Mr. R. V. Lennard. Miss E. M. Carus Wilson has shared her knowledge with me on a number of points, as have Mr. J. E. Pilgrim and Dr. W. B. Willcox. A year's attendance at the seminar of Professor R. H. Tawney and Mr. A. V. Judges in the Institute of Historical Research provided a valuable stimulus to my researches. At the Public Record Office Mr. R. B. Pugh and the late Mr. J. R. Crompton—both Wiltshiremen—helped me without stint. In Wiltshire Mr. W. L. Bown, lately Clerk of the Peace, was at pains to facilitate my access to the county records. In the final stages, I owe thanks to Professor G. N. Clark in his editorial capacity. I am grateful to the firm of Messrs. Edward Early & Son, Witney, who permitted me to observe at my leisure the processes of cloth manufacture. The work as a whole would have been impossible but for the material aid vouchsafed by the Board of Management of the Bryce Research Studentship and also by the Committee for Economics and Political Science as donors of a George Webb Medley Senior Scholarship.

G. D. R.

as from
ST. EDMUND HALL,
OXFORD.
August 1942

CONTENTS

INTRODUCTION TO THE SECOND EDITION

FEW practising historians surveying in later life a work of their youth are likely to feel that, given the time and the materials once again, they would not write it differently. This volume is not one of the exceptions. However, the arguments set forth in its pages have so far not to my knowledge been challenged, and in any case the conditions of this re-issue preclude extensive alterations. For the most part I have therefore limited myself to the correction of the few misprints and errors that have come to light in the text, and to the addition of an index which the wartime conditions of the original edition had made impracticable. Finally, I have taken the opportunity to put into an extra appendix the report of the Clothing Committee of the Privy Council dated 22 June 1622, to which reference is made *infra*, page 78. Although discussed by various historians within recent years, this document has hitherto not been available in print. My version is based on the Public Record Office copy at SP 14/131/55, with some help from the inferior British Museum copy, Stowe 554, ff. 45 *et seq.*—neither is original.

The historiographical background against which this book must now be read is very different from that against which it was written. The conditions under which the historian nowadays pursues his researches have greatly improved, both at the Public Record Office and in Wiltshire, where the county records are now well housed and available for consultation without any need for special and laborious arrangements. Even the Somerset House anomaly seems to be nearing its end. There are many more workers in the field, and we now know much more about the economic development of Tudor and Stuart England than was the case a quarter of a century ago. It may help the reader if I mention here a few of the writings that since 1943 have added most directly to our knowledge of the Wiltshire woollen industry in the sixteenth and seventeenth centuries. It must be borne in mind that anything like a complete bibliography would be much longer: those who seek more detailed guidance should consult the lists of publications bearing upon the economic history of Great Britain and

Ireland published yearly in the Economic History Review.

Pride of place must go to the *Victoria County History of Wiltshire*, in process of publication since 1953. Vol. IV covers the economic history of the county and contains authoritative surveys of the Wiltshire textile industries by E. M. Carus-Wilson and J. de L. Mann; there is also much to be learnt from the topographical volumes, especially vol. VII dealing with the industrial hundreds of Bradford, Melksham, and Potterne and Cannings. The series published by the Records Branch of the Wiltshire Archaeological and Natural History Society has also made available a great deal of relevant fresh information; vol. XIX (1963) contains an edition of *Documents Illustrative of the Wiltshire Textile Trades in the Eighteenth Century* by J. de L. Mann, whose study of 'Clothiers and Weavers in Wiltshire during the Eighteenth Century' was printed in *Studies in the Industrial Revolution* ed. L. S. Pressnell (London, 1960), 66–96. Other writings of E. M. Carus-Wilson bearing on Wiltshire clothmaking are collected in *Medieval Merchant Venturers* (London, 1954), to which should be added the same author's discussion of the Castle Combe woollen industry in 'Evidences of Industrial Growth on some Fifteenth-Century Manors', *Economic History Review* second series (henceforth *EcHR*), XII (1959–60), 190–205. Our knowledge of the clothing and landed families of Wiltshire has been deepened by G. D. Squibb's edition of *Wiltshire Visitation Pedigrees 1623* (Harleian Society, CV and CVI, 1953 and 1954). K. G. Ponting, *A History of the West of England Cloth Industry* (London, 1957), benefits from the author's practical experience in cloth manufacture. For comparative purposes must be mentioned R. Perry, 'The Gloucestershire Woollen Industry, 1100–1690', *Transactions of the Bristol and Gloucestershire Archaeological Society*, LXVI (1947 for 1945), 49–137; J. E. Pilgrim, 'The Rise of the 'New Draperies' in Essex', *University of Birmingham Historical Journal*, VII (1959–60), 36–59; and T. C. Mendenhall, *The Shrewsbury Drapers and the Welsh Wool Trade in the XVI and XVII Centuries* (London, 1953). From a general point of view, there is a suggestive essay by J. Thirsk, 'Industries in the Countryside', in *Essays in the Economic and Social History*

INTRODUCTION TO THE SECOND EDITION

of Tudor and Stuart England, ed. F. J. Fisher (Cambridge, 1961), 70–88 ; and a broad survey by H. Kellenbenz, 'Les industries rurales en Occident de la fin du Moyen Age au XVIIIe siècle', *Annales,* XVIII (1963), 833–882.

With regard to the social background in the sixteenth and early seventeenth centuries, there are two articles by E. Kerridge, 'The Revolts in Wiltshire against Charles I', *Wiltshire Archaeological and Natural History Magazine,* LVII (1960), 64–75 ; and 'The Movement of Rent, 1540–1640', *EcHR,* VI (1953–4), 16–34, repr. in *Essays in Economic History,* ed. E. M. Carus-Wilson, II (London, 1962), 208–226. The latter has a particular relevance to Wiltshire. The supply of the raw material of the woollen industry has been investigated by P. J. Bowden, *The Wool Trade in Tudor and Stuart England* (London, 1962). There is much that bears on Wiltshire in M. G. Davies, *The Enforcement of English Apprenticeship. A study in Applied Mercantilism* (Cambridge, Mass., 1957). The use of the common informer to maintain standards of manufacture has also been discussed by G. R. Elton, 'Informing for Profit', *Cambridge Historical Journal,* XI (1954), 149–167 ; and by M. W. Beresford, 'The Common Informer, the Penal Statutes and Economic Regulation', *EcHR,* X (1957–8), 221–238. E. Moir has examined in detail the activities of a clothier—no less significant because he was rather more a Gloucestershire than a Wiltshireman—in 'Benedict Webb, Clothier', *EcHR,* X (1957–8), 256–264.

It is in the marketing of Wiltshire cloth that our knowledge has especially been widened. For the sixteenth century, there are the two detailed volumes of O. de Smedt, *De Engelse Natie te Antwerpen* (Antwerp, 1950 and 1954). A picture of the situation after the downfall of the Antwerp mart is given by F. J. Fisher, 'London's Export Trade in the Early Seventeenth Century', *EcHR,* III (1950–1), 151–161. J. D. Gould has argued forcefully that the trade crisis of 1586–7 was basically of political origin in 'The Crisis in the Export Trade, 1586–1587', *English Historical Review,* LXXI (1956), 212–222, and has also investigated the major disaster of the early seventeenth century in 'The Trade Depression of the Early 1620's', *EcHR,* VII (1954–

5), 81–90; and 'The Trade Crisis of the Early 1620's and English Economic Thought', *Journal of Economic History*, XV (1955), 121–133. There is a fruitful examination of early Stuart trade vicissitudes by B. E. Supple, *Commercial crisis and change in England* 1600–1642 (Cambridge, 1959). An impressive commentary on the loss of the Baltic market has been supplied by S. -E. Åstrom, *From Cloth to Iron. Anglo-Baltic Trade in the late Seventeenth Century*. Part I (Helsingfors, 1963).

In other directions, seventeenth-century developments are discussed in two notable articles by R. Davis, 'England and the Mediterranean, 1570–1670', *Essays in Economic and Social History*, ed. F. J. Fisher *ut supra*, 117–137; and 'English Foreign Trade, 1660–1700', *EcHR*, VII (1954–5), 150–166, repr. in *Essays in Economic History*, ed. E. M. Carus-Wilson, II (London, 1962), 257–272. New light has been shed on the shipping of western cloths, some of them undoubtedly of Wiltshire manufacture, from Exeter to Rotterdam in the later seventeenth century, by W. B. Stephens in *Seventeenth-Century Exeter* (Exeter, 1958). For the Portuguese market, there are two studies, one by A. D. Francis, 'John Methuen and the Anglo-Portuguese Treaties of 1703', *Historical Journal*, III (1960), 103–124; and H. E. S. Fisher, 'Anglo-Portuguese Trade, 1700–1770', *EcHR*, XVI (1963–4), 219–233. A general survey of European textile output is to be found in C. H. Wilson, 'Cloth production and international competition in the seventeenth century', *EcHR*, XIII (1959–60), 209–221. I have myself attempted to sketch some main lines of export activity in *English Overseas Trade during the Centuries of Emergence* (London, 1957).

For specific corrections to my text, I am indebted to E. Moir, *loc. cit.*, 256; and to W. B. Stephens, 'Merchant Companies and Commercial Policy in Exeter', *Report and Transactions of the Devonshire Association*, LXXXVI (1954), 159.

G. D. R.

ST. EDMUND HALL,
OXFORD
May 1964

NOTE

DATES are assumed to be according to the Julian calendar, but the year is taken as beginning on January 1st.

ABBREVIATIONS

Add. .	.	Additional
C.P.	.	Chancery Proceedings
C.R. .	.	Proceedings in the Court of Requests
C.S.P.D. ·	.	Calendar of State Papers, Domestic Series
Dep. by Comm. .		Depositions by Commission
East. .	.	Easter term
E.C.P.	.	Early Chancery Proceedings
Ex. .	.	Exchequer
H.M.C.	.	Historical Manuscripts Commission report
Hil. .	.	Hilary term
I.p.m.	.	Inquisition post mortem
K.R. .	.	King's Remembrancer
L.P.Hen. VIII	.	Letters and Papers of the reign of Henry VIII
L.T.R.	.	Lord Treasurer's Remembrancer
Mem.	.	Memoranda Roll
Mich.	.	Michaelmas term
P.C.C.	.	Prerogative Court of the archbishop of Canterbury
S.C. .	.	Proceedings in the Court of Star Chamber
S.P.D.	.	State Papers, Domestic Series
Subs. .	.	Subsidy roll
Trin. .	.	Trinity term
Wilts. Arch. Mag.		Wiltshire Archaeological and Natural History Society Magazine

I

INTRODUCTORY: THE LOCATION OF THE WILTSHIRE WOOLLEN INDUSTRY

THE following pages embody one of the many preliminary studies which must be made before it is possible
to write the history of the west of England woollen industry
from its origins in the remote middle ages through its
hey-day in the fifteenth and sixteenth centuries and its silver
age in the eighteenth down to its collapse in the nineteenth
and its sadly attenuated existence in the twentieth century.
The main area covered by the west country woollen industry stretched roughly from Witney and Painswick in
the north to Shepton Mallet and Warminster and even
Salisbury in the south, where it merged imperceptibly into
the small local textile districts of Dorset and Hampshire.
It thus centred round the river valleys which radiated from
the Cotswolds and Mendips, though it must be remembered
that there existed a lesser though important industrial
district in Devonshire and western Somerset. But the
boundaries of this great textile area were neither stable nor
clear-cut and altered from century to century in accordance
with the variations in the demand for cloth in the markets
both at home and still more abroad. Upon the immense
importance of the west country woollen industry in the
economic development of England during a period cover-
ing over half a millennium it is not necessary to dwell;
this study is simply concerned with its history in a single
district during two of the fleeting centuries in which Wiltshire was one of the chief industrial counties of England.

Its manufacturing area extended over large portions of
at least five if not six counties, from Devon in the west to
Oxfordshire in the east, and a considerable fragment of it
lay within the frontiers of Wiltshire. The justification for
a separate study of this latter district—which was separated
from the main textile area by no very striking geographical
or economic frontier—must rest to a large extent upon the
nature of the documentary sources available to the historian, which in almost every case are divisible only upon a

county basis. This classification of the evidence does, however, reflect a real character in the administration of the county sufficient to distinguish Wiltshire from its neighbours. And it may also be pointed out that the seat of the Wiltshire woollen industry possessed, broadly speaking, a geographical unity in so far as it more or less covered the inland basin of the Bristol Avon with an extension southeast down the Wylye valley to Wilton and Salisbury—just as the Gloucestershire woollen industry existed mainly in the valleys of the steep western slope of the Cotswolds and the Oxfordshire textile centres lay chiefly along the banks of the Windrush. The Wiltshire woollen industrial area is further distinguishable from that of these neighbours in that it extended far from the Cotswold and Mendip hill country and penetrated to the villages lying beneath the edge of the downland stretching southwards from the Thames valley to the Channel coast. Of the fringes of the Berkshire and Hampshire manufacturing area which extended to Marlborough and Ramsbury no account is taken in this study; the cloths made in this district differed markedly from the products of the west country and their output in Wiltshire was comparatively slight.[1]

The seat of the woollen industry in Wiltshire lay thus almost exclusively in the western half of the county; and save for the narrow strip of industrial territory along the Wylye reaching as far south as Salisbury it centred in the north-west, above all perhaps in the hundreds of Chippenham and Melksham, though other neighbouring hundreds were scarcely less important. Here were to be found the conditions requisite for the establishment of the textile manufacture. The fuller's earth, almost indispensable for the thickening of broadcloth, was available not only in the Cotswold country along the north-western frontier but also elsewhere, notably in deposits along and under the edge of the downs, from Westbury and Edington to the Lavingtons and farther north towards Rowde and Calne.[2] The Avon and its numerous small tributaries supplied the clear water necessary for scouring cloths when they had been fulled

---

[1] Cf. *infra*, 19, n. 5.
[2] Cf. Aubrey's remarks in his *Natural History of Wiltshire* (ed. Britton, 1847), 35.

and also provided the motive power for driving the fulling mills. Some wool was grown locally, but larger and finer supplies from the Cotswolds, the Welsh marches, and the grazing counties of the midlands were conveniently available. The countryside drained by the Avon was sufficiently fertile to yield most of the foodstuffs necessary for the maintenance of what was for the sixteenth and seventeenth centuries a fairly dense industrial population, and for the rest it was possible to draw upon the overflowing granaries of Somerset-shire[1]; periods of any exceptional shortage were, however, usually marked by riots in the industrial area. Thus geography and geology both helped to transform north-west Wiltshire into a centre of the woollen industry.[2]

The industrial population was in no way restricted to the towns, but was spread in varying degrees of thickness over the countryside,[3] though Salisbury, Devizes, Chippenham, Calne, Bradford, Trowbridge, Westbury, and certain other centres were always of particular importance as homes of the woollen industry. It is, however, perhaps possible to trace during the later sixteenth and seventeenth centuries a slight tendency towards the localization of the industry in more concentrated areas. Steeple Ashton, which in the early sixteenth century had been a thriving industrial village, subsequently lost all its trade.[4] Malmesbury, Kingswood, and Castle Combe also declined in the course of the seven-teenth century.[5] On the other hand, new districts where coloured cloth was made rose to prominence; Corsley be-

[1] The threatened interruption of this trade through the activities of informers in the early seventeenth century caused some trouble—cf. e.g. S.P.D. Jas. I, cx, 122; also the quarter sessions great rolls for the period, *passim*.

[2] Cf. Stamp and Beaver, *The British Isles, a Geographic and Economic Survey* (1933), 445–7, and Kinvig, *Historical Geography of the West Country Woollen Industry, Geographical Teacher*, viii (1916), *passim*.

[3] *Infra*, ch. II, *passim*; cf. the preamble to stat. 18 Eliz. c. xvi.

[4] Knubley, *The Rise and Fall of Steeple Ashton as a Market Town, Wilts. Arch. Mag.* xxxii (1901–2), *passim*. It is not, however, possible to believe that the decline of Steeple Ashton was due merely to a disastrous fire. It may be noted that two of the sons of Robert Long, the most famous clothier of Steeple Ashton, appear to have migrated to Trowbridge, where in 1545 they were taxed for a royal benevolence—E.C.P. 332/57 and 59 and Ex. K.R. Subs. 197/230.

[5] Aubrey, *Natural History of Wilts.*, 115; Scrope, *History of the Manor and Ancient Barony of Castle Combe* (1851), 315–16; Moffatt, *The History of the Town of Malmesbury and of its Ancient Abbey* (1805), 124–5 and 161; *H.M.C. Wilts.*, 154.

B

came a textile centre after the restoration, when apparently for the first time the valuable chemical qualities latent in the waters of the Biss were discovered.[1] These geographical changes are to be related both to new needs springing from technical developments in the manufacture of Wiltshire cloth as well as to the increasingly large-scale and capitalist organization of the industry.

The history of clothmaking in Wiltshire is doubtless to be measured in millennia rather than in centuries, and in the present inquiry no effort has been made to describe the origins of the Wiltshire woollen manufacture. Its importance as an exporting industry was already great in the fourteenth century, when Wiltshire was one of the chief textile counties of the kingdom; and the cloth manufacture of Wiltshire waxed yet further in the next hundred years.[2] It specialized almost exclusively in the making of white undyed broadcloth, chiefly for the central European market, where English fabrics enjoyed favour as the finest and most expensive of all woollen stuffs. In the later middle ages the manufacture of white broadcloth had established itself in a single main area lying within the four western broadcloth counties of Gloucester, Somerset, Oxford, and Wiltshire, though there were also less important isolated branches of the industry in Suffolk and Worcestershire. Its products had acquired certain standards of its own; the famous clothing statute of 1552[3] was doubtless echoing well-worn custom in prescribing that each broadcloth should be from twenty-six to twenty-eight yards long, not less than seven quarters in breadth and that it should weigh at least forty-four pounds—these measurements were subsequently revised slightly from time to time.[4] There also came to exist within them certain accepted distinctions between the various grades of broadcloth, which were differentiated by the type of list or selvedge into broad and narrow, plain and stop-listed cloths.

---

[1] Davies, *Life in an English Village: An Economic and Historical Survey of the Parish of Corsley, in Wiltshire* (1909), 24–7.

[2] Gray, *The Production and Exportation of English Woollens in the Fourteenth Century, Eng. Hist. Rev.* xxix (1924), 34; Heaton, *Yorkshire Woollen and Worsted Industries* (1920), 85.

[3] 5 & 6 Ed. VI, c. 6.   [4] *Infra*, p. 53.

By the opening in the sixteenth century of the period with which this study is concerned, the Wiltshire woollen industry was thus long established and highly developed both in technique and in organization. It continued to manufacture its traditional products even in the later sixteenth century when the East Anglian industrial area went over to the making of 'new draperies',[1] and only in the seventeenth century was it forced in its turn to seek new markets and to develop new varieties of cloth. The following pages are devoted to an examination of the broadcloth manufacture in the days when it was at its zenith, the manner and consequences of its fall, and its phoenix-like supersession by the making of other types of cloth in the course of the seventeenth century.

[1] Cf. Unwin, *Studies in Economic History* (1927), 291–3. It is difficult to suggest any reasons for the failure of the new draperies to take root in Wiltshire during the sixteenth century save the obvious geographical one; it is possibly of significance also in this connexion that the Suffolk woollen industry had been concerned mainly with the manufacture of coloured broadcloth—Unwin, *op. cit.* 270. Cf. *infra*, p. 102.

II

THE STRUCTURE OF THE WILTSHIRE WOOLLEN INDUSTRY DURING THE SIXTEENTH CENTURY: PROCESSES AND TRANSACTIONS FROM WOOL GROWER TO CONSUMER

THE Wiltshire woollen industry in the sixteenth century may be said to have been organized on what is generally known as the domestic or putting-out system. Such a simple description, while nevertheless not actually incorrect, is somewhat misleading, for the most diverse elements went to make up the industrial edifice. There were, on the one hand, clothiers petty and great, including at least one of the most remarkable industrial capitalists of Tudor England, and there was already an industrial proletariat; and there were, on the other hand, quasi-independent spinners and weavers. Large-scale enterprise and the small free craftsman competed side by side. The varied structure of the industry may conveniently be illustrated by following the course of the wool as it passed through the hands of spinner, weaver, and clothier on its way from the sheep-grower to its ultimate consumer.

The wool which was worked up into cloth in sixteenth-century Wiltshire came from many parts of the kingdom. Clothiers indeed bought wool from local growers; Thomas Horton, the famous clothier of Bradford mentioned by Leland, purchased not long before his death £30 worth of wool from a Wiltshire farmer,[1] and a little later another grazier of Stockton agreed to sell all his wool for three years to a local capitalist.[2] But the fleeces grown on the chalk downs of Wiltshire could not always suffice, and more often the wool came from afar, even from areas where an independent local clothmaking industry flourished. A Wilton clothier contracted for a regular delivery of wool from Devonshire,[3] while Edward Horton of Iford and

---

[1] E.C.P. 642/40; Leland, *Itinerary*, ed. Smith (1906), i, 135. The farmer, John Goddard, doubtless belonged to the family of that name which flourished in north-east Wiltshire, and his wool was probably the produce of sheep pastured on the Marlborough downs.

[2] E.C.P. 1118/53–6.   [3] E.C.P. 1117/33.

Trowbridge, another member of a famous clothing family, entered into an agreement to fetch wool from a grower at Aston Magna in Worcestershire.[1] In the main, however, the evidence does not suggest that even the wealthiest clothiers habitually sought out the wool producer in distant shires. There were two largely complementary means of overcoming these geographical difficulties. One was provided by the innumerable markets which were regularly and frequently kept in every small town; those of Cirencester, Tetbury, and Castle Combe, all within the Cotswold country, were particularly notable for their sales of wool, while another important wool market was also held at Devizes.[2] To Cirencester market there had already come in the late fifteenth century even the costly wool of Herefordshire, and Wiltshire clothiers continued to make their purchases at this great centre during the sixteenth century.[3]

But for the most part the wool markets were probably haunted far less by the graziers than by middlemen, the wool broggers, whose enterprise provided another means of transferring wool from grower to manufacturer.[4] These middlemen, whose apparently unproductive business offended the still predominant medieval standards of commercial ethics, and whose activities as engrossers of wool rendered them liable to indictments for offences against both common and statute law, carried on their traffic under a darkening cloud of obloquy. In the halcyon days of the fifteenth century the merchants of the staple had traded busily with the great Cotswold woolmen—the Midwinters, the Busshes, the Thames—who had thriven by collecting the fine wools of Gloucestershire and Oxfordshire and selling them for export.[5] But the increasing demand for wool at home for the needs of the expanding native woollen industry threatened this lucrative traffic. Before the end of the century the decline of the staplers had

---

[1] C.R. 206/29.
[2] Aubrey, *Natural History of Wiltshire*, 115; C.R. 3/276; Cunnington, *Annals of the Borough of Devizes* (1925), *passim*.
[3] E.C.P. 27/353, 1116/88–9; C.R. 16/21, 202/2.
[4] 'Broker' is the modern form of the sixteenth-century noun 'brogger'.
[5] Power and Postan, *Studies in English Trade in the Fifteenth Century* (1933), 48–58.

begun. Proportionately to the rise of the merchant adventurers their trade, both export and import, dwindled away.
They accordingly began to turn more attention to the distri-
bution of wool to the home manufacturer; and after the fall
of Calais and the outbreak of serious political disturbances in
the Netherlands had thrown their ancient organization out of
gear the internal trade became their main interest.   But
already a horde of other individuals without any particular
authorization had long been engaged in this line of business.
The common wool brogger was to be found everywhere,
often ingeniously operating under cover of the staplers'
privileges or, later, of the royal licences granted to private
individuals to buy and sell wool within the kingdom.[1]

The activities of the wool dealers were, however, per-
sistently denounced by the clothiers, who in the sixteenth
century were fully conscious of the importance with which
the expanding woollen industry invested them. They protested against the continued export of the wool which was
the indispensable raw material for their continental com-
petitors; but they attacked with an even greater vehemence
the wool broggers, whether staplers or not, who intruded
themselves between grazier and manufacturer. The unprecedented rise in the cost of wool, particularly during
the second half of the century, was ascribed entirely to
their manœuvres; it was alleged that not only did they
denude the home market of wool by their exporting
activities, whether licensed or surreptitious, but that they
manipulated prices by buying up and withholding the
available stocks of wool. They were also charged with
fraudulently mixing and adulterating the wools which
passed through their hands, possibly with some justice. An
act designed to frustrate their activities by forbidding for ten
years the sale of unshorn wool in a number of counties,
Wiltshire and all its neighbours included, reached the
statute-book as early as 1489; it was re-enacted in 1530
and in 1545.[2]

---

[1] A list of the licences issued during the twenty-six years 1558–84 is to be
found in S.P.D. Eliz. CLXXV, 19.

[2] 4 Hen. VII, c. 11, 22 Hen. VIII, c. 1, 37 Hen. VIII, c. 15. The internal trade
in wool was probably expanding, as industry sought for its raw material at even
increasing distances. Numerous petitions and accusations directed against the

Nevertheless, the wool broggers played no merely parasitic part in the manufacture of Wiltshire cloth. The rise in the price of wool was probably due to their manœuvres in a very small degree; it was no doubt helped by the debasement of the coinage under Henry VIII and Edward VI and by the persistent heightening of the internal demand for wool, especially after the introduction of the new draperies, but for the most it was simply part of the great upward trend of prices general throughout Europe during the sixteenth century. The notorious ubiquity of the wool broggers despite the hostility of the government goes far alone to demonstrate how necessary their services were. They were active in Dorsetshire throughout the century, dealing, for instance, in tithe wool.[1] During the reign of Edward VI the operations of one John Stephens of Burton-on-the-Hill in Gloucestershire and his partners were said to have doubled the price of Cotswold wool. Stephens acted under a licence which he had bribed Northumberland to grant, but upon a vigorous protest by the Gloucestershire clothiers the licence was revoked[2]; and in 1552 a stringent statute was passed, which forbade the sale of wool save to authentic staplers or cloth manufacturers.[3] Shortly afterwards, in the new reign, Stephens and two other Cotswold woolmen were prosecuted in the star chamber; the attorney-general alleged that they had engrossed some thousands of sarplars of wool in a group of nine adjacent counties, from Wiltshire and Berkshire to Warwick and Leicestershire.[4] Throughout the rest of the century woolmen of the pastoral country in and around Wiltshire, in particular of the Cotswolds and midlands, were from time to time prosecuted in the courts at Westminster for

wool broggers are to be found scattered among the State Papers Domestic and in the various collections of the British Museum. Particularly informative for the historian of the Wiltshire woollen industry are—B.M. Lansdowne MS. 114, ff. 95-8, S.P. Hen. VIII, 239, f. 128, S.P.D. Eliz. cxiv, 27, S.P.D. Add. Eliz. ix, 56 and xxiv, 100. Cf. also S.P.D. Eliz. cxiv, 32, pr. in Tawney and Power, *Tudor Econ. Docs.* (1924), i, 191-2, S.P.D. Jas. I, lxxxiv, 36, and Rich, *The Ordinance Book of the Merchants of the Staple* (1937), *passim.*

[1] *Cal. Pat. Rolls Ed. VI*, ii, 148; C.R. 206/3.
[2] B.M. Lansdowne MS. 114, f. 95.
[3] 5 & 6 Ed. VI, c. 7.
[4] S.C., P. and M., 3/63.

hoarding or engrossing wool,[1] and the privy council kept
an eye on the wool traffic. But the efforts of the government met with little success; in 1576 it was reported to
the queen's secretary that the statute of 1552 had fallen
into disuse,[2] and during the rest of the century the
abounding number of wool broggers received frequent
mention.[3] John Briant of Northampton, a woolman whose
illicit activities the privy council in 1577 resolved to check,
was apparently not permanently restrained, for before the
end of the century he had become the creditor of Thomas
Yerbury, a Trowbridge clothier, for some hundreds of
pounds' worth of wool which he had sold to him at
Cirencester market.[4] If the government could not—and
perhaps would not—effectually curb even the great wool
dealer whose name was well known and whose actions took
place under its nose, still less could it hope to prevent the
ubiquitous and confidential transactions of the multitude
of small broggers of wool throughout the kingdom.

The case of the woolmen did not go undefended. During
the last two decades of the century, it was alleged, the
character of the continental cloth market had changed, and
the German and Dutch merchants no longer bought up the
coarsest broadcloths. This was particularly significant for
the Wiltshire manufacturer, since the finer fleeces, now
more necessary than ever, had to be sought outside his own
county. It was therefore claimed that the services of the
wool brogger were indispensable for the selection and dis-
tribution of these fine wools.[5] This provided an argument
additional to the main justification of the woolman—that by
supplying the local markets he saved the poorer clothier
the time and money that would otherwise have to be
expended in seeking out the distant farmer or grazier, and
that he was ready to sell wool in smaller quantities than
the growers were willing to do.[6] It is of some significance

[1] Ex. K.R. Mem. East. 6 Eliz. 77 ff.; Mich. 7 Eliz. 347, &c.
[2] S.P.D. Eliz. CIX, 37. Cf. Steele, *Catalogue of Tudor and Stuart Proclamations*,
i (1910), no. 712.
[3] *Acts of the Privy Council*, 1592, 349–50; B.M. Lansdowne MS. 48, f. 159, &c.
[4] C.R. 202/2; *Acts of the Privy Council*, 1577–8, 24.
[5] B.M. Lansdowne MS. 48, f. 157.
[6] S.P.D. Eliz. CCLXI, 63.

that almost all the twelve Wiltshire clothiers who in 1577
signed a memorandum denouncing the abuses of dealers
in wool can be shown to have been large-scale manufacturers[1]; and the same may be said of the Wiltshire
clothiers whose names eight years later were appended to
a protest against the renewal of a royal licence to buy and
sell wool.[2] A parsimonious queen would, however, be reluc-
tant to abandon the sale of these licences; and near the end
of the century an anonymous representative of the interests
of the wool middleman supported the policy of the government by pointing out that while the small broggers might
indeed enhance prices and corrupt the wools which they
bought, the responsible licensed man operating on a large
scale did not lie open to such a charge.[3] This may possibly
have indicated that the greater clothiers had tardily come
to recognize the fact that the services of intermediaries in
the wool trade were indispensable. Nevertheless, the controversy as to the rights and wrongs of the home trade in
wool which raged with a particular vehemence during the
last quarter of the century was in fact to no small degree
part of the struggle for control of the cloth industry between
the large capitalist and the small manufacturer, and its very
violence testified to the vitality and power yet remaining to
the latter.[4]

Some of the wool was, however, not bought by clothiers
or even by weavers; they raised it themselves. Apart
entirely from the normal purchase of land as an investment
by the wealthy manufacturer it is clear that agriculture and
clothmaking in sixteenth-century Wiltshire were closely
related and frequently complementary. Despite the comparative coarseness of Wiltshire fleeces, probably much land
—by enclosure or otherwise—had been turned to pasture
during the later middle ages[5]; and in the sixteenth century

[1] S.P.D. Eliz. CXIV, 27.   [2] B.M. Lansdowne MS. 48, f. 159.
[3] S.P.D. Eliz. CCLXI, 63.
[4] Cf. S.P.D. Jas. I, LXXX, 13, pr. in Unwin, *Industrial Organization in the
XVIth and XVIIth Centuries* (1904), 234–6.
[5] Cf. the map of enclosures before 1700 in Gonner, *Common Land and Inclosure*
(1912), at end; much of the parish of Christian Malford, within the industrial
area, had been enclosed before 1519—Gray, *English Field Systems* (1915), 101—
though how far the enclosures were for arable rather than pasture must admittedly
remain uncertain.

the impact of an expanding industry upon agriculture doubtless continued to be felt in Wiltshire as much as in the other clothing counties.[1] The risings against enclosures which occurred in 1548 throughout the west country were partly caused by the activities of individuals who were at once graziers and clothiers[2]; and there is no doubt that Wiltshire clothiers often owned flocks of sheep. John Flower, a clothier of Potterne, possessed over eight hundred sheep,[3] Richard Whitaker *alias* Bathe, another clothier, purchased and occupied some 160 acres of enclosed pasture and meadow with a sheephouse in Westbury,[4] while it is difficult to resist the conclusion that Richard Potticary of Stockton, who was fined by the London cloth searchers in May 1562 for bringing defective white cloth to Blackwell Hall, must from the wool of the numerous sheep he owned have manufactured the coarse blankets so many of which he later bequeathed to various individuals on his death.[5] Indeed, the frequency with which clothiers, including those dwelling within towns, left legacies of ewes, lambs, and ' chilver sheep ' sufficiently attests how often they were also graziers.

Sometimes they were actually full-blown farmers. A fulling mill was often to be found in close proximity to a grist mill and in the occupation of the same individual.[6] In the middle of the sixteenth century Robert Whitaker *alias* Bathe of Bishopstrow, who described himself as a clothman, kept not only flocks of sheep but oxen and horses, and corn and barley were growing in his fields.[7] Henry Long, a rich clothier of Whaddon, bequeathed in 1558 to his wife, among other things, a plough of eight oxen, a bull and a dozen cows, two hundred sheep, and various articles of agricultural significance.[8] A man of probably less wealth, though of greater public activity, was

[1] Tawney, *Agrarian Problem in the Sixteenth Century* (1912), 196–7 *et passim*.
[2] B.M. Lansdowne MS. 238, f. 292, pr. in Miss Lamond's edition of *The Common Weal of this Realm of England* (1893), lii–lxvii.
[3] S.C. Hen. VIII, 15/129.   [4] E.C.P. 1281/36 ; S.C. Ed. VI, 4/59.
[5] Will of Richard Potticary (Poticary) (1570), P.C.C. 1 Holney; Ex. K.R. Mem. Hil. 7 Eliz. 329.
[6] *Vide infra*, p. 18.
[7] Will of Robert Whitaker *alias* Bathe (1559), P.C.C. 27 Chaynay.
[8] Will of Henry Long (1558), P.C.C. 75 Noodes.

Henry Goldney *alias* Farnewell, who was mayor of Chippenham in 1554 when the borough received a charter of in-
corporation,[1] and who was generally named as a clothier in
the documents of the several lawsuits in which he engaged.[2]
He inherited a couple of looms from his father Nicholas,
and kept a store of oil, wool, and yarn in his house. On
one occasion he was indicted for keeping a gig-mill.[3]
Nevertheless, he described himself in his will as a yeoman,
and was designated as such when returned to parliament in
1553 as member for Chippenham—with perfect justice,
for he raised crops, worked at least one grist mill, and kept
cattle and pigs.[4] The connexion between industry and
agriculture may not have been so intimate in sixteenth-century Wiltshire as in certain other contemporary clothing
counties—in Gloucestershire or the north country, for instance—where a greater proportion of the wool was grown
in or very near the industrial areas; but it did undoubtedly
and closely exist.[5]

Closely connected with the acquisition of wool was the
sale of yarn. Carding and spinning were staple occupations
pursued in every part of the kingdom where the housewife
had leisure and wool was available; it was not necessary
to wait for transport to the clothing areas or for the commission from the clothier. In Salisbury from the middle
of the century onwards the municipality saw to the provision of work for spinsters as a measure of poor relief, the
necessary capital having been bequeathed for the purpose
by a rich citizen.[6] Wool broggers frequently dealt also in
yarn,[7] and yarn was commonly to be bought with wool in

[1] Goldney, *Records of Chippenham* (1889), 342.

[2] E.C.P. 984/9–10, 1122/15; C.R. 103/2.

[3] Ex. K.R. Mem. East. 5 Eliz. 85.

[4] Wills of Nicholas Goldney *alias* Farnewell (Affernell) (1538), P.C.C. 16
Dyngeley, and of Henry his son (1573), P.C.C. 39 Peter. Other examples of
farmer-clothiers could also be cited.

[5] Cf. Heaton, *Yorkshire Woollen and Worsted Industry* (1920), 93; Wadsworth
and Mann, *The Cotton Trade and Industrial Lancashire* (1931), 25–8. An Act of
1576—18 Eliz. c. 16—contained a clause which attempted to limit the acquisition
of land by clothiers in Wiltshire, Somerset, and Gloucestershire, but it was undoubtedly directed against investors rather than farmers. *Vide infra*, pp. 58–9.

[6] *H.M.C. Salisbury Corporation*, 222–3, 228.

[7] E.g. *Cal. Pat. Rolls Ed. VI*, ii, 148; Ex. K.R. Mem. East. 14 Eliz. 127;
B.M. Lansdowne MS. 152, ff. 213–14.

the markets; it was carried in large quantities, for instance, to Cirencester and sold to the clothier there.[1] There were also small obscure dealers in yarn—yarn badgers—who took up the thread spun locally by independent spinners who were said to buy their wool in weekly instalments in the markets.[2] Sometimes a clothier dealt in yarn.[3] But not only was the law hostile to regrators of yarn; the larger cloth manufacturers disliked the yarn badger as much as the wool brogger and for similar reasons. They complained that he raised prices, that he fummed the yarn with hot water so as to make it weigh more, that he mixed yarn made from different sorts of wool so that the cloth made from his thread shrank unevenly when fulled.[4]

But though this humble traffic between spinners and dealers nevertheless continued throughout the century, it is probable—though no figures of any sort are available—that a very large part of the wool which was subsequently manufactured into cloth in sixteenth-century Wiltshire did not pass through the hands of any dealers in yarn, but after its purchase by the clothier was cleansed with oil and mixed on his premises, and then was distributed for carding and spinning to individuals, no doubt chiefly women, who worked in their own homes for piece-rate wages. The earnings of spinners were meagre, particularly in the latter half of the century when the rise in prices was making itself felt,[5] and it is not surprising to find that, as was usually the case when the putting-out system prevailed, spinners were in Wiltshire often enough convicted of embezzling the wool which had been committed to their charge.[6] On occasion the clothier extended his posthumous charity to the poor spinners who had worked for him, either by forgiving them their small debts or even by bequeathing a tiny legacy to them.[7]

[1] E.C.P. 1116/88–9; C.R. 16/21.

[2] Cf. S.P.D. Jas. I, LXXX, 13, pr. in Unwin, *Ind. Org.* 143–6. This was doubtless no new phenomenon in 1615.   [3] Ex. K.R. Mem. Mich. 7 Eliz. 529.

[4] S.P.D. Eliz. CCXLIV, 126, and CCLXXXVII, 96; cf. also B.M. Lansdowne MS. 155, ff. 223–4.

[5] S.P.D. Eliz. CCXLIV, 126, pr. in Tawney and Power, *Tudor Econ. Docs.* i, 371–6; and *vide infra*, p. 81.

[6] Cunnington, *Annals of the Borough of Devizes* (1925), I, i, 15, 42–3, 46.

[7] E.g. wills of John Whitaker *alias* Bathe (Whitacre) (1530), P.C.C. 2 Thower, and of Thomas Scott (1553), P.C.C. 10 Tashe.

When the wool had been carded and spun, the yarn was entrusted by the clothier to the weaver, a person whose wealth and social position varied considerably. Cloth-making was often as much complementary to agriculture for him as for the clothier; and no doubt many a peasant varied his labour in the open fields by taking a turn at the loom. Sometimes the weaver owned a modest acreage of meadow and pasture upon which his sheep and cattle might graze.[1] Or he might choose to invest his capital by buying a house, as did Robert Daniell of Castle Combe, though he was indeed unable to pay off the purchase money during his life.[2] Philip White, another weaver, owned not only his house but also an orchard and some cottages.[3] There were weavers who kept two looms; Robert Marshman of Melksham actually possessed three.[4] In fact, the class of the more well-to-do weavers almost imperceptibly merged into the ranks of the meaner clothiers, in whose homes was so often to be found a loom at which they themselves pre-sumably wove; for instance, Robert Burgis, clothier of Veverne mill, Slaughterford, included among his bequests the legacy of ten shillings to 'Jhon my boye', who was doubtless employed to pass the shuttle of the broad loom to and fro for his master.[5] Between Burgis, who was clearly not in affluent circumstances, and a prosperous weaver there can have been little or no difference in wealth or social standing. Some weavers may have grown their own wool or have bought their own wool or yarn in the market and come into contact with the clothier only for the disposal of their cloth. The father of the great William Stumpe of Malmesbury was a weaver before he became a clothier,[6]

[1] E.C.P. 470/23, 792/23-6; wills of John Gonston (1586), P.C.C. 55 Wind-sor, and of Steven Curtice (1604), P.C.C. 96 Harte. Cf. also the wills of John Lucas of Broughton (1560), William Aynell of Bishopstone (1573), and John Alwaye of Keevil (1573), Salisbury Archdeaconry Register, 3, ff. 183, 184, and 207.

[2] Will of Robert Daniell (1598), P.C.C. 59 Lewyn.

[3] Will of Philip White (1595), Peculiar Court of the Dean of Salisbury, Register, 6, f. 106.

[4] Will of Walter Philipp (1567), pr. in Phillipps, *Collectanea de familiis diversis quibus nomen est Philipps* (1816-40), 285-6; wills of Thomas Lucas (1568) and of Robert Marshman (1570), Salisbury Archdeaconry Register, 5, ff. 93 and 98.

[5] Will of Robert Burgis (1580), P.C.C. 26 Arundell. The wills of clothiers often reveal that they kept looms.

[6] Aubrey, Natural History of Wiltshire, Bodl. MS. Aubrey 2, f. 143. Cf. the

the brother of Richard Batt, a wealthy clothier thrice mayor of Devizes, was a weaver,[1] and very occasionally individuals were designated as either.[2]

But while the existence of the well-to-do weaver cannot be questioned, particularly during the first half of the century, it is nevertheless clear that he was the exception rather than the rule. Most weavers lived from hand to mouth upon the meagre wages of the clothier, into whose debt they not infrequently fell; the trade crisis of 1528 was accompanied by rioting in Wiltshire[3]; a hitch in the sale of cloth at London which, during the unhappy winter of 1586–7,[4] threatened their livelihood, brought them to the verge of revolt; and in 1595 a scarcity of grain was followed by corn riots near the industrial centre of Warminster.[5] More often than to their spinners the clothiers indeed bequeathed small sums to the weavers who worked for them; customarily they at least left legacies to the 'poor people' of their own and sometimes also of adjacent parishes where presumably their employees dwelt. But whatever the charity of the clothier it is not surprising that some weavers preferred the risks and hardships of a vagabond life to the tedious poverty of existence in a small cottage with no more than a garden to cultivate, or that weavers as a class bore a reputation for turbulent and riotous behaviour.[6] Most of them had little or no property to bequeath or to defend in the law courts, so that they remain for posterity an anonymous multitude, 'the thousands of poore people that doe onlye lyve uppon clothing'.[7] Their collective history in the sixteenth century must chiefly be sought in the occasional

conclusion of Kulischer as to the origins of the clothier—*Allgemeine Wirtschaftsgeschichte*, ii (1929), 116.

[1] *Wilts. Notes and Queries*, ii (1896–8), 598, and iii (1899–1901), 35.

[2] So Thomas Yerbury of Trowbridge—S.C. Eliz. 28/25 and C.R. 202/2—if the identification be correct; or William Wodewalle—*L.P. Hen. VIII*, i, 820.

[3] *L.P. Hen. VIII*, quot. Pollard, *Wolsey* (1929), 159.

[4] Wheeler, *Defence of the Merchant Adventurers* (1601), pr. in Tawney and Power, *Tudor Econ. Docs.* iii, 292.

[5] *Acts of the Privy Council*, 1595–6, 43. *Vide infra*, p. 69.

[6] Cunnington, *Annals of the Borough of Devizes*, I, ii, 32 *et passim*; S.P.D. Eliz. xxxv, 33, pr. in Tawney and Power, *Tudor Econ. Docs.* ii, 45.

[7] This quotation is taken from B.M. Lansdowne MS. 41, f. 83; other similar references might be cited. Cf. the description of the inhabitants of Kingswood in *Acts of the Privy Council*, 1597, 221–2.

obiter dicta of contemporary writers and in the minatory or patronizing language of the statute-book.

Sometimes the weaver did not even own the loom which he worked; he rented it in his home, or went to weave in the clothier's house or wherever the latter might keep his workshop. It might seem that in the first half of the century the clothiers were beginning to collect the ownership of looms into their hands. John Flower of Potterne, for instance, kept four,[1] while Nicholas Goldney *alias* Farnewell of Chippenham owned at least three.[2] But the outstanding example of their concentration in the hands of the capitalist was provided by William Stumpe, who earned much fame by transforming the buildings of Malmesbury abbey into a workshop for his weavers.[3] Stumpe bequeathed to one son ten of his looms and the remainder to another, which suggests that he may have possessed a score or so.[4] But his spectacular exploits were unique; he had no forerunners or imitators in Wiltshire. Further experiments of a similar sort on a large scale were restricted by the passage of the act of 1555 which forebade country clothiers in future to own more than one loom and weavers to own more than two.[5] During the ensuing quarter of a century or so and particularly in the early sixties informations were laid in the common law courts at Westminster against various Wiltshire manufacturers for owning more than the statutory loom.[6] The act, however, did not apply to dwellers within cities, boroughs, or market towns—a very wide exception—and within their boundaries the clothiers continued to own more than one loom. Christopher Stokes of Castle Combe possessed at least a couple in the sixties,[7] Christopher

---

[1] S.C. Hen. VIII, 15/127, pr. in *Wilts. Notes and Queries*, viii (1914-16), 168-76.

[2] Will of Nicholas Goldney *alias* Farnewell (Affernwell) (1538), P.C.C. 16 Dyngeley.

[3] Leland, *Itinerary*, i, 132—an often quoted passage.

[4] Will of William Stumpe (1554), P.C.C. 26 Powell, pr. in *Wilts. Notes and Queries*, viii (1914-16), 391-2.   [5] 2 & 3 P. & M. c. 11.

[6] Miss M. Gay in her article on *Aspects of Elizabethan Apprenticeship* in the volume entitled *Facts and Factors in Economic History* by former students of E. F. Gay (1932) has traced sixteen such Wiltshire prosecutions in the courts of exchequer and king's bench—*op. cit.* 162.

[7] Will of Christopher Stokes (1566), pr. in *Wilts. Notes and Queries*, viii (1914-16), 390-1.

Eyre of Salisbury a little later kept weavers in his house,[1] and Henry Morris of Devizes kept at least two broad looms in a building 'at the lane end' there.[2] It is impossible to believe that the engrossing of looms could have been rigidly confined within arbitrary geographical limits, and indeed the very statute-book itself bore witness in 1576 to the existence of clothiers' workhouses in the rural districts of the west country broadcloth area.[3] Further, if the act of 1555 did not prevent the congregation of weavers here and there under one roof, still less could it be believed to have prevented the clothier from hiring out his looms for rent by private transactions of which word could not easily come to the ears of the common informer. But it may in any case be concluded that so far as the act appeared to be effective it was in fact largely superfluous, since looms were not insuperably expensive to construct. Further, the woollen industry in the sixteenth century was not sufficiently advanced in technique to make the engrossing of many looms of particular profit to the clothier save in exceptional circumstances[4]; and after the middle of the century the phase of most rapid expansion had passed.

When the cloth left the loom it was then ready for scouring, fulling, and stretching. The fabric was thickened and shrunk by being pounded in a solution of fuller's earth or some kindred substance, so that the grain ceased to be visible. In sixteenth-century Wiltshire the powerful hammers which lashed the sodden fabrics were driven by water-power; there is no evidence to suggest that fulling by hand or foot still survived. Fulling mills were to be found wherever this water-power was available; in and near the clothing town of Calne, for instance, they congregated upon Calne water.[5] In the countryside they were often placed in close proximity to grist mills; sometimes a fulling and a grist mill were worked under the same roof.[6] But whether the

[1] Will of Christopher Eyre (1582), P.C.C. 3 Rowe.
[2] Will of Henry Morris (Mores) (1572), P.C.C. 2 Peter.
[3] 18 Eliz. c. 16.
[4] Cf. Heaton, *Yorkshire Woollen and Worsted Industry*, 89–91.
[5] Ex. Depositions by Commission, Hil. 30 Eliz. 8; evidence of William Swadden of Calne.
[6] E.g. *Cal. Pat. Rolls Ed. VI*, v, 164. *Supra*, p. 12.

fulling mill was in town or country it is clear that by the Tudor period it had generally passed—save for one district —into the effective occupation of the clothier. The latter sometimes owned it outright, but more often, particularly in the rural industrial areas, he held it upon lease, for so much as forty or seventy-five years.[1] The owner was usually one of the landed gentry, though before the dissolution a number of fulling mills were in the possession of religious houses; those in Bishopstrow manor, for example, were the property of Lacock abbey.[2] Beside the fulling mill and in the hands of its occupant there was normally a piece of ground on which stood the rack upon which the shrunken cloth after leaving the mill was stretched; such no doubt was the 'racke close' which Roger Chivers, a clothier of Calne, bequeathed to his wife.[3] All these final processes, of which fulling, scouring, and stretching were the chief, were carried out if not by the clothier personally at least by his employees and no doubt under his eye.[4]

While in the organization of the woollen industry the large or middling clothier on the whole predominated from Malmesbury to Warminster and from Trowbridge to Devizes, there is one corner of the county whose industrial development was sufficiently peculiar to deserve some special attention—the Salisbury and Wilton district. Salisbury lay on the fringe of a geologically distinct area whose staple woollen products, from Newbury and Winchester to the Kentish clothing villages, were kerseys and similar narrower or coarser fabrics.[5] It had been the chief textile manufac-

[1] C.R. 63/79 and 101/39; references to the leasing of fulling mills abound. There was a fulling mill at Westbury of which a fuller claimed part ownership as late as the early years of the reign of Elizabeth—C.P. Eliz. i, W 11/55. This instance of the ownership of important industrial property by a fuller at so late a date seems exceptional.

[2] Hoare, History of Modern Wiltshire, Hundred of Warminster (1831), 70.

[3] Will of Roger Chivers (Chiver) (1602), P.C.C. 42 Montague.

[4] Clauses iii and iv of the act of 1555—2 & 3 P. & M. c. 11—forbade weavers to full and fullers to weave. There is evidence to show that many clothiers in Wiltshire continued to do both, so that although there was a very occasional prosecution at Westminster of a Wiltshire manufacturer—Ex. K.R. Mem. Hil. 14 Eliz. 95 records the indictment of Henry Phipps, a clothier of Westbury— the clause may be considered to have been practically a dead letter.

[5] To some extent Marlborough shared the characteristics of the Salisbury region; it also lay upon the fringe of the kersey area and as a textile centre was an outpost of the Reading and Newbury clothing district.

C

turing city of the kingdom at the end of the fourteenth century,[1] and it specialized during the later middle ages in the production of the famous 'Salisbury rays' which were striped and white cloths probably of the kersey type.[2] Kerseys were certainly being still made in Salisbury in the reign of Philip and Mary,[3] and their manufacture persisted into the seventies at least.[4] This Salisbury industry was not mainly dependent upon the ubiquitous clothier in the fashion of the sixteenth-century broadcloth manufacture; it was carried on chiefly by a multitude of weavers or small clothiers who probably purchased their wool or yarn, dyed and undyed, from middlemen. The fullers were independent craftsmen who competed with each other for custom.[5] In Wilton as late as the end of the reign of Henry VIII the local mill-owner fulled and stretched the fabrics of the humble clothmakers of the neighbourhood, presumably on commission.[6] This more archaic organization of the Salisbury clothing area may reflect the conditions of an earlier period in the broadcloth manufacture—it was no doubt the time and expense of carrying the latter to the distant market in London which handicapped the independent small weaver and helped to put him ultimately in the power of the clothier who marketed his cloth.[7] But in the Salisbury and

[1] Gray, *The Production and Exportation of English Woollens in the Fourteenth Century, English Historical Review*, xxix (1924), 30.

[2] Benson and Hatcher, *History of Salisbury* (1843), 113–14; Gidden, *Steward Books of Southampton*, i, 14, 18, &c. (*Southampton Rec. Soc. Publ.* xxxv, 1935).

[3] John Abyn, a merchant of Salisbury who was mayor in 1551 and M.P. in 1554—Benson and Hatcher, *History of Salisbury*, 696 and 708—bequeathed by his will—P.C.C. 48 Welles—£20 to the city, to be lent out 'as a stock to help younge beginners that be kersye makers'.

[4] Thomas Grafton of Salisbury was fined in 1573 for bringing a defective kersey for sale to Blackwell Hall—Ex. K.R. Mem. Hil. 16 Eliz. 292. Kerseys were probably made in Salisbury throughout the sixteenth century, since they were certainly being manufactured there early in the seventeenth—*infra*, p. 109.

[5] E.C.P. 67/68.

[6] S.C. Hen. VIII, 23/227. The Wilton clothiers appear to have been very small fry; William Durston merely claimed to employ his own family—E.C.P. 1117/33—while John Twyforde was by no means well off—cf. his will (1588), P.C.C. 1 Leicester.

[7] It is perhaps not without significance that Thomas Horton, the rich clothier of Bradford whose memory was still green when Leland visited the town some ten years after his death—Leland, *Itinerary*, i, 136—should have sometimes designated himself as 'merchant'—e.g. E.C.P. 411/26 and *L.P. Hen. VIII*, iv, 309.

Wilton area during the fifteenth century the market lay at hand; the cloths were sold to the merchants of Salisbury itself. These formed a rich mercantile community whose members traded directly with France and Spain.[1] Their activities were based largely on the port of Southampton, which during the fifteenth century enjoyed its brief hey-day of prosperity.[2]

At the end of the fifteenth and the beginning of the sixteenth century there flourished the last great generation of the Salisbury merchants. Richard Bartilmewe, William Webbe, Thomas Coke, and yet other burgesses of the city imported through Southampton wines, iron, fruit, oil, woad and other dyeing materials, for which wool, cloth, and other products of the neighbourhood were exchanged.[3] A diminution in this lucrative traffic had, however, already begun,[4] and during the reign of Henry VIII it shrank very considerably.[5] By the seventies only one Salisbury merchant was trading on any considerable scale through Southampton, and he dealt chiefly in Hampshire kerseys and 'cottons'; finally in 1577 he went bankrupt.[6] The port of Southampton had long since been deserted by the Venetian, Genoese, and Spanish merchant fleets, and now was sinking into three and a half centuries of quiescence and decay; and as one result, the Salisbury merchants became more completely dependent upon the London market, in which they had indeed been already wont to trade both by land and water during the fifteenth century.[7] This absorption of Salisbury within the economic hinterland of the metropolis was also

[1] E.C.P. 1089/21 and 1502/19–21; *Cal. Pat. Rolls 1478*, 145 quot. by Miss Wallis-Chapman, *Black Book of Southampton*, 7 (*Southampton Rec. Soc. Publ.* xiii, 1912).
[2] Cf. Miss Wallis-Chapman's introduction to the *Black Book of Southampton*, *passim*.
[3] Southampton Civic Centre MS. Brokage Books, 1492–3, 1493–4, *passim*. My attention was directed to this source by Miss E. M. Carus-Wilson.
[4] Wallis-Chapman, *Black Book of Southampton*, xxvi and xxiii.
[5] Southampton Civic Centre MS. Brokage Books, 1528–9 and 1543–4, *passim*. In 1595 the mayor of Salisbury plausibly assured the Privy Council that not more than three merchants of his city were engaged in the Southampton trade—*Acts of the Privy Council, 1595–6*, 208–9.
[6] Ex. K.R. Port Books, 814/10; Hamilton and Aubrey, *Books of Examinations and Depositions*, 66–70 (*Southampton Rec. Soc. Publ.* xvi, 1914).
[7] E.C.P. 224/76; cf. also E.C.P. 63/83 and 67/41.

connected with a change in the character of the cloth it produced. The remarkable expansion of the market for English cloth in the Netherlands and Germany during the fifteenth and sixteenth centuries led to an extension of the frontier of the industrial broadcloth area at home; it advanced down the Wylye valley and in the course of the sixteenth century it finally engulfed Salisbury. As a potential centre of the broadcloth industry Salisbury and its neighbourhood had many advantages to offer—there was a plentiful supply of water-power and a large population versed in spinning and weaving, while even the wool grown on Salisbury plain though inferior to that of the Cotswolds was yet of fine quality.[1] It is thus not surprising to learn that at least two clothiers migrated to Salisbury from the broadcloth district of Somersetshire during the first half of the sixteenth century.[2] In the same period Salisbury merchants were bringing broadcloth for sale to London,[3] and by the early years of the reign of Elizabeth it is certain that large numbers of white broadcloths were being manufactured there for the London market.[4] It may be surmised that the organization of the Salisbury broadcloth industry gradually assimilated itself to that of the other west country areas; the clothiers rose in civic importance and came sometimes to hold the office of mayor from the last quarter of the century onwards.[5] Thus the decay of the port of Southampton and the disappearance of the mercantile magnates was accompanied in Salisbury by a minor industrial revolution and the establishment of a new oligarchy of manufacturers.

Southampton was not the only port whose trade declined,

[1] Cf. Drayton, *Polyolbion*, song xiv, ll. 235-6.

[2] These two individuals were Thomas Whelpeley, sometime mayor of Bath—S.C. Hen. VIII, 11/63-73, pr. in Bradford, *Proceedings in the Court of the Star Chamber, Somerset Record Society*, xxvii (1911), 146—and John Compton of Beckington, *L.P. Hen. VIII*, i, 256.

[3] E.C.P. 980/33.

[4] Half a dozen Salisbury clothiers and, it is significant to notice, one *soi-disant* draper, Edmunde Wykewyke—cf. E.C.P. 1170/88-9—were fined by the London searchers for bringing defective broadcloth to the market there during the years 1561 and 1562—Ex. K.R. Mem. Hil. 7 Eliz. 329-32.

[5] The first mayor of Salisbury who can be definitely proved to have been a clothier was John Bayly, who was elected to the office in 1577—Benson and Hatcher, *History of Salisbury*, 696. Cf. Bayly's will (1581), P.C.C. 18 Darcy.

for during the sixteenth century the commercial activity of
the kingdom tended steadily to become concentrated in
London.[1] There was possibly a diminishing trickle of
Wiltshire cloths through the havens of the south-west. The
trade with Bristol also decayed. In the later middle ages
there had been close contact between Bristol and the Wiltshire clothing area in the valley of the Avon, when clothiers
had sold their wares to Bristol merchants and in return had
bought oil from Spain and woad from Toulouse[2]; but in
the Tudor period the continental broadcloth market lay
outside the trade routes frequented by Bristol shipping.
Thus there was probably little traffic in Wiltshire cloth
westwards,[3] though clothiers from time to time visited
Bristol fair and may have sold a few fabrics there.[4]

Such cloth as was exported through the ports in adjacent
counties was possibly in part dyed and dressed in Wiltshire,
as were the few fabrics sold for the local retail market.
The clothier might utilize his produce to pay by barter for
other commodities; near the beginning of the century
some tenements in Devizes were actually purchased in this
fashion.[5] No doubt such bargains were generally smaller.
Broadcloth was a common material for dress in Tudor
England, and the slight fraction of the Wiltshire output
which was dyed and finished within the county was in the
main probably consumed locally. An occasional dyer was
to be found at the chief industrial centres—in the middle

[1] The steady aggrandizement of London commerce at the expense of that of
the outports may be traced in the tables to be found in Schanz, *Englische Handelspolitik gegen Ende des Mittelalters* (1881), ii, 37–59 and 86–105. Cf. also his
calculation that the share of London in the foreign trade of the kingdom during
the reign of Henry VII was about 50 per cent., during the reign of Henry VIII
about 66 per cent., and had by 1582 risen to 86·4 per cent.—*op. cit.* 30.

[2] E.C.P. 66/58; cf. Miss Carus-Wilson's account of Bristol commerce in
Power and Postan, *Studies in English Trade in the Fifteenth Century*, 183–246.

[3] S.P.D. Eliz. CCLV, 56, pr. in Tawney and Power, *Tudor Econ. Docs.* iii,
199–210, which gives an account of the trade of the southern and south-western
ports about the year 1584, does not mention Wiltshire cloth among the many
kinds it enumerates. Between Easter and Michaelmas 1565—the first year for
which port books are available—none of the cloths exported from Bristol were of
Wiltshire manufacture—Ex. K.R. Port Books 1128/3.

[4] Cranfield papers, letter of Henry Pearce to Cranfield dated 30 January 1601/2,
&c. Cf. Lipson, *Economic History of England*, ii (1931), 252–3.

[5] Cunnington, *Annals of the Borough of Devizes*, I, i, 26. In this case, however,
the cloth was undyed.

of the century there was one in Trowbridge[1]—and gig-mills, used for dressing the cloth—the final stage—were not entirely unknown in sixteenth-century Wiltshire.[2] The dyer was an independent craftsman who owned his own dye-house, furnaces, vats, and other implements of the trade.[3] It may be assumed that he worked on commission for the clothier who himself was directly responsible for the dressing; thus Stephen Whitaker *alias* Bathe, a Westbury clothier, kept the necessary instruments in a loft above his fulling mill.[4] Walter Gray, a clothier of Wilton, owned no less than four pairs of the shears used in cloth-finishing.[5] It may be that the cloth was usually dyed immediately before or after being fulled and scoured; there is at least no evidence to suggest that the Wiltshire clothier had become familiar before the end of the century with that coloured yarn whose employment was destined to provoke such agitation a generation or so later. But in any case it is not to be expected that much information about the dyeing and dressing of cloth should be available, since every indication points to the conclusion that the vast bulk of Wiltshire broadcloth was neither shipped abroad from the nearest ports nor consumed by the local retail market, but was sent, undyed and undressed, to London for sale.[6]

The cloth, done up in packs of ten pieces, was transported from the central industrial area along the medieval road through Marlborough, Hungerford, Reading, and Maidenhead, while the products of Malmesbury probably found their way via Faringdon, Abingdon, and Henley, and those

[1] Misc. Books, D. of Lancs., vol. 108, f. 58.

[2] Clothiers were indicted at Westminster for owning gig-mills after the Act 5 & 6 Ed. VI had reached the statute-book—Ex. K.R. Mem. Hil. 4 & 5 P. & M. 94; East. 5 Eliz. 85; Hil. 14 Eliz. 95. Cf. also *Cal. Pat. Rolls Ed. VI*, iv, 20 and B.M. Lansdowne MS. 114, f. 120.

[3] This is clear from the wills of dyers—cf. those of Thomas Dashe of Calne (1598), P.C.C. 72 Lewyn, Thomas Singer *alias* Smithe of Trowbridge (1604), P.C.C. 52 Harte, and John Cabell of Salisbury (1604), P.C.C. 52 Harte.

[4] *Inquisitio post mortem* on the property of Stephen Whitaker, Ch. Ser. 179/105, quot. Hoare, *History of Modern Wiltshire, Hundred of Warminster* (1831), 42-3.

[5] Will of Walter Gray (1556), Salisbury Archdeaconry Register, 3, f. 38.

[6] Coloured cloth was very rarely dispatched from Wiltshire to Blackwell Hall in the later sixteenth century but was not utterly unknown there—in September 1574 William Lightfoot of Keevil was fined for bringing faulty red broadcloth to the market, as was less than a year later John Barnard of Westbury for plunket broadcloth—Ex. K.R. Mem. Mich. 17 Eliz. 238.

of Salisbury through Winchester, Farnham, and Guildford.[1] Often the clothier himself brought his own cloths, though he sometimes committed them to the care of one of the many carriers whose wagons plied on the main traffic arteries.[2] No doubt clothiers were anxious to spare themselves the loss of time and of money involved in the journey to London if it could be avoided; Richard Potticary of Stockton, for instance, found it convenient to offer by letter to the purchaser of his last consignment of cloths those which he had in hand.[3] William Stumpe of Malmesbury kept his own factor in London, as no doubt did a few other very rich clothiers.[4] Occasionally clothiers from the same neighbourhood did business for each other.[5] Thomas Daungerfeld, a Gloucestershire clothier, while on his way to London sometimes bought a considerable quantity of broadcloths from a widow dwelling in Devizes, whose age or sex presumably hindered her from making the journey herself[6]—though such considerations did not deter the widow of John Hedges of Malmesbury from faring to London to sell her cloths.[7] The London cloth market from the end of the fourteenth century onwards was held in Blackwell Hall in Basinghall street hard by the Guildhall; the addition to it of several annexes in the course of the century and finally its destruction and re-edification as a 'new, strong, and beautiful storehouse' in 1588 bore witness to the expanding textile industry of the kingdom.[8] The market at Blackwell Hall was open for sales every week from Thursday noon until Saturday morning only, so that clothiers from distant counties after spending Sunday at

[1] Cf. Stenton, *The Road System of Medieval England, Economic History Review*, vii (1936), 9.
[2] E.g. E.C.P. 439/36 and 1108/75; there is no dearth of references to carriers.
[3] Cranfield papers, letter of Richard Potticary to Lionel Cranfield dated 13 October 1601.
[4] C.R. 11/60; cf. also Exchequer, Barons' Depositions, 5/693.
[5] E.C.P. 1093/20; C.R. 100/53.   [6] E.C.P. 1214/5-8.
[7] She was fined by the London cloth searchers in April 1561—Ex. K.R. Mem. Hil. 7 Eliz. 330.
[8] Stow, *The Survey of London*, ed. Kingsford (1908), i, 289; Guildhall, City of London Repertories, 17, ff. 5 b, 407 b, 19, f. 66. An historical account of Blackwell Hall, for which materials in plenty exist, would be a boon to the local historian.

home should be able to reach London before it began.
Municipal regulations forbade the sale of cloth wholesale
at other times or places within the city and its liberties;
but these injunctions were not invariably obeyed. Country
clothiers were sometimes apt to let their cloth remain in
inns and private houses[1]; near the middle of the century
they were wont to trade illegally in the houses opposite the
Steelyard of the German merchants near Dowgate.[2]

The sixteenth-century clothier was, however, fortunate in
supplying a market at Blackwell Hall wider than that known
either to his medieval predecessor, whose sales were restricted to the citizens of London, or to his successor in the
eighteenth century, whose cloths were bought by the ob-
truding and hated factors alone. The country clothier from
Wiltshire—and elsewhere—not only sold his goods to clothworkers, drapers, mercers, and, far above all, to merchant
adventurers; he also traded directly with the Hansards who
from the end of the fifteenth century had secured access to
Blackwell Hall, much to the resentment of the native
merchants, who believed that their competition lowered the
standards of manufacture—and heightened prices.[3] The
Hansards were no doubt as well acquainted with the tricks
of the market as the merchant adventurers; with true
German thoroughness their young apprentices on their
arrival in the kingdom were sent to dwell with a clothier in
the country, there to perfect their English[4]—and presumably to acquaint themselves, too, with the technical
details of textile manufacture. The Hamburg merchant
Mathias Hoep regularly bought Wiltshire cloths in Blackwell Hall during the period 1566–72, while acting not only
for himself but also as agent for a number of his colleagues.
He purchased various consignments from Thomas Long and
Robert Wallis, big clothiers of Trowbridge, and was also

[1] Guildhall, City of London Repertories, 13, f. 188 b, 14, f. 87, 20, f. 410, 22, f. 93 b, 23, f. 354.
[2] Höhlbaum, *Kölner Inventar*, i (1896), 383–4.
[3] Armstrong, *A Treatise concerninge the Staple*, repr. from Pauli's edn. by Tawney and Power, *Tudor Econ. Docs.* iii, 108; Höhlbaum, *Kölner Inventar*, i, 383; S.P.D. Eliz. cvi, 5.
[4] Ehrenberg, *Hamburg und England im Zeitalter der Königin Elisabeth* (1896), 251.

a customer, among others, of William Grafton of Salisbury, Henry Chivers of Calne, and John Wilcox of Standley.[1] The importance, however, of the Hansards diminished steadily during the second half of the century. Their privileges were whittled away bit by bit; their right of access to Blackwell Hall was interrupted in 1576,[2] and with the final closure of the Steelyard in 1598 they lost their foothold in England for some years. Their presence may have been a stimulus to the market; but its backbone always continued to be the merchant adventurers, who by the last quarter of the sixteenth century had acquired very nearly a monopoly of the export trade to the Netherlands and Germany.[3]

The transaction involved in the sale of cloth to the merchant was seldom simple, and sometimes involved some complex credit conditions, the giving of recognizances, and the reception of counter-recognizances. The oil of credit indeed greased every cog in the machinery of the woollen industry, from the purchase of wool to the disposal of the cloth. Prices rose and fell with the varying needs of the clothier for ready money; in the early autumn when he required cash to pay for the wool of the midsummer shearing which he had bought upon short-term credit the wary merchant might expect to have his cloth more cheaply.[4] Sometimes the credit was spread over a long period; William Page of Devizes early in the century sold £100 worth of cloth and covenanted for payment in two instalments, one at the end of a year and the other at the end of a second year.[5] Henry Morris, another clothier of Devizes, must have been engaged in a number of such long-term transactions, for he bequeathed to his cousin 'all my billes of debtes at London'.[6] No doubt, to sell for deferred pay-

---

[1] The account books of Hoep for the years 1566–72 will be found in summary in Ehrenberg, *Hamburg u. England*, 271–6. The above identifications cannot be proved correct, but are very probably so. Others might more tentatively be made; e.g. the 'Middelgut' from whom Hoep bought cloths in 1566 was probably either Richard Middlecot of Bishopstrow or William Middlecot of Warminster.

[2] Ehrenberg, *Hamburg u. England*, 137; cf. also S.P.D. Eliz. CVI, 5.

[3] The numbers of broadcloths exported by natives, Hansards, and other aliens can be found in Ex. L.T.R. Enrolled Customs Accounts.

[4] Ehrenberg, *Hamburg u. England*, 278–2.   [5] E.C.P. 365/39.

[6] Will of Henry Morris (Mores) (1572), P.C.C. 2 Peter. There is plenty of evidence as to the use of credit, but to insist further on the point would merely

ment was better than to pawn the cloths, a course to which in a period of trade depression the clothier was sometimes forced.[1] But the written promise to pay was not always fulfilled; there were dishonest Hansards who fled abroad with the intention of evading payment of their debts,[2] and there were native rogues ready to deceive the simple clothier when the opportunity arose.[3] And even when he had received his money the clothman could scarcely yet consider himself to have escaped all pitfalls; he was still in danger of the fate which befell John Flower, a clothier of Potterne, who while on his way home with his brother was held up near Windsor Great Park and robbed of two horses and their harness, a ring of gold, and sixty pounds in coin[4]—the last being doubtless the money he had received for a pack of broadcloths.

After the cloths had passed out of the hands of the clothier, they found their way to various destinations. Some were dyed and dressed in London. These were destined chiefly for the home market, though a few were sent over-seas—in the eighties dyed Wiltshire cloths were exported to Denmark.[5] But probably the greater proportion were shipped abroad, still undyed and undressed, by merchant adventurers, interlopers, or Hansards—after the payment of export dues to the customs officials. For the first two-thirds of the century the great emporium for English cloths was at Antwerp, the commercial capital of western Europe, where the task of dyeing and dressing them gave employ-ment to hundreds of workfolk.[6] Here during the years

be to fill with superfluous detail the picture which has already been adequately drawn by Professor Tawney in his introduction to Wilson's *Discourse upon Usury* (1925), 45–6.

[1] Ehrenberg, *Hamburg u. England*, 275; *A Discourse of Corporations*, pr. in Tawney and Power, *Tudor Econ. Docs.* iii, 272.

[2] Höhlbaum, *Kölner Inventar*, i, 1, no. 7; *Acts of the Privy Council*, 1597-8, 257-9.

[3] *Acts of the Privy Council*, 1554-6, 230 and 344.

[4] S.C. Hen. VIII, 15/127, pr. in *Wilts. Notes and Queries*, viii, 168-76.

[5] Cf. the licence granted in 1589, S.P.D. Eliz. ccxxv, 53—'. . . whereas our good sister the Queene of Denmark hath . . . made request, that such mony as riseth by the sale of certain fish, which is yeerly brought out of Island into this our realm, and is imploied here in buying of Wiltshire clothes, which are died and dressed in our city of London. . . .' Cf. *H.M.C. Hatfield House*, viii, 65.

[6] Pirenne, *Histoire de Belgique*, iii (1912), 226.

1553 and 1554 the Hamburg merchant Jacob Schröder
bought large quantities of Wiltshire cloths.[1] But from 1564
onwards, for political reasons, the main commercial route
tended to shift eastwards from the line of the Rhine to that
of the Elbe. The merchant adventurers indeed sent regular
cargoes of broadcloths to the mart town which in 1587
they had established at Middelburg,[2] but the more important
branch of their trade was with the cities of north-west
Germany—Stade, Emden, and above all Hamburg—though
in the seventies both adventurers and interlopers transported English cloth as far south as Nuremberg and
Frankfort-on-the-Main.[3] While Antwerp and Cologne decayed, the dyeing and dressing of English cloths developed
into a flourishing industry at Hamburg[4]; it was both fed
either directly by the regular arrival of the fleets of the
merchant adventurers or indirectly from Stade and Emden
and by the less certain ships of the interlopers as well as
by the Hansards themselves—until the latter, before the
end of the century, were finally driven out of the carrying
trade. The finished fabrics were mostly distributed to their
various markets by German wholesale traders; in the first
half of the century the merchants of Cologne after buying
their English cloths at Antwerp sent them to Leipzig and
Thuringia, and later Nuremberg rose to importance as a
distributing centre.[5] But the chief inland market for English
cloths remained throughout the century at Frankfort-on-
the-Main, whence they were finally dispersed to their consumers in central and south Germany, Hungary, and even
Poland.[6]

Thus ended the long chain of processes and transactions

[1] Ehrenberg, *Zur Geschichte der Hamburger Handlung im 16. Jahrhundert,*
Zeitschrift des Vereins für hamburgische Geschichte, viii (1886), 153–61.
[2] Te Lintum, *De Merchant Adventurers in de Nederlanden, een bijdrage tot de*
geschiedenis van den engelschen handel met Nederland (1905), 33–4.
[3] Ehrenberg, *Hamburg u. England,* 118–19, 153; Unwin, *Studies in Economic*
History, 199 and 210–12.
[4] Statistics illustrating the growth of the cloth-finishing industry at Hamburg
are to be found in Ehrenberg, *Hamburg u. England,* 327–8. For a similar phenomenon at Emden see Hagedorn, *Ostfrieslands Handel und Schiffahrt,* ii (1912), 63.
[5] Ranke, *Kölns binnendeutscher Verkehr im 16. und 17. Jahrhundert, Hansische*
Geschichtsblätter, xxix (1924), 67–9.
[6] Dietz, *Frankfurter Handelsgeschichte,* ii (1921), 265; S.P.D. Eliz. ccxxxv,
93.

begun by the purchase of wool at Cirencester or Salisbury and continued by the spinning and weaving of the broadcloths in hundreds of homesteads throughout Wiltshire, the sale of the unfinished fabrics at Blackwell Hall, and their transport over the sea. Despite the rapid economic development of Tudor England the manufacture of cloth ' by which so many people are sett on worke and great profytte doth come to her Majestie's custome' remained until the end of the century—and long afterwards—the most important industry of the kingdom.[1] The organization of the Wiltshire woollen industry was not merely of significance in itself but also because it was almost certainly typical of the organization of the whole west country broadcloth area from the eastern Cotswolds to central Somerset.[2] Indeed, many of its characteristics were common to the woollen industry throughout the kingdom, including the north country. Despite the obvious geographical differences and their immediate effects, the great contrast between the organization of the woollen industry in Yorkshire and in the west country which was to be so striking in the early nineteenth century was as yet in germ. The large or middling clothier in Wiltshire no doubt accounted for a far larger proportion of the total output of cloths than in the West Riding, but as in Yorkshire so in Wiltshire there was to be found the small as well as the great clothier and the independent spinner and weaver.[3] The vehement controversy as to the rights and wrongs of the wool brogger and the yarn badger reflected the conflict of the large capitalist and the small manufacturer for the control of the industry—a conflict which was assuredly not decided finally during the sixteenth century.

[1] The quotation is from *Acts of the Privy Council*, 1598–9, 302.

[2] If John Smith of Nibley had compiled a list of the able-bodied men of Wiltshire with their occupations at the opening of the seventeenth century it is highly probable that such a document on analysis would—save for the comparative absence of dyers and cloth-finishers—yield results similar to those obtained from his Gloucestershire census by Mrs. and Professor Tawney in *An Occupational Census of the Seventeenth Century, Econ. Hist. Rev.* v (1934), 25–64.

[3] Cf. Heaton, *Yorkshire Woollen and Worsted Industries*, 89–123.

III

THE GREAT CLOTHIERS OF THE SIXTEENTH CENTURY: STUMPE AND HIS CONTEMPORARIES

DESPITE the very varied nature of industrial organization in sixteenth-century Wiltshire it remains true that the clothier was the pivot of the textile manufacture. There were indeed independent spinners and weavers; but even if the clothier neither grew the wool himself nor bought it from the wool brogger, even if it reached him only in the form of yarn already spun or cloth already woven, it normally became his property before it passed through the fulling mill, and he alone was responsible for its sale in the London market. The clothier was thus a very important figure in the industrial life of Tudor England. He was often a man of wealth and sometimes of considerable social standing. How the Wiltshire clothier of the sixteenth century spent or invested his money, the figure he cut in the county, his social aspirations and connexions—these are all matters concerning which there is some amount of evidence yet available.

The most remarkable clothier of Wiltshire in the Tudor period was undoubtedly William Stumpe of Malmesbury, whose history has regularly been quoted together with that of Winchcombe of Newbury as illustrative of the career of a hero of sixteenth-century *Frühkapitalismus*.[1] Little is known of his origins save that they were humble; his father was said to have been a weaver before rising to be a clothier and also to have been at one time parish clerk of North Nibley, a few miles beyond the Gloucestershire border,[2] where

[1] Ashley, *Introduction to English Economic History* (1909), ii, 230; Lipson, *Economic History of England* (1937), i, 477–8; Salzman, *Medieval English Industries* (1923), 233; Brentano, *Eine Geschichte der wirtschaftlichen Entwicklung Englands* (1927), ii, 68. Apart from the incidental references by these historians to the famous passage in Leland's *Itinerary*, i, 132, and to Turner's *Selections from the Records of the City of Oxford* (1880), 184–6, the only notable account of Stumpe's activities is that provided by Canon F. H. Manley in an important series of short articles on the family history of the Stumpes contributed to *Wilts. Notes and Queries*, viii. Canon Manley in particular summarized the wills and *inquisitiones post mortem* of Stumpe and his family and also drew upon the manuscripts of the College of Arms and of Charlton House.

[2] Aubrey, Natural History of Wilts., Bodl. MS. Aubrey 2, f. 143.

his brother Thomas apparently continued to live as a comparatively lowly tiller of the soil.[1] But as early as 1524 William Stumpe was one of the four richest men dwelling in Malmesbury,[2] and thenceforth it is certain that he invested much money, particularly after the fall of the monasteries, in the purchase of land both in north-west Wiltshire and in eastern Gloucestershire. He was sufficiently unscrupulous on one occasion to attempt to appropriate four mills and twenty-six acres of adjacent land, all formerly the property of Kingswood abbey and belonging to an individual of no importance inhabiting a distant shire—if the plea of the latter is to be credited.[3] At his death in 1552 he owned an immense aggregation of property in the Cotswold area and the adjoining vale country, from Tewkesbury and Woodchester to Warminster and Wootton Basset.[4] As he was twice impleaded in chancery by aggrieved copyholders whom he had evicted from holdings in manors under his control it may be surmised that he was one of the landlords of the new style whom immemorial custom did not restrain from exploiting their possessions as business investments.[5]

Most notable among the many fragments of monastic property which came into his hands was the site of Malmesbury abbey itself, for which, together with some neighbouring lands formerly also belonging to the abbey, he paid into the court of augmentations in 1544 some fifteen hundred pounds odd.[6] He had already begun his famous experiment by installing his looms and weavers in the vacant monastic buildings, and no doubt it was largely his activities which were responsible for raising the annual production of cloths in Malmesbury to the remarkable figure of three thousand.[7] It may be assumed that the establishment of this workshop was at least for the moment a profitable

[1] The will of Thomas Stumpe, husbandman, who survived his wealthy brother by a few years, was abstracted by Canon Manley from the original at the Probate Office, Gloucester, *Wilts. Notes and Queries*, viii, 531.

[2] Ex. K.R. Subs. 197/153.

[3] E.C.P. 1080/26–31.

[4] *I.p.m.*, pr. *Wilts. Notes and Queries*, viii, 391–5.

[5] E.C.P. 1111/19–21 and 1319/63–5.

[6] *L.P. Henry VIII*, XIX, i, 167, 502; ii, 414.

[7] Leland, *Itinerary*, 8, 132; *vide supra*, p. 17.

venture, since in 1546 minutes of an agreement were drawn up between Stumpe and the city of Oxford with a view to his utilizing similarly the empty buildings of Osney abbey, and he even began subsidiary negotiations with the dean and chapter of the new cathedral there with regard to their rights in the lands and streams near by.[1] But though this grandiose project never came to fruition—possibly owing to the failure of Stumpe to find the two thousand skilled employees for whose engagement the agreement stipulated [2]—there is other evidence which suggests that his industrial interests were not confined to Wiltshire. On one occasion a dispute with his factor in London revealed that he owned some thirty-two red stop-listed broadcloths which, it is significant to notice, were in the keeping of a cloth-worker there.[3] These cloths may have been woven at Malmesbury; but the presumption is that they were finished if not dyed for him in London. There is no evidence that any other contemporary Wiltshire clothier ever embarked upon such an industrial venture beyond the orthodox limits of his broadcloth manufacture. At one time Stumpe fell foul of a Berkshire cloth-maker with whom he may or may not have had dealings.[4] On yet another occasion he was charged by his neighbours the bailiff and burgesses of Tetbury with a design to usurp the control of their market, reputed to be one of the best for wool and yarn in Gloucestershire, in order to destroy it.[5] No doubt Stumpe preferred that the spinners and weavers of the district should take their wool and yarn from his hands and as his employees rather than that they should have an opportunity of buying small quantities for themselves in the open market from broggers; the case is of great interest as illustrating Stumpe in the role of a protagonist in the persistent class warfare raging between the large clothier and the small independent manufacturer.

Stumpe's activities as a wealthy industrialist were matched by his importance in a wider sphere. He sat as one of the

[1] Bodl. MS. Top. Oxon. c. 22, ff. 42 a and 69–72. The reference given by Turner, *Selections from the Records of the City of Oxford*, 186, is incorrect.

[2] This has been plausibly suggested by R. W. Jeffery in the *V.C.H. Oxfordshire*, i, 244.

[3] C.R. 11/60.   [4] E.C.P. 1049/43.   [5] C.R. 3/276.

burgesses for Malmesbury in the reformation parliament and very probably also on other occasions. He was appointed to the commission of the peace for Wiltshire in 1538 and was usually thenceforth one of the justices for both Wiltshire and Gloucestershire.[1] At the same time he also held many other administrative offices; he served on commissions of array and of gaol delivery, he was a subsidy collector and a commissioner appointed to take evidence from local witnesses on behalf of the courts at Westminster.[2] In 1545 he was appointed escheator for Gloucestershire and the marches of Wales.[3] His name was pricked as sheriff of Wiltshire not long before his death, and it perhaps throws some light on his character that his tenure of the office was marked by his refusal to pay the customary fees to the clerk of the peace for the delivery of prisoners from the county gaol.[4] In short, Stumpe rose to enter that select oligarchy of a dozen or so country gentlemen to whom the king committed the government of Wiltshire—no mean achievement for a self-made man and a clothier.

The evidence does not permit the making of any estimate of the factors to which Stumpe's advancement in the county was due; probably his wealth and personality and possibly also the direct favour of the king were chiefly responsible. There can be little doubt that he was personally acquainted with Henry VIII. A pleasant tale relates how on one occasion he entertained the latter with his retinue to an impromptu feast at Malmesbury[5]; the story even if legendary is none the less *ben trovato*. It may at least be surmised that it was due to the intervention of the king that in 1537 he was appointed to the office of receiver for north Wales to the court of augmentations; it may not have been

---

[1] *L.P. Hen. VIII*, XIII, 138 *et passim*.
[2] *L.P. Hen. VIII, passim*; Ex. K.R. Subs. 197/230; C.R. 18/157—Stumpe's signature, in a large round hand, was appended to the minutes of the evidence. The letter to Richard Scrope of Castle Combe dated 11 Nov. 34 Hen. VIII concerning arrangements for the collection of the tenths and fifteenths—B.M. MS. Add. 28,212, f. 45—was certainly written by an amanuensis.
[3] *L.P. Hen. VIII*, XX, 447.
[4] E.C.P. 1346/61.
[5] The story was repeated by Aubrey, Natural History of Wiltshire, Bodl. MS. Aubrey 2, f. 143, and by Fuller, *Worthies of England* (1662), 853, in his somewhat garbled account of Stumpe.

one of the plums, for north Wales was hardly rich in houses of religion, but it carried with it certain profits and a yearly salary of twenty pounds.[1] Possibly the regular presentation of accounts involved him in too much labour, for a few months before his death he resigned the office in exchange for an annual pension of forty pounds.[2] There is no reason to suppose that his connexion with north Wales was ever at all close, though shortly after his appointment to the receivership he acquired the leasehold of some property formerly belonging to Conway abbey.[3] But how long he continued to own this distant land in Carnarvonshire is not known.

As to his way of living there is little to be discovered. He kept in his household a French priest who was also a good gardener,[4] and who may therefore have planned for him the grounds of the Abbey House, a pleasant piece of mid-sixteenth-century domestic architecture which he caused to be erected inside the walls of the dissolved monastery. Here too within the abbey precincts there lived some of his weavers and workmen, though he probably did not build the 'street or two' for their accommodation which, when Leland visited Malmesbury, he was credited with the intention of erecting.[5] His munificence was illustrated by his gift of the great nave of the abbey church for parochial use; and it was mainly owing to his exertions that the licence necessary for the creation of the new parish was obtained from the archbishop of Canterbury.[6] On his death he conventionally forgave his weavers and tenants dwelling within the site of the monastery their debts, and he left the unusually large sum of forty pounds to be distributed among the poor people of Malmesbury.[7] Stumpe possessed

---

[1] *L.P. Hen. VIII*, XIII, i, 573; cf. also xx, 676 and Ex. Aug. Enrolments of Leases, 223, f. 391.

[2] Ex. Aug. Enrolments of Leases, 222, f. 375.   [3] *L.P. Hen. VIII*, XIII, i, 584.

[4] Page, *Letters of Denization and Acts of Naturalization for Aliens in England, 1509–1603* (1893), 28.

[5] Canon Manley, who is well acquainted with the site, believes that it was William Stumpe who erected the Abbey House but that he did not build the projected 'street or two'—*Wilts. Notes and Queries*. viii (1914–16), 389.

[6] Leland, *Itinerary*, i, 132; *Wilts. Notes and Queries*, viii (1914–16), 388.

[7] Will of William Stumpe, P.C.C. 26 Powell (1554), pr. *Wilts. Notes and Queries*, viii (1914–16), 390–1.

D

imagination and enterprise; and though he was probably a hard-headed and unscrupulous man of business it is perhaps not unduly fanciful to discern a touch of the *grand seigneur* in his character.

The history of his family serves to illustrate his social ambitions. He married three times. His first wife belonged to a younger branch of the house of Berkeley, and by her he had two sons, James and John.[1] Of his second wife, the widow of William Byllyng of Deddington in Oxfordshire, little is known; he was sued with her by her stepson for defrauding him of his inheritance.[2] His last wife was another widow, and he married her only two years before his death, when he left a third and infant son, William.[3] It may be inferred that he wished his eldest son, who was knighted during his own lifetime and to whom he bequeathed the bulk of his possessions, to be the founder of a county family, while his remaining two sons, to whom he left his looms and other comparatively small legacies, should follow him by earning their livings in the woollen industry. Of William, who was brought up in Norfolk, no information is readily forthcoming,[4] but John continued to live as a clothier at Malmesbury of which he was one of the borough trustees and which he represented in the parliament of 1584.[5] Sir James fulfilled almost completely what may be presumed to have been the hopes of his father; he enjoyed the favour of Queen Katherine Parr[6] and the friendship of the earl of Pembroke,[7] and until his early death in 1563 he in his turn was one of the more important county

[1] Smyth, *Lives of the Berkeleys* (1883), i, 267, quot. *Wilts. Notes and Queries*, viii (1914–16), 389.

[2] E.C.P. 948/85–7.

[3] *Wilts. Notes and Queries*, viii (1914–16), 389; cf. *Cal. Pat. Rolls Ed. VI*, iv, 66.

[4] *Wilts. Notes and Queries*, viii (1914–16), 484–7.

[5] C.R. 42/47; John Stumpe was fined by the London searchers for bringing defective cloth to Blackwell Hall in May 1561 and May 1562—Ex. K.R. Mem. Hil. 7 Eliz. 329–30. But it is often impossible to be certain as to the identity of the various John Stumpes whose names crop up from time to time in the records of the second half of the sixteenth century; there was not only the great clothier's second son but also his brother, who long survived him, and his nephew, the latter's youngest son, who were all called John.

[6] *L.P. Hen. VIII*, XXI, 472.

[7] S.P.D. Ed. VI, XIV, 57.

grandees. His first marriage, to the daughter of Sir Edward Baynton, allied him to a powerful Wiltshire family; his second wife was no less than the widow of Sir Edward and the half-sister of Queen Katherine Howard.[1] His only daughter and heiress married Sir Henry Knevett, and their three daughters, co-heiresses of the Stumpe fortune, married the earls of Suffolk, Lincoln, and Rutland,[2] so that in the seventeenth century the blood of the parvenu clothier was carried into the noblest families of the kingdom.

It is scarcely necessary to emphasize the very exceptional nature of Stumpe's career, though it differed more in degree than in kind from those of other clothiers in Tudor Wiltshire. Far more representative in many ways of the generality of his colleagues was his younger contemporary Matthew Kyng, another clothier of Malmesbury. Like Stumpe, Kyng was probably not by birth a native of the borough[3]; possibly he came from Bremhill, if it was his father William Kyng who at one time acquired a copyhold in the manor for the lives of his three sons John, Matthew and Robert.[4] It is probably not unjust to conclude that it was a turbulent and unscrupulous character that brought Matthew Kyng into the law courts with a most unusual frequency; on one occasion he was alleged to have acquired some twenty-three pounds worth of yarn from a Northampton merchant by sharp practice,[5] on another he fell foul of a carrier whose services he had hired for the transport of a score of cloths from Tetbury to London,[6] on a third occasion he was sued for debt in London,[7] and yet again

---

[1] *Wilts. Notes and Queries*, viii (1914–16), 448–50.

[2] Of the three daughters of Sir Henry Knevett and Elizabeth Stumpe the eldest married firstly Richard, son of Lord Rich, and secondly the first earl of Suffolk; the second married the third earl of Lincoln; the youngest married firstly Sir William Bevill of Kilkhampton, Cornwall, and secondly the sixth earl of Rutland —*Wilts. Notes and Queries*, viii (1914–16), 449–50. The genealogy given by Aubrey in his Natural History of Wiltshire, Bodl. MS. Aubrey 2, f. 144, is thus defective.

[3] At least, no member of the Kyng family was assessed in Malmesbury for the 1524 subsidy—Ex. K.R. Subs. 197/153—and there is no evidence that anybody bearing the name dwelt previously in Malmesbury. Matthew Kyng of Malmesbury must not be confused with his namesake and contemporary who for many years was clerk of the check in Ireland.

[4] C.P. Eliz. II, 107/4.   [5] E.C.P. 1115/88–9; C.R. 16/21.

[6] E.C.P. 1108/75.   [7] E.C.P. 1093/20.

he was charged with having attempted to facilitate the sale
of his own goods by appropriating the cloth-mark of a
Gloucestershire clothier.[1] Between December 1560 and
December 1562 he was fined by the London searchers of
cloth for bringing defective fabrics to sell at Blackwell
Hall no less than four times—no other Wiltshire clothier
was fined more often within the same period.[2]

But though the stigma of deceitful dealing may cling to
his name Kyng was a man of some standing; he represented
Malmesbury in the first parliament of 1554 and again in
1555 and 1557, he probably owned a fair amount of land,[3]
and he himself claimed more than once that he set many
of the king's subjects on work.[4] The lawsuits in which he
engaged over titles to property both real and personal were
indeed quite as numerous as those concerning his trade;
he defended his right to a tenement and garden in Malmesbury,[5] he was sued for taking possession by violence of
twenty-four acres of pasture at Garsdon,[6] he was alleged to
have withheld the title-deeds of a hundred acres of land near
Malmesbury belonging to John Stumpe,[7] and another time
he was charged with seizing plate and household goods to
the value of over eighty pounds which had belonged to a
Malmesbury resident who had recently died, and in defiance
of the latter's heirs.[8] This last case is of particular interest
since the plaintiff, a weaver of Wotton-under-Edge, alleged
that he could get no justice in the common law courts as
the essential witnesses were the friends or employees of
Kyng and his confederates and refused to give evidence—
such was the power of a clothier in an industrial area. But
the most famous of Kyng's quarrels must undoubtedly have
been his feud with a certain Ralph Bolton, a farmer of Cole
Park; Kyng and his allies were alleged to have raided
Bolton's house more than once and inflicted serious damage
on both his property and his person; there was a scene in

---

[1] Ex. K.R. Mem. East. 4 Ed. VI, 5.   [2] Ex. K.R. Mem. Hil. 7 Eliz. 329–32.
[3] He bought considerable property in Bisley from Sir James Stumpe in 1552—
Cal. Pat. Rolls Ed. VI, iv, 259.
[4] C.R. 16/21.   [5] E.C.P. 1240/69.
[6] C.R. 18/157—the plaintiff alleged that he was 'a man of dissolute and
luxurious lyving'.
[7] C.P. Eliz. II, 158/47.   [8] E.C.P. 1207/30–1.

the market-place at Malmesbury during the fair there, in
the course of which Kyng and Bolton came to blows, and
the matter was then pursued from court to court at Westminster.[1] Eventually Kyng was bound over by the privy
council in a hundred marks to keep the peace towards
Bolton[2] and the whole dispute was subsequently referred
to the arbitration of Sir James Stumpe. His award was
that Bolton should deliver twenty pounds in money and
three kine to Kyng and that Kyng should then give him a
discharge of all debts, strifes and controversies.[3] This did
not, however, prevent further litigation,[4] and the upshot of
this *cause célèbre* is unknown. It may have been still proceed-
ing when Kyng died; with a final characteristic touch he
left his affairs out of order and the ownership of his large
accumulation of property in and around Malmesbury was
disputed by his daughter and her husband John Stumpe—
possibly the second son of the great clothier—and one John
Kyng, citizen and tallow-chandler of London, who may have
been a relative.[5]

A third Malmesbury clothier of importance and contemporary with William Stumpe and Matthew Kyng was
John Hedges. Practically no light can be thrown upon his
industrial activity, though he was once pursued in the star
chamber by a weaver whom he in turn impleaded in chancery.[6]
In May 1561, not long before his death, he was fined two
pounds by the London cloth searchers for bringing to market
some cloth lacking the statutory breadth.[7] But already in 1524
he was a citizen of substance, though not, indeed, nearly so
rich as Stumpe,[8] and at his death he was lord of the manors
of Easton Grey and Shipton Moyne—there were still villeins
attached to the latter—though he actually lived in Malmes-

---

[1] S.C., P. & M. 4/56; Ex. K.R. Mem. East. 4 & 5 P. & M. 49–50; S.P.D.,
P. & M. VIII, 45.

[2] *Acts of the Privy Council*, 1554–6, 240.

[3] S.P.D. Add. Eliz. XI, 6.   [4] C.P. Eliz. II, 28/52.

[5] C.P. Eliz. II, 107/49; John Kyng alleged that Matthew Kyng had sold and
conveyed to him and his heirs all his property in Malmesbury and the neighbourhood—possibly it was another instance of the latter's double-dealing. There was
no *inquisitio post mortem* on the property of Matthew Kyng, and a search for his
will has proved fruitless.

[6] E.C.P. 1068/36.   [7] Ex. K.R. Mem. Hil. 7 Eliz. 331.

[8] Ex. K.R. Subs. 197/155.

bury, where he owned a house.[1] His legacies in money amounted to over a hundred and fifty pounds—including twelve pounds to the 'poore people' of Malmesbury, so many of whom had no doubt been in his employment.[2] He represented Malmesbury in the two parliaments of 1554 and was commonly referred to as a 'gentleman'. After his death his widow and his son Thomas, by whom the bulk of his property was inherited, continued, at least for a time, in the clothing business[3]; the latter subsequently married a wealthy heiress and migrated to Gloucestershire.[4] Of the trio of Malmesbury clothiers of whom some account has now been given John Hedges was undoubtedly the most typical of his class; he was neither a genius like Stumpe nor—as far as the evidence goes—a scoundrel like Kyng.

Further south, in the main industrial area of the county, there was to be found a notable group of such well-to-do manufacturers. There was Alexander Langford of Trowbridge, who was made known to the traveller Leland by his Christian name as a great clothier there[5]; he was in fact the first member of a prosperous clothing family and an ancestor of the lord chancellor Clarendon.[6] Another even more celebrated Wiltshire industrial family was founded by Thomas Yerbury, whose activities were divided between Trowbridge and the neighbouring Bradford.[7] Both the Langfords and the Yerburys intermarried with a third famous clothing family, the Hortons, who were established at Bradford and Iford, hard by the Somersetshire border, and also at Westwood, a local hamlet. The first member of this family to rise to eminence in the woollen industry was Thomas Horton the elder, who described himself as

[1] I.p.m. Ch. Ser. 134/218 and Ex. Ser. ii, 1001/8.

[2] Will of John Hedges (1561), P.C.C. 2 Streat.

[3] Thomas Hedges was fined by the London cloth searchers in July 1561 and 'Wydoo Hedges' in April 1562—Ex. K.R. Mem. Hil. 7 Eliz. 329–31. *Supra*, p. 25.

[4] Information concerning Thomas Hedges is to be found in C.P. Eliz. ii, 14/76, 91/8, and 97/9; Thomas Hedges of 'Underedge' in Gloucestershire was fined in 1569 for bringing defective cloth to the market at Blackwell Hall—Ex. K.R. Mem. Mich. 13 Eliz. 263.

[5] Leland, *Itinerary*, i, 136. The surname Alexander was unknown at Trowbridge in the sixteenth century, while Alexander Langford was indubitably a very wealthy clothier—the evidence of the subsidy rolls alone is decisive.

[6] *Wilts. Notes and Queries*, i (1893–5), 155–9, 166.

[7] The will of Thomas Yerbury (1573) will be found in P.C.C. 12 Peter.

the second son of John Horton of Lullington in Somerset
and who flourished as a clothier at Bradford in the opening
decades of the sixteenth century. He managed to accumulate much landed property in Somerset, Wiltshire and
Gloucestershire and he also built—presumably as investments—what Leland later described as 'dyvers fair houses'
in Trowbridge.[1] His munificence was exemplified by the
chantry, school and church house which he set up at Bradford,[2] where his memory was perpetuated by a memorial
brass in the parish church. Though in 1530 he died child-
less his collateral descendants were later to be found
mingled among the chief industrial families of the county.[3]
It is indeed tempting to discern towards the middle of the
sixteenth century something like an oligarchy of large
capitalist families in central Wiltshire—the Langfords,
Yerburys and Yews of Trowbridge, the Batts and Flowers
of Devizes, the Barkesdales and Blagdens of Keevil, the
Chiverses and Formans of Calne, the Hortons and Baileys
of Bradford, the Longs of Steeple Ashton, the Whitakers of
Westbury—whose close social cohesion is suggested by
their frequent intermarriages [4]; through the Longs of Whaddon they were even connected with the Berkshire Winch-
combes, the family of Jack of Newbury.[5]
The social origins of these capitalist families were
diverse; the Hortons and the Longs were probably drawn
from the class of small landowners, while it may be con-
jectured that the Batts, the Whitakers and the Yerburys
were as humble in their beginnings as the Stumpes.[6]

---

[1] Leland, *Itinerary*, i, 136. *Infra*, p. 44.   [2] *Infra*, p. 43.

[3] Further information about Thomas Horton may be found in—Jones, *Bradford-on-Avon, passim*; Stote, *Abstract of Copies of Court Rolls and Other Documents Relating to the Manors of Bradford and Westwood, Wilts. Arch. Mag.* xli (1920–2), 242; *Wilts. Notes and Queries*, ii (1896–8), 336; iii (1899–1901), 372; iv (1902–4), 168; *L.P. Hen. VIII*, I, i, 210; IV, i, 309; E.C.P. 319/27, 411/26, and 642/40. His will—P.C.C. 20 Jankyn—has been summarized in *Wilts. Notes and Queries*, iv, 165.

[4] Genealogical tables of the Long family will be found in *Miscellanea Genealogica et Heraldica*, New Ser. iii (1880), and of the Bradford and Trowbridge clothing families in Jones, *Bradford-on-Avon: a History and Description*, ed. Beddoe (1907).

[5] The will of Henry Long (1558), P.C.C. 75 Noodes, mentions his brother-in-law Harry Winchcombe—husband of his sister Agnes.

[6] The ancestry ascribed to the Whitakers by Sir R. C. Hoare—*History of Modern Wiltshire, Hundred of Westbury*, 43—is demonstrably fabulous.

Industrial connections offered no bar to their ascent of the social ladder; the Chiverses and the Hortons illustrated a characteristic of English social history by entering the ranks of the county families, Flowers and Longs and Yerburys were eventually to be found in every walk of life, while the Yews dropped back into the peasantry from which they had sprung.[1] Meanwhile, in the hey-day of their clothing activity, they lived in fair comfort, often with a staff of domestic servants. They slept on the newly introduced luxury of feather beds, they loaded their tables with tankards, goblets, and other pieces of silver plate, and they kept their stores of silken finery—no doubt Henry Long of Whaddon cut an impressive figure when he strolled abroad clad in his 'best satin doublet' and his 'gown faced with taffeta'.[2] Such prosperous clothiers provided carefully for their children. Christopher Stokes of Castle Coombe, who gave two hundred pounds as a dowry for his daughter on her marriage, was no exception.[3] The sons usually were put to follow the trade of the father, but sometimes a cadet was sent to make his fortune in London. At least one such entered the ranks of the merchant adventurers when in 1588 William Swadden, a clothier of Calne, apprenticed one of his sons to Richard Sheppard, later the master and father-in-law of Lionel Cranfield; the young Swadden served as a factor for some years overseas, while his father continued to sell his cloths to Sheppard.[4] A Forman of Calne rose to be lord mayor of London in 1538.[5] Other clothiers' sons were sent to study the law; a son and namesake of Henry Long of Whaddon entered the Inner Temple in 1552,[6] and in 1561 Edward Langford, son of

[1] Manley, History of Great Somerford, Wilts. Arch. Mag. xxxi (1899-1900), 288-9.
[2] Much information as to the way of living of the sixteenth-century clothier is to be found in wills.   [3] C.P. Eliz. II, 171/91.
[4] Cranfield papers, ledger-book of Richard Sheppard, passim; C.P. Eliz. I, s 4/41.
[5] Aubrey, Natural History of Wiltshire, 79; Beaven, The Aldermen of the City of London, i (1908), 131.
[6] Cooke, Students admitted to the Inner Temple 1547-1660 (1877), 13; cf. Miscellanea Genealogica et Heraldica, new ser. iii (1880), where Henry is erroneously stated to have been the eldest son. This Henry Long was the grandfather of Sir Walter Long, a minor politician and opponent of the king in the early seventeenth century.

Alexander Langford, was admitted to Lincoln's Inn,[1] whither he was followed in 1594 by Nash Whitaker of Tinhead.[2] The latter, however, subsequently returned home to take up his father's trade—apparently with success, though in 1606 he was presented by the local searchers for illegally stretching his cloths.[3]

It was not merely through their industrial activities or their way of living that the larger clothiers left their imprint upon English social history; the manner in which they spent or invested their wealth contributed much to their influence. In the early part of the century they gave generously to the church, not only by bequeathing money for the singing of masses and by the foundation of chantries but also by paying for the erection of new church buildings. At the end of the fifteenth century John Stokes, a clothier of Seend, gave an additional north aisle to his parish church,[4] and a little later the magnificent perpendicular church at Steeple Ashton was erected at the cost of two local clothiers, Walter Lucas and Robert Long.[5] Thomas Horton the elder not only founded a chantry and school at Bradford which he endowed with an annual income of over ten pounds from land but he also built a large church house there *ex lapide quadrato*.[6] But after the middle of the century the stream of benefactions almost dried up; the conscience of the clothier was usually satisfied with the perfunctory legacy of a few shillings to Salisbury cathedral and to his parish church.[7]

[1] C.R. 129/26; *Lincoln's Inn Admission Register* (1896), 68. This Alexander Langford was a son and namesake of the clothier mentioned by Leland : *supra*, p. 40.

[2] *Lincoln's Inn Admission Register*, 116. The will of Nash Whitaker, P.C.C. Wingfield 98, will be found summarized in *Wilts. Notes and Queries*, iv (1902–4), 111–12.

[3] Cunnington, *Records of the County of Wilts.* (1932), 14.

[4] His generosity was duly inscribed upon his memorial brass there.

[5] Leland, *Itinerary*, v, 83. The clothiers' gift was recorded in an inscription inside the church.

[6] Leland, *Itinerary*, i, 136; *L.P. Hen. VIII*, IV, 309; cf. Jones, *Bradford-on-Avon*, 115–16.

[7] One notable exception was Adam Archard of Malmesbury, who left £1 'to be imployed and bestowed in the churche of Malmesburie in writing uppon the wall in the most convenient places the Lordes prayer and other places (*sic*) and sentences of scripture'. His will (1588) is to be found in P.C.C. 29 Rutland. Cf. also the restoration of the chantry chapel of St. Laurence, Warminster, in which at least one clothier took part—Hoare, *History of Modern Wiltshire, Hundred of Warminster*, 31.

The witness of his wealth was henceforth to be sought in secular rather than in ecclesiastical buildings. Already in the first quarter of the century Thomas Horton had built his 'dyvers fair houses' in Trowbridge, and other clothiers were also engaged in building.[1] The Abbey House built by William Stumpe at Malmesbury was a forerunner of not a few fine Elizabethan manor houses erected in country villages by successful clothiers; thus the wealth accumulated in the woollen industry was among the influences directly forwarding the progress of English architecture.

These secular building activities furnished in part a convenient outlet for the clothier's capital; but various means of investing wealth other than by the erection of houses lay open to him. The practice of giving and receiving casual loans of money upon interest was widespread in sixteenth-century England; it was in one sense, indeed, an extension of that highly developed system of credit on which the whole conduct of the woollen industry was based. The Wiltshire clothier was sometimes a borrower,[2] but probably more often he was a lender. John Grafton of Salisbury and Adam Archard of Malmesbury were two large clothiers who were indicted before the court of exchequer for breaking the usury laws[3]; the operations ot both were probably fairly extensive.[4] No doubt the affluent lent money whenever a profitable opportunity was offered; in the thirties a clothier lent fifty pounds to secure the election of a certain abbess of Wilton,[5] and a little later a mercer of Salisbury borrowed twenty-nine pounds from another clothier.[6] Certain transactions of Thomas Yerbury of Bradford and of Edward Horton of Westwood suggest that the impoverished country gentleman upon occasion fell into the debt of the rich manufacturer.[7] The

---

[1] Leland, *Itinerary*, i, 136.

[2] E.C.P. 1452/55–8; C.P. Eliz. II, 244/77; C.R. 223/102. Some information as to the business of a Wilton money-lender is to be found in S.C. Jas. I, 3/22.

[3] Ex. K.R. Mem. Mich. 10 Eliz. 159 and Mich. 16 Eliz. 126.

[4] Cf. Hammond and Aubrey, *Books of Examinations and Depositions*, 68 (*South. Rec. Soc. publ.* xvi), and C.P. Eliz. I R 8/32.

[5] E.C.P. 902/34.   [6] C.P. Eliz. II, 207/70.

[7] Jones, *Bradford-on-Avon: a History and Description*, ed. Beddoe, 250; Ex. Extents on Debts, 25 Eliz. 6.

security for such loans was sometimes land, but plate was also accepted; Henry Morris of Devizes, rich man as he was, was not above retaining a couple of silver spoons 'for pawnes'.[1]

But the building of houses, the purchase of plate and the lending of money were far less important as a means of investing wealth than the acquisition of land. The connexion between industry and agriculture in Tudor Wiltshire was very intimate, and it is often impossible to be certain how far the clothier purchased land in order to stock it with his sheep or even to raise crops upon it and not merely to let it for rent to someone else.[2] There is, however, no doubt that clothiers did acquire much landed property purely as an investment. There were admittedly few clothiers so rich as Thomas Long of Trowbridge, who possessed no less than nine manors[3]; but it was not uncommon to find clothiers exercising their rights as the owner of an advowson by presenting to country livings.[4] Although church property was comparatively seldom bought directly from the crown by country clothiers, yet it is probable that when the royal favourites and speculators had realized their profits a considerable proportion of the sometime monastic and chantry land found their way ultimately into their hands, if not by direct tenure at least upon long lease.[5] The accumulation of land by clothiers was certainly sufficiently large to arouse the fears of the country gentry, who procured the insertion into an act of 1576 of a clause by which their future acquisitions in Wiltshire, Somerset, and Gloucestershire were to be so limited that each clothier

[1] Will of Henry Morris (Mores) (1572), P.C.C. 2 Peter.
[2] *Vide supra*, pp. 11–13.
[3] I.p.m., Ex. ser. II, 1001/11.
[4] Examples can be found, e.g. in Aubrey, *Wiltshire Topographical Collections*, ed. Jackson (1862), 38 and 283—the clothiers being Henry Chivers, Roger Vince, and John Yew.
[5] William Stumpe of Malmesbury and John Adlam of Westbury bought monastic property directly from the crown—*vide supra*, and also *Ninth Report of the Deputy Keeper of the Public Record Office* (1848), 152, and *L.P. Hen. VIII*, XX, 420. Henry Goldney of Chippenham similarly bought chantry lands—Ex. K.R. Mem. Mich. 2 Eliz. 178. Cf. the fate of the lands of Lacock abbey as related by Baskerville, *English Monks and the Suppression of the Monasteries* (1937), 196–7; the Robert Bath mentioned as sharing in the spoils was Robert Whitaker *alias* Bathe, a clothier of Bishopstrow—*v. supra*, p. 12.

should own no more than twenty acres.[1] There is, however,
no evidence to suggest that any serious attempt to enforce
this curious piece of legislation was ever made, and its chief
interest lies in the illustration it affords of the class jealousy
subsisting between clothiers and country gentry in the west
country textile area.[2]

This class feeling was possibly more acute by 1576 than
it had been earlier in the century, for there are signs which
suggest that social distinctions in Wiltshire were hardening
during the reign of Elizabeth. The first heralds' visitation
of the county of which records survive took place in 1565;
several indubitably clothing families were actually accepted
as armigerous, but a number of clothiers were summoned
before Clarenceux king-of-arms where they 'disclaymed
the name of a gentelman', and a few, including so notable
an industrialist as Henry Goldney *alias* Farnewell of Chippenham, were even 'disgraded'.[3] But the social effect of
nascent antiquarian and legalistic currents of opinion[4] was
possibly less important than the final collapse in the early
sixties of that exceptionally high prosperity which had
generally prevailed in the broadcloth industry during the
reign of Henry VIII; there were indeed rich clothiers in
Wiltshire during the last four decades of the century, but
there was no one of the calibre of William Stumpe whose
greatness could overleap the barriers of class. The landed
gentry practically monopolized not only the administration
of the country but also its parliamentary representation—
a change of great significance whose cause has yet to be
explored. In the period before 1560 the parliamentary
representation of the boroughs lying within the industrial
area of Wiltshire, as far as can be surmised, was still open
to the industrial class, and large clothiers, particularly if

[1] 18 Eliz. c. 16.
[2] A calendar of the Wiltshire feet of fines for the sixteenth century is to be
found in *Wilts. Notes and Queries, passim*. On the question of the friction between
clothiers and gentry in the west country during the later sixteenth century there
are some illuminating remarks in Unwin, *Studies in Economic History*, 187–9.
[3] *Genealogist*, new ser. xiii (1896–7), 91–4. For Henry Goldney *alias* Farnewell, *v. supra*, p. 13.
[4] The part played by the college of arms as a defensive weapon of the aristo-
cracy and gentry in heightening class consciousness is a subject which has yet to
be investigated.

they lived within a parliamentary borough, sometimes sat in the commons.[1] But from the accession of Elizabeth onwards Wiltshire clothiers were rarely to be found in the house. John Scott sat for Chippenham in 1572 and John Stumpe for Malmesbury in 1584, but they were exceptions; and the last instance of the election of a clothier occurred when the borough of Calne returned John Noyes to the first parliament of James I.[2]

But although the Wiltshire clothiers practically ceased to be directly represented in parliament by one of their number, and thus incidentally laid themselves open to the vexatious albeit ineffective act of 1576, there is no reason to believe that their influence with the government at all diminished; throughout the period they continued to fight on equal terms before the privy council their battles of controversy with the merchant adventurers, and towards the end of the century their power may even have increased. No government could close its eyes to the clothiers; not only did they support the livelihood of so many families throughout the kingdom, but their activities also contributed in more than one way to the royal revenue. The woollen industry was subject to the aulnage dues, and a tax was levied upon the export of cloth. Further, the wealth of the individual clothier furnished a reserve upon which throughout the century the government did not scruple to draw; several Wiltshire clothiers were assessed in 1522 for a forced loan of fifty pounds each,[3] and among the seventy-five Wiltshire gentlemen who at the hour of need in 1588 lent twenty-five or fifty pounds each to the queen there was a fair sprinkling of clothiers.[4] Clothiers were sometimes to be found acting as collectors of tenths and fifteenths and subsidies,[5] though any such administra-

---

[1] This is a tentative conclusion from the returns for the reformation parliament and the parliaments of the reign of Mary I, which alone have survived, and it may well be modified if ever further information becomes available. Cf. Notestein, *The Winning of the Initiative by the House of Commons* (1924), 62.

[2] His colleague William Swadden belonged to a clothing family and may very possibly also have been a clothier.

[3] *L.P. Hen. VIII*, III, 1049.   [4] B.M. Stowe MS. 165, f. 29.

[5] William Stumpe was frequently a subsidy collector; a generation later Alexander Langford of Trowbridge was on one occasion bound as such to pay £140 to the queen in discharge of his office—Ex. K.R. Mem. East. 17 Eliz. 189.

tive help as they may have given was far less important than the high figures at which their own contributions were frequently assessed. For the unparliamentary subsidy of 1545, for instance, the whole hundred of Malmesbury was rated at £11. 5s. 8d., of which exactly seven pounds was furnished by Stumpe and his two colleagues, John Hedges and Matthew Kyng.[1] Elsewhere at the same time certain other clothiers were assessed for sums considerably higher than the £3. 6s. 8d. at which Stumpe's contribution was fixed; thus Richard Batt of Devizes and Alexander Langford of Trowbridge were rated at £4, while Anthony Passion and Thomas Long, both also of Trowbridge, were assessed for £7 and £8 respectively.[2] Few country gentlemen paid much more. Whether these clothiers were really so much richer than Stumpe or whether their wealth, which was possibly invested less in land than in movable goods, was merely believed to be more readily taxable, must be a matter for conjecture only.

It is at least certain that throughout the century a high proportion of the money collected for subsidies in the hundreds of the Wiltshire industrial area was contributed by clothiers[3]; and it is difficult to resist the conclusion that either they were being immoderately fleeced for the ultimate benefit of the landed gentry or else that they did not play that part in the political and social life of the county to which their wealth and economic importance corresponded —or possibly and even probably both.[4] In the industrial districts of sixteenth-century Wiltshire a new capitalist order had come into existence, but the social and political privileges characteristic of a bygone age still remained and were even accentuated in the course of the century. A government solicitous for the tranquillity of the industrial districts indeed gave ear to the country clothiers, the strength of whose influence in the council chamber has already been remarked; but with the rarest exceptions the offices of dignity and power in local administration were

[1] Ex. K.R. Subs. 197/230.   [2] Ex. K.R. Subs. 197/230.

[3] Trowbridge clothiers, e.g. were again assessed at very high figures for the subsidy of 1587—Ex. K.R. Subs. 259/21.

[4] Cf. Cheyney, *A History of England from the Defeat of the Armada to the Death of Elizabeth*, ii (1926), 238–43.

withheld from their grasp. And so although the landed gentry from time to time recruited their numbers from the prosperous clothing families it yet remains true that the Wiltshire clothier was sustaining a conflict on two fronts— on the one side against his own workfolk, and on the other against the county families whose preponderant position rested on the ownership of land.

IV

CUSTOM AND COERCION IN THE WILTSHIRE WOOLLEN INDUSTRY BEFORE THE COCKAYNE EXPERIMENT

HOW far the persistent interference of successive Tudor governments was a help rather than a hindrance to the progress of the woollen manufacture is a question of some complexity. But it is at least certain that even by itself the broadcloth industry was not without some means of maintaining the calibre of its products. The cloth merchant in London no doubt scrutinized as closely as he could the quality of his purchases—the prices paid for cloth certainly varied greatly. And although few may have gone to the trouble of wetting and examining the packs of cloth, each containing ten pieces over two dozen yards long, yet probably many merchant adventurers were wont to do as Richard Sheppard, who exacted a signed declaration of the goodness of his cloths from every clothier with whom he did business.[1] It would in fact appear that these guarantees were abused, for in 1601 it was enacted that merchants should not in future take advantage of clothiers' signatures, but that cloths which were subsequently found to have been unduly stretched might be returned to their maker at the latter's costs.[2] But in any case the word of the clothier was in all likelihood less esteemed than the reputation of his cloth-mark.

At Blackwell Hall the price of each pack of ten broadcloths varied according not only to the quality of the fabric but also to the reputation of the maker whose mark it bore.[3] The employment of a cloth-mark was enjoined in particular by an act of 1536,[4] and the privy council on one occasion intervened to enforce the law.[5] But the use of the cloth-

[1] Cranfield papers, ledger-book of Richard Sheppard, *passim*.
[2] 43 Eliz. c. 10.
[3] The history of the cloth-mark in the woollen industry has been related in Schechter, *The Historical Foundations of the Law relating to Trade-marks* (1925), 78–100.
[4] 27 Hen. VIII, c. 12.
[5] *Acts of the Privy Council*, 1591, 98–9.

mark—usually a simple geometrical device with the initials of the owner—was undoubtedly long anterior to any statutory enactment, and its maintenance depended less on the authority of the government than upon the needs of the individual clothier, for whom the possession of an honoured cloth-mark constituted a valuable advantage which he would not lightly forgo. William Wilkins, a Trowbridge clothier, when driven by trade losses to sell his cloth-mark, received for it £20—a considerable sum.[1] The fabrics of Nicholas Passion of Westbury, long after they had left his hands, were known by their mark in the distant Hamburg market where the merchant adventurer or the Hansard *Englandsfahrer* trafficked with the German wholesale importer.[2] Sometimes a clothier owned more than one mark; John Grant of Monkton Farleigh worked his device in different colours for coarse or fine cloths,[3] while Robert Ray of Salisbury employed both the 'red castle' and the 'golden arrow'.[4] Cloth-marks were not infrequently bequeathed in wills.[5] The shrewd merchant adventurer no doubt did as Richard Sheppard, who usually noted in his ledger the marks of the various consignments of cloth which he purchased.[6] It is not surprising that the dishonest clothier should sometimes have attempted to appropriate the mark of a successful rival; thus in 1551 Matthew Kyng of Malmesbury was indicted before the barons of the exchequer on the charge of having counterfeited the cloth-mark of a Gloucestershire clothier.[7] The cloth-mark, in fact, was a convenient and quasi-automatic device by which the responsible manufacturer was encouraged to improve the standard of his fabrics; and there can be little doubt that as a result it helped to maintain the quality of the national output of cloth.

[1] C.R. 115/51.
[2] Ehrenberg, *Hamburg u. England*, 279. This identification is, of course, no more than very probable.
[3] Cranfield papers, ledger-book of Richard Sheppard, *passim*.
[4] Cranfield papers, account dating from April 1605.
[5] E.g. the wills of the family of Whitaker *alias* Bathe, pr. in *Wilts. Notes and Queries*, iv, 108–11.
[6] Cranfield papers, ledger-book of Richard Sheppard, *passim*. As a result, this precious volume contains a magnificent collection of cloth-marks.
[7] Ex. K.R. Mem. East. 4 Ed. VI, 5; *supra*, p. 38.

E

But the insufficiency of these trade safeguards by themselves was one of many motives which led to the progressive interference of the government with the conduct of the industry—an interference whose origins can be traced far back into the middle ages. Much industrial legislation had already been enacted during the reign of Edward IV; and under the Tudors a vast body of laws deeply affecting the maker of broadcloth reached the statute-book. Some account of the sporadic efforts of the government to eliminate or at least to control the middlemen who dealt in wool has already been given,[1] and an estimate has also been made of the effect upon the Wiltshire woollen industry of the act of 1555 limiting the ownership of looms.[2] These were, however, but two instances of the attention of the government. Hardly a phase of the industrial process, from the winding of wools to the use of gig-mills for raising the nap on cloth, escaped legislative interference. As early as 1511 an act defined in detail the relationship of the clothier and his various employees,[3] and much subsequent legislation was repeated and codified in 1563 by the famous act of apprentices.[4]

Foremost among the subjects of regulation was the length, breadth and weight of broadcloths. The first enactment enjoining the measurement of cloth dated from the end of the twelfth century; a hundred years later Edward I created the office of the aulnager—who was to measure all cloths before they were offered for sale—and in the reign of Edward IV the aulnagership was further developed. During the greater part of the sixteenth century the farm of the Wiltshire aulnage was held by successive generations of the Dauntsey family, and their deputies were to be found in the chief clothing centres of the county. It does not seem that the aulnagers in general throughout the kingdom did their work with any approach to thoroughness during the reign of Henry VIII; in 1534 they were ordered by proclamation to be diligent and circumspect,[5] but within less than two years the governor of the merchant

---

[1] *Supra*, pp. 7 ff.   [2] *Supra*, pp. 17–18.   [3] 3 Hen. VIII, c. 6.
[4] 5 Eliz. c. 4.
[5] B.M. MS. Harl. 442, f. 127, pr. *L.P. Hen. VIII*, VII, 549.

adventurers was reiterating the familiar complaints of the faulty manufacture of English cloths.[1] It would actually appear that in Wiltshire the Dauntseys and their deputies, without any inquiry into the calibre of the broadcloths, were simply in the habit of agreeing with the clothier for what amounted to the sale of the aulnage seals, which were then affixed to the cloth by the latter and in his own good time.[2] In fact, the importance of the aulnager under the Tudors had come to be chiefly fiscal rather than industrial.[3]

Since, therefore, the aulnager system failed to fulfil the purpose for which it had been designed, it is not surprising to find that during the reign of Henry VIII attempts were made to discover other means of providing that regulation which the London cloth merchants believed to be indispensable for the manufacture of honest cloth. These at first chiefly took the form of efforts to stimulate by legislation the use of cloth-marks and of seals indicating the place of manufacture which were to be affixed to each cloth.[4] In 1536 there was enacted a statute sponsored by Sir Richard Gresham and other merchant adventurers which included among its clauses a revision of the standard sizes of broadcloths and kerseys; for this reason it provoked some three years later from a number of clothiers a protest of which the privy council took account.[5] Such measures were by themselves found eventually to be insufficient, and during the last parliament of the reign a bill was read in the house of lords for the true making of cloths in the west country broadcloth area.[6] This bill not improbably embodied some of the provisions of the subsequent statute of 1550 by which, through the appointment of overseers of cloth by justices of the peace in the industrial districts, the first step was taken towards building up new machinery for the enforcement of legislative regulation.[7] This momentous innovation

[1] S.P. Hen. VIII, cv, 250.

[2] Ex. Dep. by Comm. Hil. 30 Eliz. 8. Cf. in particular the evidence of John Dauntsey and of John Webb *alias* Rawlyns.

[3] This point has been made, though hardly stressed, by Lohmann—*Die staatliche Regelung der englischen Wollindustrie* (1900), 59.

[4] 14 & 15 Hen. VIII, c. 3; 26 Hen. VIII, c. 16; 27 Hen. VIII, c. 12.

[5] 27 Hen. VIII, c. 12; *Acts of the Privy Council*, 1540-2, 156, 192.

[6] *Lords' Journals*, i, 286, quot. *L.P. Hen. VIII*, xxi, ii, 389.

[7] 3 & 4 Ed. VI, c. 2.

was further developed by the great act of 1552, which
enjoined the appointment of cloth searchers upon the chief
officer of every town[1]; thus the supervision of textile manufacture was embodied as a function of the new system of
local government which was in process of development
under the Tudors. Other clauses of the act of 1552 exactly
specified the size and weight of standard broadcloth by
measurements; they were subsequently modified in 1558,
1585 and 1607.[2]

Nevertheless the temptation to economize in the use of
wool by over-stretching the cloth on tenters to the required
length remained, and the immediate efficacy of the act of
1552 is at least highly doubtful[3]; in 1558 many clothiers
feared to attend Bartholomew Fair at London lest their
cloths should be seized and forfeited for faulty manufacture.[4] It is certain that the mercantile interests whose
activity may be suspected to have supplied the driving
force in the enactment of the statutes of 1550 and 1552
were still unsatisfied; and a further expedient to secure
their ends was made possible by the predominance, amount-
ing almost to monopoly in the case of broadcloths, of the
London market. Practically all Wiltshire cloths save the
few consumed locally, for instance, had ultimately to pass
through the bottle-neck of Blackwell Hall, together with
the output of many other textile areas; and to have the
cloths undergo a second examination there must have seemed
much preferable to a mere continuance of their trust in the
local aulnagers and searchers. That cloths already searched
locally had been recently exempted by statute from further
search at Blackwell Hall did not restrain the cloth merchants.[5]
And so in the summer of 1559 they brought pressure to
bear upon the rulers of the city of London; a committee
of aldermen was appointed to debate with them touching
the enforcement of the act of 1552, a visit was paid in May

[1] 5 & 6 Ed. VI, c. 6.
[2] 4 & 5 P. & M. c. 5; 27 Eliz. c. 17; 4 Jac. I, c. 2. The official prescription
of the size of cloths embodied, of course, no new policy.
[3] Section 12 of the Act of 5 & 6 Ed. VI, c. 6, forbade the use of any tenters
with 'wrinche rope or ringe' or of any other 'Engyne unlawfullye to streyne or
tretche any Clothe'.
[4] *Acts of the Privy Council*, 1556-8, 379-80.
[5] 4 & 5 P. & M. c. 5, sect. xvii.

1560 to the city recorder at his chamber in Sergeant's Inn for perusing the title of the city to the measuring of cloths, and the case of the city was laid before the barons of the exchequer.[1] Action was then taken. A grant of special privileges for the London aulnager had already been obtained from the queen by letters patent in the previous January,[2] and in the autumn the existing aulnager and his staff were pensioned off.[3] One John Flete was thereupon appointed aulnager for the city with five assistant cloth searchers,[4] and the new guardians of the law were established in offices hard by Blackwell Hall with instructions to search all cloth brought there for sale.[5] Thus ingeniously had the drapers and merchant adventurers caused their trap to be laid.

As a result, the country clothiers who arrived at Blackwell Hall with their wares in December 1560 found to their anger and dismay that they were required to pay aulnage dues to the city—one halfpenny per cloth—that their cloths were liable to search and that fines might be exacted from them for shortcomings in size or weight. For the most part it would seem that they submitted, though with a bad grace, in the hope that their cloths would at least not be plunged into water to discover whether they had been over-stretched—a process of great inconvenience to the clothier even if at the end his cloths were found sufficient.[6] However, from December 1560 onwards some hundreds of manufacturers from all parts of the kingdom, and not infrequently including notable Wiltshire clothiers, were fined in the course of each year by the London aulnager for bringing defective cloth to Blackwell Hall; and subsequently, upon the request of the mayor and aldermen of the city of London, lists of the offenders' names were

---

[1] Guildhall, City of London Repertories, 14, ff. 52, 54, 61, 163, 333.

[2] *Ibid.* 14, f. 396-7; 15, f. 64.

[3] *Ibid.* 14, ff. 364 b, 386 b. Cf. Ex. Bills and Answers, 48/73.

[4] Guildhall, City of London Repertories, 14, ff. 397, 399. The five cloth searchers were George Clough, Francis Langley, John Leake, Robert Nicholls, and Walter Spencer.

[5] These offices were soon afterwards 'amended' for their use—*ibid.* 14, f. 501.

[6] Many clothiers could recollect a generation later their feelings when the London searchers claimed to examine their cloths—Ex. Dep. by Comm. Hil. 30 Eliz. 8

from time to time put on record in the court of exchequer.[1] It is probable that for some years the new broom swept fairly clean and that the acts of 1552 and 1558 were in general enforced upon cloth sent to London from the country, though, indeed, it was known that the searchers acted with a certain amount of discretion lest dangerous disorders should be provoked.[2] Nevertheless, it would seem that the pristine efficiency of the five London cloth searchers eventually declined; after the first couple of years they certainly exacted fines less often. In 1572 one of them protested at the amount of false and deceitful cloth which his colleagues allowed to pass.[3] Possibly it may be that the clothiers of Wiltshire and the neighbouring counties had learnt their lesson at least for the moment, for a little later John Leake, another London searcher, while tacitly admitting the charges, pointed out that west country broadcloths were usually less strained than other fabrics.[4]

Yet however mild the activities of the cloth searchers at Blackwell Hall may ultimately have become, the resentment of the country clothiers did not abate. They would readily have agreed to compound for the payment of aulnage in London, so as to avoid the searching of their cloths.[5] Some of them succeeded in eluding molestation by sending complaints to Burleigh[6]; others escaped by quietly evading or defiantly confronting the searchers.[7] It is possible that the grievance was felt all the more acutely as time passed and the local system of supervision came to work less ineffectively. In 1589 the common council of the city of London resolved to prosecute two or three clothiers for not paying aulnage, as a test case[8]; a lawsuit accordingly ensued when

[1] The first and longest list is therefore to be found in Ex. K.R. Mem. Hil. 7 Eliz. 329–32; it was utilized by the author of the manuscript economic history of Wiltshire written for the Victoria County History and now deposited at the Institute of Historical Research, University of London. Later lists are in Ex. K.R. Mem. Trin. 9 Eliz. 206, Mich. 11 Eliz. 484, Hil. 12 Eliz. 513, &c.

[2] B.M. Lansdowne MS. 60, f. 53.   [3] B.M. Lansdowne MS. 14, ff. 95–6.

[4] Leake's Treatise on the cloth industry, S.P.D. Eliz. CXI, 38, pr. in Tawney and Power, *Tudor Econ. Docs.* iii, 217.

[5] B.M. Lansdowne MS. 60, f. 58.   [6] S.P.D. Eliz. CXX, 70.

[7] Ex. Dep. by Comm. Hil. 30 Eliz. 8, especially the evidence of William Webb of Kingswood.

[8] Guildhall, City of London Repertories, 22, ff. 25 b and 130 b.

Roger Chivers, a large clothier of Calne, was thus forced
formally to challenge the right of the London authorities
to exact aulnage from him and to search his cloths. His
case, together with those of some other clothiers, was tried
before the barons of the exchequer; a number of Wiltshire
clothiers testified that they had never been subjected to the
jurisdiction of the London aulnager and searchers until
1560, and due evidence was also given that Chivers had
already paid aulnage and had his cloths searched at Calne.[1]
When subsequently the barons of the exchequer had given
an order in favour of a couple of clothiers there at once ensued a general refusal on all sides to recognize the authority
of the London aulnager.[2] The ringleaders among the Wiltshire clothiers, besides Roger Chivers of Calne, were
Edward Horton of Bradford, Geoffrey Whitaker of Tinhead,
and Henry Long, possibly of Trowbridge—probably all
men doing business on a large scale. They sustained pro-
tracted litigation in the court of exchequer,[3] during which
country cloths presumably continued to enter London scot
free. When at length in 1591 the London searchers again
dared to lay hands upon west country broadcloths entering
the city there ensued a shrill protest; the injured clothiers
petitioned the privy council for relief against the exaction
of aulnage fees by the London searchers, and for the right
to compensation from the latter when their cloths had been
'wetted' and then found true. Their case was referred to
the attorney general, and on his advice the council virtually
assented to the demands of the clothiers—though the city
authorities did not give way without a final struggle.[4] It is
quite certain that the government was ready to protect the
country clothier from unfair molestation, and, indeed, when
a few years later the London searchers attempted to lay
hold of broadcloths belonging to some Suffolk clothiers
they were prosecuted by the attorney general in the star

---

[1] The evidence tendered by the clothiers will be found in Ex. Dep. by Comm.
Hil. 30 Eliz. 8. Cf. also Ex. Books of Decrees and Orders, Eliz. xv, f. 269.

[2] B.M. Lansdowne MS. 60, ff. 57–8. This document contains Leake's apologia
for the work of the London searchers.

[3] Ex. Bills and Answers, 48/73 ; Ex. Books of Decrees and Orders, Eliz. xviii,
ff. 32, 37, 76, and xix, f. 57.

[4] *Acts of the Privy Council*, 1591, 97–100, 128 ; 1591–2, 242.

chamber.[1] All doubts were ultimately set at rest by a statute passed in 1607, which withdrew from the London aulnager and his searchers all rights to inspect cloths which had already been duly sealed.[2] Thus after a struggle lasting for nearly half a century the country clothiers won their freedom, and a notable incident in the history of the broadcloth industry was closed.

The first infliction by the Dutch government in 1591 of the much resented custom of the 'tare' or inspection of cloth upon the merchant adventurers trading to the Netherlands[3] may have made the latter regret all the more keenly the abandonment of the search in Blackwell Hall; but in any case the activities of the London searchers had represented only one aspect of the supervision to which the manufacturer was nominally subject. A method of controlling the woollen industry less direct but more fundamental than the simple inspection of cloth was afforded by the legislation regulating its personnel, organization, and geographical situation, which reached the statute-book early in the second half of the sixteenth century. The manner in which this legislation served the ideals or necessities of Tudor government is not a subject for the purely local historian to discuss, though it may, in fact, be observed that the ultimate legal effect of the series of statutes culminating in the act of apprentices was to enclose the woollen industry in an economic strait-waistcoat superficially of medieval design.[4] But how far this restrictive code was actually effective in Wiltshire—and elsewhere—is a matter for examination.

It has already been suggested that the effort to restrict the number of looms owned by clothiers who lived outside towns met with only a partial and largely fortuitous success,[5] and it is practically certain that another clause of the act of 1555 which attempted to prohibit the further spread

---

[1] S.C. Eliz. A 8/4 and A 25/27. Cf. S.P.D. Eliz. CCXLIV, 106.

[2] 4 Jac. I, c. 2. The fate of the diligent and unlucky Leake, the main instrument of the cloth merchants in the whole affair, does not appear. In 1595 he held the office of keeper of Leadenhall and was characteristically fighting for the keepership of the Green Yard—C.R. Eliz. 43/52.

[3] Te Lintum, De Merchant Adventurers in de Nederlanden, 34–5.

[4] 3 & 4 Ed. VI, c. 22, 5 & 6 Ed. VI, c. 6, 5 & 6 Ed. VI, c. 8, 2 & 3 P. & M. c. 11, 4 & 5 P. & M. c. 5, 5 Eliz. c. 4.   [5] Supra, pp. 17–18.

of industry over the country-side proved almost entirely
vain. For some twenty years Wiltshire clothiers were very
occasionally prosecuted at Westminster for cloth-making in
districts where it was alleged that the art had not previously
been practised[1]; but there were no organized interests to
profit by enforcement of the law and it thus remained largely
a dead letter. Even the indictments were not always effective. For instance, in 1560 an information was laid in the
court of exchequer against George Drinkwater, a clothier
who had established himself in Semington; he was able
plausibly to assert in his defence that the charge was frivo-
lous in that he had not introduced the industry into the
parish,[2] and in fact it is clear that there were other clothiers
in Semington.[3] Probably the informer, a Devizes weaver,
had simply attempted to make trouble; another information
which he laid against a Bromham cloth-maker provoked the
intervention of the attorney general on behalf of the latter.[4]
There were a couple of prosecutions in the court of exchequer in 1568,[5] but the Wiltshire woollen industry was in
the main left free to develop where it listed until in 1575
a certain mischief-making clothier of Frome, by name Peter
Blackborrow, indicted a number of west country broadcloth
makers, including five notable Wiltshire clothiers, for breaking the law.[6] Such a stroke at once brought powerful interests into play, the prosecutions were stopped by order of
the privy council, and in the following year parliament was
invoked to pass an act which somewhat grudgingly legalized
the activities of the country clothiers in Gloucestershire,
Somerset, and Wiltshire, though putting restriction upon
their acquisition of land.[7] It was a clear defeat for the policy
of regulation.

[1] Miss Gay has counted twelve such prosecutions in the courts of exchequer and king's bench—*Aspects of Elizabethan Apprenticeship*, 162.
[2] Ex. K.R. Mem. East. 2 Eliz. 76.
[3] Two other Semington clothiers were fined by the London cloth searchers in March 1561/2—Ex. K.R. Mem. Hil. 7 Eliz. 329.
[4] Ex. K.R. Mem. East. 2 Eliz. 77.
[5] Ex. K.R. Mem. East. 10 Eliz. 308 and Trin. 10 Eliz. 183.
[6] Ex. K.R. Mem. East. 17 Eliz. 96–8. The clothiers were Henry Long of Whaddon, Edward Long of Mounton, Robert Blackborough of Tinhead, John Middlecot of Bishopstrow, and Edward Horton of Westwood.
[7] 18 Eliz. c. 16. *Vide supra*, pp. 45–6. Cf. *Acts of the Privy Council*, 1575–7,

Less unsuccessful was the attempt to enforce a preliminary seven years of apprenticeship upon all who practised the major arts connected with the woollen industry. It was imposed by law upon weavers in 1552 [1]; and in the same period limits were set to the number of apprentices which any master weaver might concurrently keep.[2] Finally in 1563 the statute of artificers extended the obligation of apprenticeship to all persons exercising ' any art, mystery or manual occupation . . . now used within the realm '[3]— a very comprehensive enactment, although spinning and a few minor textile crafts such as burling remained unaffected.[4] A decision in the court of king's bench in 1580 further laid it down that clothiers also were immune from the apprenticeship obligation so long as they did not personally engage in manual labour.[5]

The vitality of the apprenticeship laws probably rested as much upon the survival of the medieval tradition of craftsmanship as upon mere technical exigencies. There are indications that in the small industrial Wiltshire boroughs the custom of apprenticeship was established long before the passage of the statute of artificers[6]; and doubtless the convention was not restricted to the towns. During the reign of Elizabeth, although weavers were but seldom indicted at Westminster for practising their art without having been apprenticed to it,[7] yet there are other signs which suggest the fairly widespread observance of the apprenticeship laws. In Chippenham apprenticeship was regulated

16, 73, 121 and S.P.D. Eliz. cxv, 47. For further information about Blackborrow *vide* Appendix I.

[1] 5 & 6 Ed. VI, c. 8.

[2] 3 & 4 Ed. VI, c. 22, 2 & 3 P. & M. c. 11; cf. also 4 & 5 P. & M. c. 5.

[3] 5 Eliz. c. 4.

[4] *H.M.C. Wilts.*, 135.

[5] Ex. K.R. Mem. Hil. 22 Eliz. 65, quot. by Miss Gay, *Aspects of Elizabethan Apprenticeship*, 161. Only five Wiltshire clothiers or cloth-makers were indicted after the enactment of the act of 1563 during the reign of Elizabeth in the courts of exchequer and king's bench for offending against the apprenticeship laws—Gay, *op. cit.* 163.

[6] Cunnington, *Annals of the Borough of Devizes*, I, xvi, &c.

[7] Miss Gay has traced only four informations each against Wiltshire weavers and fullers and three against dyers, in the courts of exchequer and king's bench after the passage of the act of 1563.—*Aspects of Elizabethan Apprenticeship*, 163. In 1560 a tanner and a shoemaker of Salisbury were indicted for weaving—Ex. K.R. Mem. Mich. 2 Eliz. 112–13.

by a borough ordinance,[1] in Bradford-on-Avon—as doubtless elsewhere—the parish saw to the apprenticing of
foundlings,[2] in such a mere village as Castle Combe an
inhabitant was on one occasion presented at the manor court
for illegally keeping a loom,[3] and it is highly probable that
Robert Daniell of Castle Combe and Jherome Potticary of
Stockton were but two of many fathers who made careful
provision for the due apprenticing of their sons.[4] In general
it may be assumed that in a period of erratic trade conditions
the weavers of every town and village were ready to invoke
the law at local sessions or in manor or borough courts to
secure their own livelihood against illegal competition.

It might well have been expected that in the epoch of
comparative prosperity which marked the opening of the
seventeenth century unauthorized intruders should have
entered the woollen industry; and it is clear that it was
precisely during these years that the apprenticeship laws
were being enforced by the Wiltshire justices at quarter
sessions. In 1600 they arranged a special procedure for
the laying of informations for breaches of the apprenticeship
laws.[5] Subsequently various individuals were from time to
time prosecuted accordingly; in particular the years 1602
and 1603 were marked by the indictment of such offenders
—among whose ranks clothiers so notable as Isaac Self of
Melksham and William Chivers of Bromham were included.[6]
It was doubtless the commotion aroused by these presentments which induced the justices at Michaelmas sessions
1603 to give their assent to a formidable code of orders in
amplification and for enforcement of the existing apprenticeship laws.[7] Even this, however, did not suffice, for a

---

[1] Goldney, *Records of Chippenham*, 5–6.
[2] Merriman, *Extracts from the Records of Wiltshire Quarter Sessions*, *Wilts. Arch. Soc. Mag.* xx (1882), 348.
[3] Scrope, *History of the Manor and Ancient Barony of Castle Combe* (1851), 332.
[4] Wills of Robert Daniell and Jherome Potticary (Pottecarye) (1598 and 1596), P.C.C. 59 Lewyn and 46 Drake.
[5] Merriman, *Extracts from the Records of Wiltshire Quarter Sessions*, *Wilts. Arch. Soc. Mag.* xx, 341.
[6] Devizes, county muniment room, quarter sessions great rolls for 1602 and 1603. Cf. also Merriman, *op. cit.* 101 and *H.M.C. Wilts.* 71.
[7] Devizes, county muniment room, quarter sessions great rolls, Michaelmas 1603, 'Orders agreed upon for thoccupation of the weavers'. This remarkable document will be found abstracted in *H.M.C. Wilts.* 74–5.

little over a year later the justices formally resolved to confer
with farmers and others touching the enforcement of the
statute of artificers.[1] In 1611 they issued a special order
to churchwardens and overseers of the poor to see to the
binding of young people as apprentices.[2]

Thus while possibly occasional individuals managed to
elude the provisions of the restrictive legislation, it seems
an inescapable conclusion that the apprenticeship laws were
being enforced during the early years of the seventeenth
century by the Wiltshire justices of the peace. It can hardly
be doubted that their most valuable allies in this were the
smaller clothiers and the other textile craftsmen, who stood
to suffer if their trades were overrun by unapprenticed
intruders during a necessarily impermanent period of prosperity, and whose interests were therefore so well served by
the informers whose indictments provoked the issue of the
apprenticeship order of Michaelmas 1603; this remains
true though we do not know whether any organized body
of the lesser industrial fry supported these informers.

The suspicion that there may have been some rudimentary
combination among the master weavers of central Wiltshire
is very compatible with the issue in 1602 of a detailed table
of wage rates payable to textile and other workers by the
justices in somewhat belated fulfilment of the statute of
apprentices.[3] This table had previously been agreed upon
by the weavers and clothiers at Trowbridge; it was supplemented in 1603 and 1605 and remained nominally in force
apparently as both a maximum and a minimum rate during
the first half of the century.[4] But although it was regularly
confirmed every year its effectiveness may well be doubted.
At Trinity sessions in 1605 over forty clothiers were presented for not paying their weavers according to the appointed rates—though without any apparent result.[5] It is

---

[1] Merriman, *op. cit.* xxii, 4.

[2] Devizes, county muniment room, quarter sessions great roll, Michaelmas 1611.

[3] There is no evidence to suggest that this was not the first wage assessment for
Wiltshire as a whole, though in 1595 a table of wage rates for Salisbury had been
proclaimed by the privy council—Steele, *Catalogue of Tudor and Stuart Proclamations,* i, no. 878. Cf. the enactment of stat. 1 Jac. I, c. 6.

[4] These wage rates have been printed in *H.M.C. Wilts.* 162–8.

[5] Devizes, county muniment room, quarter sessions great rolls, Trinity 1605
and Hilary 1606.

certain that when the Wiltshire woollen industry entered
upon its phase of depression later in the reign of James I
wages were freely reduced.[1] In any case, the value of a
fixed table of wages in a period of rising prices must have
been slight; the most that can be said is that it represented
an ethical standard to which both employer and employee
might appeal. In 1613 it was asserted that in Wiltshire
wages had not risen during the previous forty years although
prices had almost doubled,[2] and much the same was urged
in a petition to the justices during the hard winter of 1614–
15.[3]

More directly important than the enforcement of the apprenticeship laws was the effective examination, on the part
of the searchers appointed by the justices of the peace, of the
cloths after they had been fulled and were awaiting trans-
portation to the market. As to this there is for the opening
years of the seventeenth century no lack of evidence. The
searchers made frequent presentments for the manufacture
of cloths short in weight or in measure or stretched to a
deceitful length. The names of those who were thus presented suggest that both great and small were liable to the
same penalties ; so well-connected a clothier as Henry Long
of Whaddon was not spared, nor were Henry Chivers of
Calne and Edward Stafford of Chippenham.[4] Nash Whitaker
of Tinhead, who had once been entered as a student at
Lincoln's Inn, failed to avoid the arm of the law when he
employed an illegal tentering device to stretch his cloth.[5]
It is, indeed, not surprising to learn that the searchers were
on occasion liable to meet with violence when they visited
a cloth mill[6] or that a dishonest clothier thought it worth
his while to attempt to counterfeit the searchers' seals.[7]

It was thus entirely in accordance with the temper of the

---

[1] *Infra*, p. 81.
[2] *Acts of the Privy Council*, 1613–14, 457–8.
[3] Devizes, county muniment room, quarter sessions great rolls, Hilary 1615—
undated petition bearing about a hundred names.
[4] Devizes, county muniment room, quarter sessions great rolls, Hil. 1603, &c.
Cf. Cunnington, *Records of the County of Wilts* (1932), 2 *et seq.*
[5] *Ibid.* 14. Cf. *supra*, p. 43.   [6] *Ibid.* 9–10.
[7] Devizes, county muniment room, quarter sessions great rolls, Easter 1606—
presentment of Edward Carpenter of Tinhead by the searchers of cloth for Westbury hundred.

county administration that in 1612 the Salisbury company
of cloth-workers was confirmed and strengthened in its
privileges by the city[1] and that in 1614 the textile workers
of Devizes were organized into a 'company of drapers' for
whose constitution a stringent body of ordinances was enacted.[2] It is indeed difficult to resist the impression that as
far as was reasonably possible the Wiltshire woollen industry
was subject to regulation in the spirit of the Elizabethan
industrial code during the early years of the seventeenth
century. Yet such was hardly the opinion of contemporaries.
The merchant adventurers in 1613 made no exception of
Wiltshire when they complained to the privy council of the
false making of cloth,[3] nor did contemporary pamphleteers
and projectors in their descriptions of cloth-searchers as
being—if indeed they were ever appointed—entirely under
the thumb of the local clothiers.[4] The conclusion must be
that however honest and active the county justices of the
peace and their nominees may have been in their efforts to
enforce the law, yet no water-tight system could have been
found for doing so, and that seventeenth-century industrial
administration had been set a task for which its technique
was insufficiently developed.[5]

[1] Benson and Hatcher, *History of Salisbury*, 323 and 340.
[2] The first order-book of the Devizes drapers' company is preserved in the
library of the Wilts. Arch. and Nat. Hist. Society. On ff. 42–4 is a stringent
order concerning apprenticeship.
[3] *Acts of the Privy Council*, 1613–14, 208–9. A proclamation enjoining observance of the clothing laws was published in December 1613—Steele, *Catalogue of
Tudor and Stuart Proclamations*, i, no. 1140.
[4] E.g. May, *The Estate of Clothing* (1613), 17–34.
[5] It has been well remarked by Heckscher—*Mercantilism* (1935), i, 250—that
'the state placed superhuman demands on the J.P.'s, and that they could not
possibly carry them all out'.

V

TRADE FLUCTUATIONS: THE GREAT CRISIS OF THE EARLY SEVENTEENTH CENTURY

THE golden age of the English broadcloth industry fell within the reign of Henry VIII. Under the combined influence of many factors the continental market grew with a considerable rapidity; the annual export of white undressed cloths from London in the fifteen-forties was nearly double the average of thirty years earlier.[1] Such textile expansion indeed carried with it its attendant dangers; merchants, jealous for the good name of their wares abroad, complained that clothiers were sacrificing quality to quantity, and it was actually during the last period of the boom that much of the restrictive industrial legislation of the century reached the statute-book. In this quickening industrial activity Wiltshire must undoubtedly have taken its share; probably little short of a quarter of the white broadcloths sent to the London market were woven on its looms. It was an age when the astute man of business—a famous example was William Stumpe—could make his fortune on an unprecedented scale, and when even a bold rogue of the type of Matthew Kyng of Malmesbury might also rise to wealth and power as a clothier.

This epoch of prosperity came to an end after the middle of the century. There had from time to time been periods of depression in the past; such years of crisis occurred in 1520–2 and again, owing to the political conflict with the ruler of the Netherlands, in 1529–31. In 1529, indeed, the accumulation of unsold cloths at Blackwell Hall grew so dangerously large that cardinal Wolsey intervened and ordered the merchants to buy them up.[2] There were serious fears of a ' verray slack sale' of cloths in 1535 which happily proved unfounded[3]; nevertheless there was a comparatively lean year in 1543. But though any serious industrial collapse

---

[1] This is clear from the figures which Schanz took from the L.T.R. enrolled accounts—*Englische Handelspolitik gegen Ende des Mittelalters*, ii, 86.

[2] Guildhall, City of London Repertories, 7, f. 246 b.

[3] S.P. Hen. VIII, xcv, 150–1.

was in fact averted until the fifties, yet when it came it was thorough, and the broadcloth industry of the kingdom took a long time to recover. In the year 1563 the export of white undressed broadcloth from London sank almost to the lowest level it had ever reached during the reign of Henry VIII, and during the five summer months from May to September 1565 the number of Wiltshire cloths assessed for export duty at London was less than nine thousand[1]—a very low figure indeed, when it is remembered that a little over twenty years earlier the annual production of cloths in Malmesbury alone had been estimated at three thousand.[2] The distress in Wiltshire must have been very great, and it is not surprising that in 1564 a workhouse was established in Salisbury.[3]

To this very serious decline a number of independent factors contributed, and some of its causes may have been of long standing.[4] The central European market for white broadcloth had begun to enter upon a period of decay. Possibly the failure hitherto to supervise dishonest manufacturers effectively may have tarnished the reputation of Wiltshire fabrics, while the imposition of the restrictive laws in the fifties later helped to diminish output. The dissolution of the monasteries, which threw so much land upon the market, may have encouraged the richer clothier to abandon the industrial struggle for profits and live at ease on his rents; it may well be imagined that the death of William Stumpe, for instance, was a serious blow to the prosperity of Malmesbury. The boom in the export of broadcloths had been powerfully stimulated by the currency inflation in the later years of Henry VIII, the crisis was intimately connected with the deflation which culminated with the rehabilitation of the coinage achieved not long after the accession of Elizabeth and which must undoubtedly have raised the price of English cloths abroad. Another

[1] Ex. K.R. Port Books 2/1—the exact figure being 8,905. Probably the total number of Wiltshire cloths exported during the year was therefore well under fifteen thousand.

[2] Leland, *Itinerary*, i, 132.

[3] Benson and Hatcher, *History of Salisbury*, 283. The actual word 'workhouse' was not used in the corporation minute book.

[4] The crisis is fully discussed in Fisher, *Commercial Trends and Policy in Sixteenth-Century England, Economic History Review*, x (1940), 95–117.

most important factor in the occurrence of the depression
at this juncture was subsequently supplied by the collapse
of the mart of the merchant adventurers at Antwerp. Though
it was not indeed until November 1563 that the regent of
the Netherlands forbade the import of English goods, yet
already for some time relations had been strained; as far
back as February 1560 the merchant adventurers had complained of their treatment at the hands of the authorities
at Antwerp.[1] For some years the export machinery for
cloth was thrown out of gear, and it was not until 1567 that
an alternative mart town was found at Hamburg[2]; general
and political causes meanwhile contributed to the further
prolongation of the crisis.[3]

But even after the recovery the total annual shipments
of broadcloth from London climbed only slowly in the late
seventies and early eighties to something like their former
size.[4] Another but less severe crisis in the early months of
1587 was possibly caused in part by an overproduction
which glutted the market, though a further contributory
factor was the political difficulties of the merchant
adventurers at their mart towns of Emden and Middelburg,
while the Spanish military successes on the Rhine also helped
to dislocate trade.[5] The chief Wiltshire clothiers to suffer
from a hitch in the sale of their wares were Edward Horton
of Westwood, Richard Potticary of Stockton, Edward Stafford of Chippenham and half-a-dozen others who can for the
most part be identified as large capitalists[6]; possibly they had
continued to expand their business beyond the limits of

[1] *Cal. S.P. For.* 1559–60, 371; cf. Brugmans, *Engeland en de Nederlanden in
de eerste jaren van Elizabeth's Regeering* (1892), 50–66.

[2] The fullest account of the dislocation caused to the export trade in cloth
during the sixties by the severance from the customary mart at Antwerp is that
given by Ehrenberg, *Hamburg u. England*, 64–89; cf. Unwin, *Studies in Economic
History*, 176–9.

[3] Scott, *The Constitution and Finance of English, Scottish and Irish Joint-stock
Companies to 1720* (1912), i, 47–63. Apparently the woollen industry entered its
period of depression before the country as a whole.

[4] These trade fluctuations may be traced from the figures given in the Ex.
L.T.R. enrolled customs accounts; I have made use of a transcript of these kindly
lent to me by Mr. F. J. Fisher. An account of the fluctuations in the price of
cloth at Blackwell Hall during the seventies and eighties will be found in S.P.D.
Eliz. cxcv, 36.

[5] Ehrenberg, *Hamburg u. England*, 180; Scott, *Joint-stock Companies*, i, 88–9.

[6] S.P.D. Eliz. cci, 29.

F

prudence. Already before the end of December 1586 the west country clothiers had made complaints against the merchant adventurers for failing to buy up their cloths; their case was subsequently argued by the attorney general before the privy council, with the result that the merchant adventurers were ordered to purchase the unsold cloths on threat of losing their monopoly to the staplers and Hansards.[1] The prosecutions of clothiers then pending in the exchequer were also suspended by the government.[2] These measures however did not suffice to conjure away the crisis; it persisted throughout the spring of 1587, and in March particularly large quantities of west country broadcloth lay unsold at Blackwell Hall.[3] It was said that a number of clothiers were ultimately forced to abandon their business, and there was certainly much misery and discontent in Wiltshire and Gloucestershire.[4] In May the government took drastic steps to free the export trade in cloth from all restrictions,[5] but it was not until June or July that the market began to recover[6]—no doubt owing to the successful return of the merchant adventurers to their former mart at Hamburg, where 1587 and 1588 proved record years for the dyers and clothdressers.[7] But the crisis had nevertheless ushered in a fresh period of trade depression which did not end until the coming of a new and somewhat higher wave of prosperity in the very late nineties and the early years of the seventeenth century.

Yet despite these trade fluctuations the Wiltshire woollen industry made some headway during the half century or so following the accession of Elizabeth. The ancient white broadcloth manufacture of East Anglia never completely recovered from the crisis of the sixties and was in part

[1] S.P.D. Eliz. cxcv, 68; *Acts of the Privy Council*, 1586-7, 272-4, pr. in Tawney and Power, *Tudor Econ. Docs.* i, 214-16.

[2] B.M. Lansdowne MS. 60, f. 53.

[3] S.P.D. Eliz. cxcix, 62.

[4] *A Discourse of Corporations*, pr. Tawney and Power, *Tudor Econ. Docs.* iii, 272; Wheeler, *Defence of the Merchant Adventurers*, pr. Tawney and Power, *Tudor Econ. Docs.* iii, 292.

[5] S.P.D. Eliz. cci, 21-2; cf. Steele, *Catalogue of Tudor and Stuart Proclamations*, i, no. 793.

[6] S.P.D. Eliz. cci, 45.

[7] Ehrenberg, *Hamburg u. England*, 328.

replaced by the production of the 'new draperies', so that the proportion of white broadcloths of Wiltshire origin shipped from London probably increased during the reign of Elizabeth from less than a quarter to over a third of the total export; it may thus be assumed that the production of Wiltshire cloths had more than made good the set-back of the sixties by the beginning of the seventeenth century. Nevertheless, the march of the Wiltshire woollen industry in the later decades of the sixteenth century was pitched in a distinctly minor key. The cost of wool rose out of proportion to the gradual advance in the price received for cloths,[1] and the profits of the capitalist were thus threatened; the less remunerative trade conditions were no doubt closely connected with the increased class consciousness of the Wiltshire landed gentry in helping to relegate the Elizabethan clothier to a position of more marked social inferiority than his grandfather had known. But the clothier was able to diminish his loss of profits by exploiting more thoroughly the labour of his employees, whose misery was liable now as much as ever to vent itself at times of particular stringency in corn riots[2]; it was asserted in 1613 that wages had not risen during the previous forty years although during that period prices had almost doubled.[3] The expansion of the Wiltshire woollen industry during the reign of Elizabeth was therefore—in a sense—paid for at least in part by a lowering of the standard of living of the industrial worker.[4]

Probably by the end of the reign of Elizabeth only a minority of Wiltshire clothiers could afford to be generous to their employees; even when trade grew brisk at the very end of the sixteenth century the humble clothier was sometimes constrained to ask for payment in advance and thus to subsist upon what was indistinguishable from

[1] *Vide infra*, p. 74.
[2] *Supra*, p. 16. Cf. Cheyney, *History of England*, ii, 3–36.
[3] *Acts of the Privy Council*, 1613–14, 457–8.
[4] Professor J. U. Nef, with his eye mainly on the heavy industries, has in his article on *Prices and Industrial Capitalism in France and England, 1540–1640*, *Economic History Review*, vii, 155–85 (1937), disputed the view of Professor E. J. Hamilton that the rapid increase of prices in the sixteenth and seventeenth centuries helped to stimulate the growth of capitalism by cheapening labour costs. The history of the Wiltshire woollen industry hardly bears out his conclusions.

borrowed capital—a process the reverse of that which had prevailed a century earlier. Lionel Cranfield in the first years of the seventeenth century dwelt near Blackwell Hall; he bought cloths from Wiltshire clothiers great and small, both from such large capitalists as Roger Chivers of Calne and Edward Horton of Westwood and from a number of obscure and humble manufacturers,[1] and consignments of cloth from Wiltshire were constantly travelling to him and money or bills of credit passing in the opposite direction. His clothiers were often very anxious to be paid on the nail if not before,[2] and he was doubtless far from being the only merchant adventurer to be harassed by importunate country clothiers for the loan of money—whether allegedly to buy such a trade requisite as a 'hogshede of oyle' or for an entirely unspecified purpose.[3] No doubt most of these requests were not granted; on one occasion however Cranfield certainly paid forty pounds in advance to Thomas Ray of Salisbury—the money to be returned if the cloths were not liked.[4] Cranfield had without a doubt chosen his man shrewdly; for Ray, who had humbly begun his industrial career in 1584 as the recipient of a charitable loan of twenty-five pounds from the city upon the benefaction of Sir Thomas White, rose to be mayor of Salisbury in 1611.[5] Altogether, while Cranfield's activities presuppose a busy industrial activity in Wiltshire in the opening years of the seventeenth century, they also suggest that the preceding period of depression had been a rather lean one for some clothiers; for they had not been able to put by sufficient capital to meet the demands of an expanding industry.

Other facts also lead to the inference that the very

---

[1] Two lists of clothiers from whom Cranfield bought cloths *c.* 1602 are to be found in the Cranfield papers.

[2] Cranfield papers, e.g. letters of Henry Pearce of Calne, 30 Jan. 1601/2, and of William Bridge of Bremhill, 12 April 1602 (?).

[3] Cranfield papers, e.g. letter of William King of Bremhill, 18 April 1600 (?), and letters of Walter and William Gray of Wilton, 19 Feb. and 7 July 1601 (?).

[4] Cranfield papers. letter of Thomas Ray, 9 March 1600/1.

[5] Benson and Hatcher, *History of Salisbury*, 292 and 696. It was no doubt Ray's sense of gratitude which impelled him in turn to bequeath property to be applied for the benefit of Wiltshire clothiers—Hoare, *History of Modern Wiltshire*, *Hundred of Westbury* (1830), 23.

early seventeenth century was a period of considerable prosperity for the Wiltshire woollen industry—albeit the last for many a long year. In 1606 the number of white undressed broadcloths made in Wiltshire and shipped abroad by the merchant adventurers from London rose to over forty-five thousand—well over half the total export of these commodities[1]—and presumably the numerous Wiltshire clothiers who in previous years had lent twenty-five pounds each to the king were well able to afford it.[2] A little earlier, Nicholas Archard, a large Malmesbury clothier, had erected on a tributary of the Avon a new fulling mill with two stocks, doubtless to deal with the expanding business under his care.[3] There were indeed transient troubles, but with these the normal administrative machinery of the county was able to deal; when in the winter of 1603-4 the plague came to Devizes, Calne, and Westbury and caused much distress there, and when in 1610-11 it visited Bradford and Chippenham, the justices of the peace enacted sanitary regulations and saw to the provision of relief.[4] Again, when in 1607 certain weavers complained of being discharged from work by the clothiers their case was duly taken up by the justices of assize.[5] At the very end of this comparatively calm period, in 1614, the export of Wiltshire broadcloths was only four thousand less than it had been in 1606.[6]

The broadcloth industry was ultimately brought to disaster not at first through general causes but by the whim of the king. James I was led by a strange mixture of motives —in which a reasonable and canny economic foresight was mingled with impulses largely prompted by the shady circle of courtiers and financiers by whom he was surrounded— to tamper with the broadcloth trade. In order that the dyeing and dressing of English broadcloths should be

---

[1] Friis, *Alderman Cockayne's Project and the Cloth Trade* (1927), 129.
[2] S.P.D. Jas. I, XVII, 86—the clothiers on the list of lenders included Robert Batt of Devizes, Nicholas Flower of Steeple Ashton, and John Yerbury of Bradford.
[3] Ex. Dep. by Comm. 3 Jas. I, East. 12; Ex. Bills and Answers, 48/189.
[4] *H.M.C. Wilts.* 73-4, 81, and 84; Cunnington, *Records of the County of Wilts.* 11, &c.
[5] Merriman, *Extracts from the Records of Wiltshire Quarter Sessions, Wilts. Arch. Soc. Mag.* xxii, 223-4.
[6] Friis, *Alderman Cockayne's Project*, 130.

performed at home rather than in Holland and Germany the privileges of the merchant adventurers were in 1614 suspended and in their place was installed a new company, the 'king's merchant adventurers', whose leading member was alderman Cockayne. This was a merchant whose interests had hitherto lain chiefly with the Eastland company in the Baltic, and he rashly undertook to find a market for the broadcloths after they had been dyed and dressed in London. The execution of this scheme met with bitter and understandable hostility abroad and it finally collapsed with ignominy when in 1617 the old merchant adventurers were restored to their former privileges. But by then the damage had been done; the whole cloth trade had been thrown out of gear and it was generally believed that the prolonged hitch in the export of English cloth had given a strong impulse to the production of the native commodity in Germany and Holland.[1] To crown all, the religious wars which were to ravage central Europe for thirty years broke out in 1618, and thenceforth the German market shrank disastrously; the cumulative effect of this distant strife was in the long run far more catastrophic for the Wiltshire woollen industry than even the Cockayne episode.

The reaction of this series of events upon the woollen industry in Wiltshire could not fail to be profound. A foretaste of the troubles to come was provided during the corn shortage of 1614 which was severely felt over all the industrial area of the county and which indicated the socially shallow nature of the years of prosperity. There were doubtless others to do as the weaver of Christian Malford who was forced to pilfer grain to sustain his wife and children.[2] Yet more serious were the corn riots which broke out in Seend, Westbury, and Warminster during May 1614; several weavers of Seend desperately confessed that they would rather die themselves than see their wives and children starve.[3] It was

[1] The Cockayne episode has been exhaustively described by Dr. Friis in *Alderman Cockayne's Project*, of which much use has been made in the above paragraph and elsewhere.

[2] Devizes, county muniment room, quarter sessions great roll, Trinity 1614—examination of Walter Geale, weaver, of Christian Malford, 20 June 1614.

[3] *Ib.*, examinations of Henry Swayne, John Ford, and Daniel Parker, weavers, of Seend, and of James Greenland and William Smith, weavers, of Westbury.

reported too that the inhabitants of Malmesbury had been driven to great want and misery by the dearth of corn.[1] At quarter sessions numerous licences were issued for middlemen to transport foodstuffs to the afflicted areas and in December the privy council ordered the justices to put some restriction upon the malting of grain, but the crisis was hardly at an end even in the following January. It is notable that the lords of the council believed the trouble to have been largely caused by the 'turbulent and seditious spirits of some idle and clamourous persons' though on the other side it was pointed out that for many years the prices of foodstuffs had been rising while wages remained stationary.[2] It is probable that considerable class bitterness had been aroused; and the whole episode formed an inauspicious prelude to the major industrial crisis which was soon to descend upon the west country woollen industry.

But even the most serious grain shortage could in due course be tided over. It would not appear that the Cockayne experiment had an immediately catastrophic effect upon the Wiltshire woollen industry—a fact which speaks volumes for the complex organization of the cloth market[3]—and there ensued a short lull before the storm. Yet even in 1615 the inability of Cockayne and his associates to dispose of the accumulating broadcloths caused a stop in the market with the result that the clothiers began to give vent to petitions and complaints[4]; and in 1616 the situation caused the new company increasingly acute embarrassment from which it only escaped by giving way to the restoration of the old merchant adventurers.[5]

The cries of distress from the clothing districts of the

---

[1] *Ib.*, undated petition from the inhabitants of Malmesbury signed among others by William Hobbes and Nicholas Archard, two large clothiers.

[2] *Acts of the Privy Council*, 1613–14, 652–3; Devizes, county muniment room, quarter sessions great roll, Hilary 1615—undated petition bearing about a hundred names. In this document is an attempt to disclaim any importance for its bearer Richard Moore as 'the stirrer and setter on of these complaints'—an admitted ringleader could presumably expect scant mercy.

[3] *Infra*, pp. 131 ff.   [4] S.P.D. Jas. I, LXXX, 38 and 108.

[5] Cf. *Acts of the Privy Council*, 1615–16, 17–19, for the expedient proposed by the king's merchant adventurers in September 1616, and Friis, *Alderman Cockayne's Project, passim.*

west country reached the privy council, and on 11 September 1616 Sir Julius Caesar gloomily noted at the council table that in Gloucestershire, Worcestershire, and Wiltshire either half or a third of the looms were abated.[1] On the next day the council sent for information about the numbers of cloths manufactured in these three counties which remained unsold in London, either in Blackwell Hall or in the storehouse there or elsewhere on deposit or on pawn —with other details.[2] The report disclosed two days later that comparatively few cloths in fact remained unbought, though no less than ninety Wiltshire cloths had been pawned by the hard-hit clothiers.[3] A week later the council wrote to the justices of the clothing counties asking them to verify discreetly the complaints of the clothiers about the plight of their industry and also to investigate the numbers of the unemployed. As in 1614, it is clear that the lords of the council were not swayed by any prepossessions in favour of the textile workers, for they added that the inquiries of the justices were not to be too public, lest complainants should be encouraged.[4] Measures were also taken to bring down the price of wool, which despite the depression had remained high.[5] But this activity of the council in no way served to alleviate directly the distress in the industrial areas, and in October Sir Julius Caesar surmised—and his estimate was probably very conservative—that in Wiltshire the unemployed numbered some three thousand.[6]

However, in November the government opened negotiations with the former merchant adventurers who in the following January were restored to their ancient privileges; and in the course of the year 1617 the market for broadcloth improved, although there was no return to the conditions of earlier years. The merchant adventurers had lost much capital and were thus the more timid. Further, by an untimely royal act, the export duty on cloth was during the next few years increased, and thus the harassed industry had no real

[1] Friis, *Alderman Cockayne's Project*, 468.
[2] *Acts of the Privy Council*, 1616–17, 12–13.
[3] S.P.D. Jas. I, LXXXVIII, 83; quot. Friis, *op. cit.* 321.
[4] *Acts of the Privy Council*, 1616–17, 21.
[5] *Ib.* 35; Friis, *Alderman Cockayne's Project*, 335–6 and 473.
[6] Friis, *op. cit.* 477.

opportunity of recovering from one severe ordeal before the
dwindling of the German market plunged it into another
and far more prolonged crisis.[1] In Wiltshire the period of
acute depression was indeed over for the moment, though
the precarious condition of the woollen industry was well
illustrated by a petition signed by several justices of the
peace and forwarded to the privy council in August 1618;
the object of the petitioners was to secure special protection
for Benedict Webb, a large clothier of Kingswood, in a
lawsuit in which he was then engaged—so that his numerous
employees should not be thrown out of work.[2] It must be
inferred that despite his undoubted enterprise and experience
Webb lacked the capital necessary to weather the storm,
and it is also clear that the justices were very nervous about
the social effects of Webb's possible bankruptcy. Such a
petition could hardly have been sent to the privy council in
a previous generation.

There is also evidence which suggests that in the general
demoralization induced by the crisis the system of cloth
inspection—such as it was—was appreciably weakened in
Wiltshire.[3] Little significance is probably to be attached to
the demand of the 'king's merchant adventurers' in 1616
for the establishment of a more efficient method of cloth
searching.[4] But in April 1618 the council upon the request
of the merchant adventurers agreed to the issue of a proclamation enjoining the enforcement of cloth-searching
throughout the kingdom—which for the moment apparently
achieved its purpose—and it also determined to proceed
against delinquent searchers in the star chamber.[5] A chief
agent in procuring these resolutions was doubtless Edward
Misselden, merchant adventurer and economist, who in the
previous year had bought from a Bremhill clothier ten
broadcloths, duly sealed, which upon examination were

[1] Friis, *op. cit.* 382-3; Scott, *Joint-stock Companies*, i, 169.
[2] S.P.D. Jas. I, xcviii, 81.
[3] It is perhaps worth noting that from the teens onwards the presentments of
cloth-searchers are no longer to be found in the Wiltshire quarter sessions great
rolls. *Supra*, p. 63.
[4] Friis, *Alderman Cockayne's Project*, 313-14.
[5] *Acts of the Privy Council*, 1618-19, 112-13; S.P.D. Chas. I, clxxx, 74.
The proclamation was apparently not published until November—Steele, *Catalogue of Tudor and Stuart Proclamations*, i, no. 1223.

found to be 'exceeding false and defective in waight, in breadth and in length'; Misselden had refused to pay the clothier and had therefore been sued in the king's bench by the latter; upon this he had brought the matter to the privy council, which at once summoned clothier and searchers to receive its censure. Misselden shortly afterwards quoted the case in a pamphlet in which *inter alia* he lamented the failure of cloth searchers in general to fulfil their duty honestly.[1] Throughout these years indeed the merchant adventurers continued to insist that the failure to execute the cloth-searching laws was a major cause of the industrial depression.

It was in 1620 that distress again descended upon the Wiltshire clothmakers. At Easter quarter sessions the justices were petitioned by workless spinners and weavers and upon inquiry they learnt that over a hundred and thirty looms were known to be standing idle; so that the number of unemployed could not be less than two thousand six hundred. These facts they reported in a letter to the privy council with the comment that these poor people could not live unless they were supplied with work. The council was also more directly supplied with information by a tremulous petition purporting to come from the weavers of Bromham, Chippenham, and Calne. In this more lurid document it was stated that the idle looms numbered many hundreds and that in Bromham alone there were the incredible number of twelve thousand carders, spinners, weavers, and tuckers, out of work and therefore on the brink of starvation.[2] Although the latter figure was doubtless highly exaggerated, the plight of the unemployed was probably for the most part little short of desperate; the lords of the council after taking consultation accordingly attempted on the one hand to arrange for the merchant adventurers to buy up the cloths in Blackwell Hall while on the other they

---

[1] *Ib.* 25-7, 42; Misselden, *Free Trade* (1622), 48-9. There can be no doubt that in the latter Misselden was quoting his own squabble with Francis Hawkins of Bremhill, though he mentioned no names. Cf. also S.P.D. Jas. I, cxx, 95.

[2] S.P.D. Jas. I, cxv, 20 and 58. It is unfortunately impossible to identify the organizers of the weavers' petition. The figure of twelve thousand unemployed is justifiably queried by Lohmann—*Die staatliche Regelung der englischen Woll-industrie*, 17.

ordered the Wiltshire justices to see to it that the clothiers
gave work to as many of their former employees as possible
and that the remainder were maintained by the raising of
public stocks for their employment.[1] Unhappily these
simple and abrupt methods did not suffice to conjure away
the spectres of distress and disturbance; it is highly improbable that the Wiltshire justices were able to execute the
orders of the privy council with real thoroughness, and, as
the merchant adventurers a little later pointed out, it was
simply not possible for trade to return to its normal channels
as long as war continued to rage in Germany.[2] The cloth
exports from London in the financial year 1621–2 were
over twenty per cent. lower in value than they had been
nine months earlier, and to offset the increase in new
draperies the decline in broadcloths should probably be
reckoned as very considerably more intense.[3]

Meanwhile, the depression continued to afflict the industrial areas, and there was a perceptible increase in petty
thefts of wool and foodstuffs in Wiltshire.[4] In the winter of
1621–2 there were rumours elsewhere of violent rioting in
Wiltshire and Devonshire by unemployed textile workers,[5]
and the corn scarcity in 1622 and 1623 undoubtedly made
these years of particularly acute suffering. In February
1622 the lords of the council again attempted to compel
the merchant adventurers to buy up the cloths in Blackwell
Hall and they reiterated their scarcely very effective com-
mands to the justices of the peace in the clothing counties
to see that wool was not hoarded, that clothiers did not
dismiss their workfolk, and that public stocks of wool and
yarn were provided for the unemployed.[6] At Easter
quarter sessions the Wiltshire justices received another
petition from the Bromham weavers stating that in their
parish no less than forty-four looms had fallen idle within

[1] *Acts of the Privy Council*, 1619–21, 200–1 and 205–6.
[2] S.P.D. Jas. I, CXVI, 23.
[3] Figures are to be found in Misselden's *Circle of Commerce* (1623), 121 and
127. Cf. Friis, *Alderman Cockayne's Project*, 421.
[4] This is a general inference drawn from a perusal of the quarter sessions great
rolls for these years.
[5] Williams, *The Court and Times of James I* (1848), ii, 291–2; S.P.D. Jas. I,
CXXVII, 102.
[6] *Acts of the Privy Council*, 1621–3, 131–3; S.P.D. Jas. I, CXXVII, 76.

the previous six months with the result that over eight hundred persons were in imminent danger of starvation, and a similar outcry from the weavers and spinners of Rowde indicated that they were in the same plight.[1] A social upheaval must have seemed not far away. Here and there corn was seized violently by mobs while on its way to market; by the end of April the unemployed in Wiltshire were estimated at over eight thousand, and the justices feared that they would take the law into their own hands and commit further outrages. The council was informed that the clothiers had been compelled to continue the dismissals of their workfolk.[2] A month earlier three hundred and forty-three Wiltshire cloths whose market value may be estimated at little less than two thousand pounds had lain unsold in Blackwell Hall—a matter which was none the less serious because they were for the most part the property of small and obscure clothiers.[3]

The gravity of the situation was realized by the government and in the summer of 1622 the council consulted busily with clothiers, justices, and merchant adventurers concerning the causes of the crisis and the possible remedies; but little of any fundamental utility could be done. The clothing committee of the council agreed with the merchant adventurers that a decline in the standards of clothmaking due to the failure of the local searchers honestly to perform their work was a major contributory factor to the depression, while the clothiers blamed chiefly the wool dealers and hoarders. Ultimately various measures were taken of which one of the most important was a partial loosening of the monopoly of the merchant adventurers, which became effective in July 1624.[4] Meanwhile, as early as May 1622, detailed instruc-

---

[1] Devizes, county muniment room, quarter sessions great roll, Easter 1622. Both petitions are undated; that from Rowde was apparently written by the incumbent, who, together with the constables and overseers of the poor, also signed it. Summaries of the Bromham petition are to be found in *H.M.C. Wilts.* 94, and also in Cunnington, *Records of the County of Wilts.* 71.

[2] S.P.D. Jas. I, cxxix, 79. [3] S.P.D. Jas. I, cxxviii, 76.

[4] *Acts of the Privy Council,* 1621–3, 153, 190, 201–2, 391; Friis, *Alderman Cockayne's Project,* 382–431, *passim.* For the views of the clothing committee of the council and of the merchant adventurers on the causes of the crisis see S.P.D. Jas. I, cxxix, 12, cxxxi, 55, cxxxiii, 35, and also Misselden, *Free Trade,* 41–53. The views of the clothiers are to be found in B.M. Stowe MS. 354, f. 65.

tions were sent from the lords of the council to the Wiltshire justices for relief of the unemployed in each parish;
with these was coupled an injunction to appoint a provost-
marshal for the apprehension of the mischievous agitators
whom the justices alleged to be fanning the flames of discontent.[1] The justices also attempted to combat the corn
shortage of the years 1622 and 1623 by the customary
issue of licences to middlemen to transport foodstuffs from
the markets to the districts where famine was threatened,
as well as by continuing to restrict the malting of corn.[2]

Though by the autumn of 1623 the bitterest period was
over, the broadcloth industry had in fact now entered upon
an epoch of chronic depression and was being forced pain-
fully to adapt itself to the circumstances of its shrunken
continental market. Wiltshire cloths were reported as lying
unsold at Blackwell Hall in January 1624 and again a year
later, though admittedly not in large quantities.[3] The spirit
of discontent doubtless remained strong; and there were
other trials in store.[4] There were further visitations of the
plague in 1625 in London and in 1627 in Wiltshire; on the
first occasion a serious dislocation of the cloth industry was
threatened and on the petition of the Wiltshire clothiers
the lords of the council were brought to the point of medi-
tating a temporary removal of the cloth market from London
lest a further cessation of purchases should lead to more
unemployment.[5]

Of the great hardships endured by the industrial workfolk of Wiltshire during these years there can be no doubt,
although there was no eyewitness to chronicle their misery.
Those presumably escaped lightest whose staple occupation

---

[1] *Acts of the Privy Council*, 1621–3, 214–15.
[2] Devizes, county muniment room, quarter sessions great rolls for 1622 and
1623, *passim*; S.P.D. Jas. I, CXXXVIII, 54. Cf. Cunnington, *Annals of the Borough
of Devizes*, I, ii, 70.
[3] S.P.D. Jas. I, CLVII, 15; and CLXXXV, 21.
[4] The Wiltshiremen who were pressed for the army in 1624 and among whom
were a number of weavers and tuckers made mutinous and unreliable soldiers—
though here there were other important factors to be considered—*Acts of the Privy
Council*, 1623–5, 424 and 446; S.P.D. Jas. I, CLXXXI, 25, and CLXXXV, 21; cf.
S.P.D. Chas. I, xv, 14.
[5] *Acts of the Privy Council*, 1625–6, 135, 138, 161–2, 211; *H.M.C. Wilts.*
96–7.

was agricultural and whose weaving and whose wives' and daughters' spinning were subsidiary items in the household economy; but these may safely be estimated as being well in the minority. There were doubtless many like the weaver of Langley Burrell who in 1624 was reported by his neighbours as having of late fallen into 'distress'.[1] For such there existed the poor law; but while its administration may have sufficed for ordinary times it proved unequal to the unprecedented emergency. The overseer of the county house of correction at Devizes had been accustomed to providing wool for his charges to convert into cloth as an ordinary business venture, but when the bad times came his profits vanished and in April 1622 he was forced to petition the justices for an increase of his stipend to cover his losses.[2] At Salisbury in 1623 a municipal brewhouse was established, the profits of which were to be applied for the relief of the poor, while at the same time the organization of the city workhouse was overhauled;[3] and rather more than three years later the mayor and burgesses of Devizes set aside twenty pounds for the provision of a stock of wool to be spun into yarn by the unemployed in the charge of the governor of the house of correction.[4] Over the countryside the provision of labour for the workless must have proved a difficult task. Here and there honest and persistent efforts were doubtless made to do so; in Steeple Ashton the raising of a stock for the poor was a problem which seems perpetually to have haunted the parish authorities.[5] But in general it is improbable that the repeated injunctions of the privy council to the justices to see to the provision of work for the unemployed by furnishing public stocks of wool in

---

[1] Devizes, county muniment room, quarter sessions great roll, Easter 1622—undated petition of the inhabitants of Langley Burrell.

[2] Ib., petition of the overseer of the house of correction, dated 30 April 1622; entries in the quarter sessions minute book show however that in the previous half dozen years he had more than once asked for money from the justices on one plea or another.

[3] Benson and Hatcher, *History of Salisbury*, 336 and 349.

[4] Cunnington, *Annals of the Borough of Devizes*, I, ii. 81.

[5] *Wilts. Notes and Queries*, vii (1911–13), *passim*. Cf. Assize Order Book, Western Circuit 1629–41, confirmation of Steeple Ashton poor rate, 4 Mar. 14 Car. I.

each parish were for long seriously obeyed, and there must have been quite sufficient misery to provoke the threats and the rioting without attaching particular importance to the alleged mischief-makers whose activities troubled the minds of both the justices and the lords of the council.

Even those lucky enough to remain in their precarious employment suffered. In the prosperous years before the crisis real wages had probably been steadily sinking,[1] and with the onset of the depression there is evidence that this process was accelerated. The mayor of Devizes in February 1623 reported to the privy council that the clothiers had lowered wages because of their smaller profits;[2] and there seems little doubt that the decline in the price of broadcloths was greater in proportion than the fall in the cost of wool.[3] At Easter sessions in the same year the justices were petitioned on behalf of the woollen textile workers of the county; it was alleged that wages had been reduced to starvation level and that clothiers compelled their employees to perform the most menial of tasks 'without giving them bread drinke or money for many dayes labours'. The justices acceded to the ensuing demand for an inquiry and ordered that the wage assessments should be enforced and that the rates fixed for weavers, spinners, and tuckers should be openly published next market day at Devizes.[4] The efficacy of such measures must be doubted, though there may well have been clothiers of the type of Thomas Hulbert of Corsham who died in 1632 and who was commemorated in his epitaph as

> a master milde
> Who never did the needy poor contemne
> And God enrich'd him by the hands of them.[5]

Yet though in the case of Thomas Hulbert virtue met its material reward it is certain that the capitalist class itself

[1] *Supra*, p. 69.
[2] Cunnington, *Annals of the Borough of Devizes*, I, ii, 71; S.P.D. Jas. I, cxxxviii, 54.
[3] B.M. Add. MS. 34,217, f. 14.
[4] Devizes, county muniment room, quarter sessions great roll, Easter 1623. This remarkable petition was written in a neat hand and was clearly not the work of a labouring man. It has been printed in *H.M.C. Wilts.* 94. It is possibly of significance that at this sessions, contrary to normal practice, a formal confirmation of the wage assessment was entered in the justices' minute book.
[5] Inscription in Corsham parish church.

did not come unscathed through the crisis. The clothiers who were also farmers were doubtless able to quit their business or to reduce its proportions and others may have been in a position to retire and live upon their savings; as early as 1620 the Wiltshire justices reported that many clothiers had abandoned their trade either wholly or in part.[1] In later years Christopher Potticary of Stockton, whose business was on a large scale, actually took credit for having continued his trade during these lean years.[2] Many clothiers must have gloomily watched their stocks of cloth accumulate unsold and lie upon their hands. Thomas Randle, a small clothier of North Bradley, left behind him in his mill at his death in 1628 a store of over a hundred pounds' worth of white cloths—a quantity which a manufacturer would hardly have allowed to accumulate in the busy days before the Cockayne crisis. Much the same might be said of John Francklin of Calne, another small clothier, who died in 1630; of rather more than four hundred pounds' worth of movable goods in his possession at his death wool accounted for over a hundred and fifty pounds, yarn for more than forty, and unsold cloths for a hundred and fifteen pounds.[3] Such unhappy accumulations of both raw materials and of the finished product well illustrate the deadness of the cloth market. Thus it is not surprising that Wiltshire should in 1622 have been numbered among the counties which were backward in contributing to the cause of the elector palatine[4] or that five years later some clothiers should have excused themselves from contributing to the forced loan by pleading poverty.[5] As early as 1617 Henry Curtis, once a well-to-do clothier of Seend, had been reduced to penury by reason of the slack trade,[6] and there was at least one spectacular crash when in

---

[1] *Acts of the Privy Council*, 1619–21, 192; S.P.D. Jas. I, cxv, 20.

[2] S.P.D. Chas. I, clxxxiv, 65. Potticary secured release in 1621 from unfair rating for poor relief, by order of the justices at quarter sessions—Devizes, county muniment room, quarter sessions minute book iv, entries under Oct. 1618 and Oct. 1621.

[3] Salisbury, Diocesan Registry, inventories of the goods of Thomas Randle and John Francklin.   [4] *Acts of the Privy Council*, 1621–3, 302.

[5] S.P.D. Chas. I, lxxix, 91. No doubt for other reasons this was not an unfamiliar phenomenon elsewhere.

[6] Information as to the plight of Curtis is to be found in *H.M.C. Wilts.* 88 and

1622 Nicholas Archard of Malmesbury was forced to sell up his mills. Archard had in his day been a considerable landowner in north-west Wiltshire, and he appears to have been rescued from utter disaster only by the timely intervention of his sons, one of whom was a London leather-seller.[1]

But other and possibly richer or more enterprising clothiers adapted themselves to changed conditions; Hulbert and Potticary were but two of a number who successfully persisted in their trade, and indeed the latter subsequently claimed that his employees numbered nearly a thousand.[2] Some gratified their social ambitions in the thick of the crisis by paying the fees of Clarenceux king-of-arms when in 1623 the heralds' visitation of Wiltshire took place. Some few clothiers, including Thomas Sumner of Passion's Mill and Robert Flower of Littleton, were indeed content formally to disclaim nobility of birth, but many industrial families were then accepted as armigerous, some for the first time; among the latter were Wallis and Yerbury of Trowbridge. A notable example was afforded by Henry Chivers, a rich clothier of Calne, whose grandfather and namesake had been 'disgraded' at the previous visitation in 1565, but who was now admitted as a gentleman.[3] Possibly the lines of distinction between the richer industrialists and the landed gentry were becoming less sharp in these days than they had been in the later sixteenth century;[4] though it is certain that the same cannot be said of the clothing capitalists and their employees. Fears of a social upheaval had genuinely disturbed both clothiers and gentry;

also at Devizes, county muniment room, quarter sessions minute book IV, entry under January 1618.

[1] Fry, *Abstracts of Wiltshire Inquisitiones Post Mortem returned into the Court of Chancery in the Reign of Charles the First* (1901), 320–1. As to Archard's property information is to be found in C.R. 168/39 and 182/20, C.R. Eliz. 1 S 8/42, and C.P. Jas. I, 11 376/29, and Ex. Dep. by Comm. 3 Jas. I, Easter, 12.

[2] S.P.D. Chas. I, CLXXXIV, 65.

[3] Marshall, *The Visitation of Wiltshire in 1623* (1882), 37 and 103–4; on Chivers see Bodl. MS. Aubrey 2, Natural History of Wilts. II, f. 144. Two of his sons later matriculated at Brasenose College, Oxford—and they were not the only clothiers' sons to be sent to the university in this period: cf. Phillipps, *Matriculationes Oxonienses pro Com. Wilts.* (n.d.), 3, &c.

[4] Perhaps the prosperous years at the beginning of the century might help to account for this.

in all probability the great depression of the sixteen-twenties may be considered as a landmark in the history of that growing cleavage between the capitalist and the working classes which can be traced from the middle ages onwards.

Yet the industrial depression ushered in by the Cockayne crisis and which was rendered chronic by the outbreak of the thirty years' war in central Europe was notable not merely as an episode in social history—indeed it would be difficult to overestimate its importance in the evolution of the Wiltshire woollen industry or even in the larger field of English economic history as a whole. It marked the end of an epoch, the decay of the exclusive and ancient broad-cloth manufacture which had evolved on its own lines since the fourteenth century. It precipitated widespread changes in the organization and technique of the west country woollen industry. Perhaps most important of all, it powerfully stimulated the release of English textile manufacturers from their preponderant reliance upon the Dutch and German markets and so took its place in the chain of events which was forcing clothiers, merchants, and government to turn their eyes more fixedly to other quarters of the globe— to the Mediterranean and Levant, to the middle east and to the west.

VI

GOVERNMENT AND INDUSTRY DURING THE
PERSONAL RULE OF CHARLES I

DURING the years of the personal rule of Charles I
the government showed a deep interest in the county
administration and the privy council provided an effective
driving force to spur the Wiltshire justices of the peace to
fulfil their duties. Regular reports were sent by the latter
to London upon the enforcement of the poor-law—the
binding of apprentices, the provision of foodstuffs, the
punishment of vagrants, and the like.[1] In 1630 the justices
resolved to levy a rate for the erection of three new houses
of correction at Malmesbury, Marlborough, and Fisherton
Anger, in addition to the repair of the already existing one
at Devizes;[2] and in 1637 the council gave its support to
Salisbury corporation in its project of again establishing a
workhouse for the city.[3] The justices continued to proclaim
wage-rates every year,[4] and, whatever the effectiveness of
these proclamations may have been, the council showed
itself ready to intervene if it found that insufficient wages
were paid.[5] Its concern over agricultural depopulation and
the enclosure question resembled the attitude of protector
Somerset.[6]

Wiltshire must have attracted the attention of the lords
of the council all the more since the shadow of depression
still hung over the west country broadcloth industry. The
inhabitants of Bradford—ever a centre of the woollen industry—in 1632 plausibly pleaded poverty as an excuse for

[1] These reports are to be found scattered among the S.P.D. for the reign. Cf.
also Leonard, *Early History of English Poor Relief* (1900), 246–66. At Calne
money was first set aside for the use of the poor in the borough accounts for 1629
—Calne, Corporation Minute Book 1565–1814, f. 59.

[2] Cunnington, *Records of the County of Wilts.* 99.

[3] Privy Council Register, 24 Nov. 1637.

[4] In *H.M.C. Wilts.* 9 it is misleadingly stated that the wage assessments were
not formally approved during certain years : the orders are sometimes to be found
in the sessions great rolls if not in the minute books.

[5] e.g. Privy Council Register, 2 Oct. 1636.

[6] The 1632 commission included Wiltshire—S.P.D. Chas. I, ccxxix, 112. Cf.
Tawney, *Agrarian Problem in the Sixteenth Century*, 351–77.

their failure to repair the local bridge over the Avon.[1] Despite the new houses of correction, idle and disorderly vagrants swarmed over the county in such numbers that at Michaelmas quarter sessions 1633 it was resolved that in future any two justices might commit at sight such persons to prison until next sessions; but this also proved insufficient to quench the evil.[2] In the same year it was credibly stated that in Gloucestershire only liberal credits availed to keep many broadcloth clothiers going at all.[3] When in 1634 the Wiltshire justices reported to the council that a number of the largest clothiers were proposing to retire from business the latter in alarm required to be informed of their reasons for taking this course.[4] Five years later, when a renewed crisis was threatened, it was demanding regular reports on the state of the market at Blackwell Hall.[5]

In the twenties the persistence of the depression had always been ascribed in large measure to the loss of reputation which English broadcloth had suffered owing to the failure of the local cloth searchers to perform their duties effectively, and it would appear that the laxity that possibly had crept in with the crisis long continued to prevail.[6] In 1627 the contents of a pack of ten Wiltshire cloths exported to Holland and duly bearing the searchers' seals were found by their Dutch buyer to be hopelessly lacking in length, breadth, and weight.[7] In February 1631 the lord mayor of London on the order of the privy council took samples of various cloths from the market at Blackwell Hall; out of twenty-nine white broadcloths of various

---

[1] Assize Order Book, Western Circuit 1629–41, entry for 27 Feb. 7 Car. I. Four years earlier the inhabitants had nevertheless complained of excessive tippling by workfolk in the alehouses of the town—Cunnington, *Records of the County of Wilts.* 89–90.

[2] Devizes, county muniment room, quarter sessions great roll, Michaelmas 1633. Cf. Goldney, *Records of Chippenham*, 55–6, and Cunnington, *Records of the County of Wilts.* 123.

[3] S.P.D. Chas. I, CCXLIV, 1 (v)—my attention was drawn to this document by Dr. W. B. Willcox.

[4] Privy Council Register, 10 Oct. 1634.

[5] S.P.D. Chas. I, CCCCXXXVIII, 84.

[6] *Supra*, pp. 75–6.

[7] Posthumus, *De nationale organisatie der lakenkoopers tijdens de republiek* (1927), 213–14.

types only six upon examination were found true.[1] The
merchant adventurers continued to press meanwhile for
reform and various schemes of regulation were canvassed
in London, from a revival of the long obsolete duties of the
aulnager to Misselden's plan for the erection of centres of
cloth inspection in the chief towns of the clothing counties—
he enumerated fourteen such for Wiltshire.[2] The situation
was one with which a strong government might well concern itself.

For various reasons, the government of Charles I was
disposed actively to intervene. In the autumn of 1630 a
weighty remonstrance of the merchant adventurers urged
upon the council *inter alia* the appointment of some skilful
person who should go to the west country broadcloth region with authority to see to the enforcement of the cloth
laws;[3] and eventually on October 29 there was issued a
commission 'for reformation of the abuses in clothmaking'
to a certain Anthony Wither and Samuel Lively.[4] By its
terms these two individuals received general powers of in-
vestigating the observance of the clothing laws in Oxfordshire, Gloucestershire, Wiltshire, and Somerset. They were
authorized to inquire into the types of men appointed as
searchers of cloth and the manner of their appointment,
to have the unsuitable replaced, and to establish a water-
tight and detailed system of cloth inspection for the future.
They were to report all obstinately delinquent or refractory
persons to the privy council and were to be entitled to all
possible assistance from the justices of the peace. The justices of assize were also instructed to give them full support.[5]

[1] S.P.D. Chas. I, CLXXXIV, 45; cf. Privy Council Register, 31 Jan. and 16
Feb. 1631.
[2] S.P.D. Jas. I, CXXIX, 12, CXXXI, 55 and CXXXIII, 35; S.P.D. Chas. I, LXXXIII,
54, CLXV, 34 and CLXXX, 69; Misselden, *Free Trade*, 127–35. The fourteen
centres were—in alphabetical order—Beckington, Bradford, Bremhill, Calne,
Castle Combe, Chippenham, Devizes, Malmesbury, Salisbury, Trowbridge,
Warminster, Westbury, Wilton, and Wootton Bassett.
[3] S.P.D. Chas. I, CLXXX, 74.
[4] Privy Council Register, 29 Oct. 1630; S.P.D. Chas. I, CLXXXIV, 97.
[5] Privy Council Register, 4 Mar. 1631. The account of the execution of the
commission in Wiltshire in the following pages is indebted to Mrs. Barford's
article on *The West of England Cloth Industry: a Seventeenth Century Experiment
in State Control*, in *Wilts. Arch. Mag.* xlii (1922–4), 531–42, although not all her
conclusions are accepted.

The commissioners who received this extensive authority were presumably the nominees of the merchant adventurers; but it can hardly be said that the latter were fortunate in their choice. After a short time Lively indeed ceased to figure in the activities of the commission[1] but Wither remained for some years the stormy petrel of the west country broadcloth industry. His past connexions would seem to have been fairly varied. He had at one time been a member of the Virginia company[2] and had also been associated with Cockayne in his ill-fated project; subsequently he had entered the ranks of the merchant adventurers, though his opinion of the latter as a body had in 1621 been somewhat critical, and he had engaged chiefly in the trade to the Spanish Netherlands.[3] In 1623 he had been for a short time imprisoned in the Fleet at the behest of the privy council.[4] As he had now accepted appointment as one of the two clothing commissioners it may be surmised that his career as a merchant had not been very successful. Subsequent events were to illustrate how far his zeal could outrun his discretion, though he had admittedly taken no easy task upon himself. But in order to understand the nature of the hornets' nest into which Wither now boldly thrust himself it is necessary to consider certain changes in the organization of the Wiltshire woollen industry which had taken place within the previous twenty or thirty years.

In the sixteenth century the smaller clothiers and independent weavers had been supported by a miscellaneous trade in wool and yarn for the suppression of which the larger clothiers had vainly battled.[5] The struggle continued in the new century upon slightly different ground. In 1615, on the eve of the great depression, it was estimated that over half the output of the west country broadcloth industry was manufactured by small clothiers who bought

---

[1] The privy council finally resolved to drop him as being unfit—Privy Council Register, 27 Feb. 1633.

[2] S.P.D. Chas. I, CCVI, 57,

[3] Friis, *Alderman Cockayne's Project*, 282, 326, 332, 404, 406. It is, however, impossible to be certain that these references all concern the same individual.

[4] *Acts of the Privy Council*, 1623–5, 102, 125.

[5] *Supra*, pp. 7 ff.

their yarn in the market from independent spinners who in turn had acquired their wool from dealers.[1] The days, however, of many of these independent spinners who refused to work for the small wages of the clothier were numbered, for within the confused ranks of the wool and yarn middlemen there existed an increasingly important class of industrial organizers—the badgers of yarn. Their emergence as an independent force was no doubt partly due to their ability to exploit more distant labour for the markets as well as to the increasing refinement of the processes of manufacture; at first, too, they served much the same classes as the wool broggers and in the later sixteenth century they had joined the latter as the objects of the clothiers' attacks.[2] Legislation against the yarn badgers of the west country was contemplated as early as 1593,[3] but it never reached the statute-book; their position was indeed as secure as that of the dealers in wool. In 1600 it was ordered at the Wiltshire Michaelmas quarter sessions that all charges depending against yarn badgers should be dropped and that for the present no more should be received.[4] By 1613 their activities had developed to such an extent that they provoked a petition to the privy council purporting to come from the clothiers of Wiltshire who in it complained forcibly of the illegal engrossing and re-sale of yarn.[5]

The ensuing industrial crisis could not fail to exert a profound influence upon the organization of the woollen industry. The first to feel the action of the government were the staplers, upon whom was cast the blame for the enhanced price of wool. After a prolonged inquiry by the privy council into their activities their continental staple was finally abolished and replaced by a number of English towns; of these, Devizes, Cirencester, and Tetbury were in or near the Wiltshire industrial area.[6] During the next few

---

[1] S.P.D. Jas. I, LXXX, 13, pr. in Unwin, *Ind. Org.* 234–6.   [2] *Supra*, pp. 13–14.
[3] S.P.D. Eliz. CCXLIV, 126–30; cf. Tawney and Power, *Tudor Econ. Docs.* i, 371–6.
[4] Merriman, *Extracts from the Records of Wiltshire Quarter Sessions, Wilts. Arch. Mag.* xx, 341.
[5] *Acts of the Privy Council, 1613–14,* 12.
[6] *C.S.P.D.* 1611–18, 452; S.P.D. Jas. I, XCII, 28; *Acts of the Privy Council,*

years there followed a vigorous though unsuccessful effort
on the part of the larger wool dealers to monopolize the
internal trade in wool;[1] no doubt the epoch of depression
offered a particular opportunity to the big merchants whose
small rivals lacked the reserves of capital necessary to tide
them over the period of falling prices and slack markets.
It is very possible that a similar evolution occurred in the
yarn trade. When neither clothier nor weaver came to
purchase his yarn the spinner was presumably glad to sell
it, for what he could get, to the yarn badger, whose business thus increased greatly. Small bundles of yarn indeed
continued to be offered for sale in the markets by independent spinners, but by the later twenties it was estimated—perhaps a trifle generously—that two-thirds of the
thread used for making cloth passed through the hands of
the badgers of yarn who—as the chief 'market spinners'
—had thus risen for the moment to high importance in the
woollen industry.[2] In particular they had laid their hands
upon the trade in imported dyed wool.[3] It was possibly
due in part to the fact that middlemen had withdrawn both
wool and yarn from Devizes market that in 1630 its keeper
was excused payment of some of the rent for his office on the
plea that his tolls for weighing wool and yarn at the common
beam had much diminished.[4] The small independent
market spinner of the sixteenth century was thus by then
completely dwarfed by his larger and capitalistic namesake, though he had by no means ceased to exist.[5]

The feelings with which the larger clothiers viewed the
progress of the market spinners may well be imagined.
There may indeed have been some truth in their familiar

1616–17, 181 ; cf. Jenckes, *The Origin, the Organization and the Location of the Staple of England* (1908), 50–7.

[1] *Acts of the Privy Council*, 1619–21, 207–8, 246–7.

[2] S.P.D. Chas. I, XIV, 15 ; possibly this document, which is undated, has been assigned to a date a few years too early. It is very similar in contents to S.P.D. Chas. I, CLXXX, 71. Cf. Cunnington, *Annals of the Borough of Devizes*, I, ii, 81.

[3] S.P.D. Chas. I, CCXLIII, 23. Dr. W. B. Willcox has pointed out that in Gloucestershire, where this wool was probably little used, the market spinners remained smaller fry—cf. S.P.D. Chas. I, CCXLVIII, 1.

[4] Cunnington, *Annals of the Borough of Devizes*, I, ii, 85. The industrial depression was doubtless also responsible for this.

[5] Cf. the case of John Hiscock of Potterne who in 1640 was a 'yarnman' in apparently poor circumstances—Cunnington, *Records of the County of Wilts.* 132

and reiterated charges against the latter, whom they asserted to falsify the yarn by mixing wools and against whom no legal redress was possible since it was often alleged that the unevenness of the yarn could only be discerned after weaving, and certainly the clothier and not the yarnmaker was held responsible for untrue cloth—though it must be remembered that some clothiers themselves dealt in yarn.[1] But the broadcloth manufacturers had another more real though less advertised grievance. During the twenties a new industry had come to take root in Wiltshire—the production of coloured cloth from dyed wool sometimes of Spanish origin.[2] As the justices of the peace in 1633 pointed out, the market spinners supplied much of the yarn used by the 'coloured' clothiers, who were wont to pay more for their thread than their 'white' colleagues, doubtless because they were less uncertain of their market; and so the 'white' clothier who employed his own spinners was forced by the competition of the market spinners to pay to them higher wages than he would otherwise have done.[3] The existence of market spinners may have as much as halved the capital necessary for the maintenance in trade of a clothier and was thus a stimulus to the development of the manufacture of the coloured cloths.[4] The Wiltshire woollen industry was in fact moving steadily away from its exclusive concentration upon white broadcloth and was probably in a greater state of flux than it had ever previously been. The tension of conflicting interests must have been fairly high when early in 1631 Wither entered this little world with all its rivalries and hatreds as the king's commissioner for clothing.

From the very first there was trouble. Among the county magnates it is true that Wither received some encouragement from Sir John Danvers, an old friend of his,[5] but the justices of the peace were decidedly hostile to the fulfilment of the commission which from the first they doubtless felt as an unwarrantable intrusion upon their offices and dignity.

---

[1] e.g. S.P.D. Chas. I, CLXXX, 71. Cf. supra, p. 14.   [2] Infra, pp. 102 ff.
[3] S.P.D. Chas. I, CCXLIII, 23.
[4] The Clothier's Complaint (1682), 9.
[5] S.P.D. Chas. I, CCVI, 57. As Mrs. Barford has pointed out, this document has been placed out of chronological order—The West of England Cloth Industry, Wilts. Arch. Mag. xlii, 538.

In July 1631 special letters were sent by the privy council
to the justices of the four broadcloth counties requiring
them to support the commissioners.[1] Even this did not
suffice; in December the council was compelled to summon
four of the Wiltshire justices, of whom the ringleader was
Sir Edward Baynton, to explain their conduct, and Thomas
Hulbert, a clothier of Corsham, was likewise examined.
There had also been similar though less acute trouble in
Gloucestershire. A royal command now again peremptorily
enjoined the immediate execution of the commission in the
clothing area—it mentioned in particular Chippenham.[2] A
year had thus practically been lost in bickering with the
justices; however, the commission had been duly notified
in the four industrial counties and the clothiers had been
warned to amend their ways before the commissioners again
arrived. When they did return they met with a hot reception. Wither while inspecting a consignment of cloths at a
Bradford fulling mill was seized and flung into the Avon at
a place where it was twenty feet deep and where a number
of cloths were floating on the surface—so that, as he pointed
out, if he had risen under any of them he would inevitably
have been drowned.[3] The news of this outrage stirred the
lords of the council to action; they ordered that the delinquents should be arraigned in the star chamber and also
that Wither should there prosecute Baynton, Hulbert, and
the other offenders of the previous year.[4] Baynton was
however not quelled, and his seat at Bromham continued
in the next year to be a centre of open opposition to Wither.[5]
How far this persistent hostility of the justices was determined by their sheer dislike of what they may have considered overweening interference from Whitehall and how
far by their social or economic ties with the cloth manufacturers it is impossible to say.

Meanwhile Wither had set about his investigation of the
cloth searchers and their ways. He found much to reform

[1] Privy Council Register, 7 July 1631.
[2] Privy Council Register, 21 Dec. 1631.   [3] S.P.D. Chas. I, ccxv, 56.
[4] Privy Council Register, 18 April, 9 and 16 May 1632. Horne was later
indicted before quarter sessions on eight separate charges for making false cloth
—Devizes, county muniment room, quarter sessions minute book VII, entries under
January and October 1633.   [5] S.P.D. Chas. I, ccxlii, 53.

—although it must be remembered that the existing system was by no means entirely ineffective. Searchers of cloth were normally appointed by the local justices in each hundred where broadcloth clothiers were to be found; there were no less than ten in the hundred of Whorwelsdown, within the borders of which lay Keevil, Edington, and other industrial centres.[1] As recently as 1630 there had been presentments for the illegal stretching of cloth.[2] Nevertheless Wither was soon able to unearth corruption and negligence in the execution of the clothing laws. Some of the searchers were ignorant of their duties, and he caught others who acted in collusion with the clothiers. The searchers of Slaughterford were under the thumbs of two large Castle Combe clothiers both by name Thomas Cullimore, father and son, to whom they delivered without inquiry the seals of their office. At Bradford the searchers were found to seal cloths without inspecting them, and at Calne they were simply evaded.[3]

According to his own word Wither acted promptly. He caused searchers to be properly sworn into their office and to give recognizances as security for the efficient discharge of their duties and he also furnished them with information concerning their statutory duties; the names of delinquents were delated to the council for prosecution in the star chamber. It does not appear that the swearing-in of the searchers met in Wiltshire with the difficulties which were raised in Gloucestershire against it.[4] The justices themselves were spurred on directly by the privy council to overhaul their administration of the cloth-searching laws,[5] and in April 1633 a long proclamation embodied directions for them to follow.[6] From 1637 onwards recognizances were actually taken from searchers upon printed forms, which indicates that their exaction was now an established practice.[7]

---

[1] This appears from the answers of the constables of the various hundreds sent to the justices of the peace in November 1632—Devizes, county muniment room, quarter sessions great rolls, Michaelmas 1632.

[2] *Ib.* Easter 1630—presentments of Thomas Page, 8 April 1630.

[3] S.P.D. Chas. I, ccxv, 56 and ccxxi, 27.   [4] S.P.D. Chas. I, ccxv, 56.

[5] Cunnington, *Records of the County of Wilts.* 103–4; Privy Council Register, 7 Nov. 1632.

[6] Coll. Procs. Chas. I, 163, listed in Steele, *Catalogue of Tudor and Stuart Proclamations*, i, no. 1657.   [7] *H.M.C. Wilts.* 102.

It would seem that the machinery of inspection was duly cranked up to the pitch of activity which it had reached in the early years of the century. Absolute efficiency could not be expected; even Wither himself when he had lit upon some faulty cloth once proved susceptible to the plea of distress—or to the money which was perhaps offered and taken —of the clothier, and accordingly withdrew his prosecution.[1] On the other occasions, however, he did not show himself so complaisant.[2]

The work of the cloth searchers was necessarily limited to the detection of untrue cloth and the suppression of mechanical devices for illegally stretching the fabric—these latter were, however, chiefly to be found in Gloucestershire and were rare in Wiltshire. The clothiers themselves had other matters to draw to the attention of Wither. They made the old complaint of the appropriation of reputable cloth-marks by inferior manufacturers.[3] An attempt was made to deal with this in the proclamation of April 1633 by ordering that each clothier should adopt and confine himself to a single cloth-mark, and in November of the same year the attorney-general was ordered to prosecute a Wiltshire clothier who had sold broadcloth bearing no seal or mark.[4] Actually, this part of the proclamation—so far as it received notice—was probably more of a nuisance than a help, since many clothiers used different cloth-marks for the various types of cloth they made.[5] With another complaint the government could not deal at all—the persistent embezzlement here and there of a few pounds of wool from clothiers by their spinners, who attempted to make up for the consequent lack of weight by adulterating the yarn with grease or dirt—and the theft of small quantities of wool or yarn continued to form the commonest type of wrongdoing with which the justices had to deal at every quarter sessions.[6]

[1] Devizes, county muniment room, quarter sessions great rolls, Easter 1633— letter from William Gibbens to the clerk of the peace, 11 April 1633, countersigned by Wither.   [2] S.P.D. Chas. I, cccvii, 61.

[3] S.P.D. Chas. I, clxxx, 71, ccxxi, 28, and ccccviii, 15.

[4] Privy Council Register, 19 Nov. 1633.

[5] S.P.D. Chas. I, ccxli, 36 quot. Barford, *The West of England Cloth Industry*, *Wilts. Arch. Mag.* xlii, 537. *Supra*, pp. 50-1.

[6] S.P.D. Chas. I, ccxliii, 23, and ccccviii, 15.

Far more momentous, however, were the charges brought by the clothiers against the now powerful market spinners. In enforcing the laws of cloth inspection and in attempting to protect the reputable clothier against his dishonest rival Wither had the support, both moral and practical, of the law. But by endorsing the complaints of the clothier against the market spinner Wither was merely backing one side against another in a tangled economic dispute, and events were soon to show that the threatened interests were as able to exert pressure in high places as he. Nevertheless from the very beginning he boldly championed the cause of the broadcloth clothiers; in his report of April 1632 he expounded the clothiers' point of view that the market spinners took advantage of their legal irresponsibility to mix and adulterate the wools which they used,[1] and he subsequently again urged this story upon the lords of the council in a memorandum countersigned by fourteen west country clothiers.[2] The crux of the matter was clearly whether the clothier could detect mingled and falsified yarn upon purchase; Wither accepted the view that he could not, but the Wiltshire justices of the peace upon inquiry found reason to believe that he could and that therefore the best remedy for the alleged malpractices of the market spinners was for the clothier to refrain from buying their bad yarn.[3] Since Wither thus took his stand upon somewhat uncertain ground it may well be asked whether he had any special motive for doing so. Was he concerned specially to see that the new coloured cloth with which the market spinners were specially identified was made from reliable yarn, since it was unregulated by any statute? There is no evidence which directly suggests this. Or, more plausibly, was he supporting the makers of white broadcloth so doggedly because they were the chief purveyors of his masters the merchant adventurers? Here again information is completely lacking.

In the event, it was the affair of the market spinners

[1] S.P.D. Chas. I, ccxv, 56.
[2] S.P.D. Chas. I, ccccviii, 15. Mrs. Barford has pointed out that this document has been placed out of order among the state papers domestic—*The West of England Cloth Industry, Wilts. Arch. Mag.* xlii, 536. Among the signatories were Christopher Potticary and William and Christopher Brewer—*infra*, p. 105.
[3] S.P.D. Chas. I, ccxliii, 23.

which was to cause his undoing. At first Wither received full support from the privy council in this as in his other activities; it set up in November 1632 a special committee to consider the abuses in the manufacture of cloth and in the following month its report entirely corroborated Wither's statements. As far as market spinners were concerned, the committee suggested that in future they should be forbidden to sell yarn which had not been spun in their own homes —a proposal which if put into operation would have killed their business. The council confirmed the report and the attorney-general was ordered to draw up a proclamation embodying its terms.[1] But at this point there occurred a hitch. Sir John Danvers succeeded through his brother the earl of Danby in getting the matter held up, so that when the proclamation directed against the frauds used in cloth-making was published in April 1633 it contained no mention of market spinners.[2] The council had resolved to seek information farther afield, and it referred the question of the market spinners to the justices of the peace in the four broadcloth counties.[3] It sent a special order to the Wiltshire justices to fix their next Midsummer sessions not at War-minster but in the centre of the industrial area at Chippen-ham so that—with the assistance of Wither—they might hold an inquiry into the matter which the clothiers could conveniently attend.[4]

Under the chairmanship of Sir Francis Seymour the inquiry was duly held and the justices sent to the council a report which by no means confirmed the views of Wither and of the merchant adventurers. This cogent document on the whole supported the market spinners in their business. It gave scant credence to the complaints of the clothiers and was concerned to point out how at the back of the trouble lurked the rivalry of the ' white ' and ' coloured ' clothiers for the labour of spinners and the con-

[1] Privy Council Register, 12 Dec. 1632.
[2] Coll. Procs. Chas. I, 163; S.P.D. Chas. I, ccvi, 57. S.P.D. Chas. I, dxxxv, 152 probably belongs to the early months of 1633.
[3] Privy Council Register, 28 Feb. 1633.
[4] Privy Council Register, 31 May 1633. The copy of this letter in the county archives at Devizes has been printed in Cunnington, *Records of the County of Wilts.* 316–17.

sequent maintenance of the wages of the latter at a higher
rate than would otherwise have been the case.[1] The reception of this report must have tended to shake Wither's credit
with the council, and no doubt it also helped to protect the
market spinners. In Somerset the latter actually came to
an agreement with the clothiers,[2] but there is no trace of
any such concordat for Wiltshire; as far as it was concerned,
Wither's activities tended henceforward to degenerate into
the pursuit of a personal squabble with Sir Francis Seymour
and the other justices. In May 1634 the latter charged
Wither before the council with attempting dishonestly to
extort a declaration against market spinners from five
Salisbury clothiers ; possibly there was some truth in the
allegation, though it may be observed that one of these
clothiers had been brought to the brink of disaster through
the seizure a little earlier of his allegedly untrue cloths by
Wither and so was doubtless a willing tool in the hands of
his enemies.[3] Wither had his own countercharges to bring;[4]
but these did not spare him during the next month a couple
of days in the Fleet and in November he was again imprisoned there for libelling Sir Francis Seymour, to whom
he was forced to make a formal apology.[5] It is scarcely surprising that in the next year the merchant adventurers secured
his removal from the commission ; his successor was one
John Holland of whose activities nothing has come to light.[6]

But although Wither thus ultimately came to grief the
government remained determined to take action with regard
to the questiom of market spinning. In July 1634 the privy
council informed the justices of the four broadcloth counties
that while it did not propose to suppress the market spinners

[1] S.P.D. Chas. I, CCXLIII, 23; *supra*, p. 91. It is difficult to accept the account
of the Chippenham inquiry as given by Wither in S.P.D. Chas. I, CCVI, 57.
Dr. W. B. Willcox has drawn my attention to the fact that the Gloucestershire
justices also reported in favour of the market spinners—S.P.D. Chas. I, CCXLVIII, 1.
[2] S.P.D. Chas. I, CCLXXXII, 81, quot. Barford, *The West of England Cloth
Industry, Wilts. Arch. Mag.* xlii, 538.
[3] Privy Council Register, 2 May 1634 and 13 March 1635; S.P.D. Chas. I,
CCLXVII, 17. The clothier in question was Edward Downes.
[4] S.P.D. Chas. I, CCLXII, 15.
[5] Privy Council Register, 11 and 13 June, 22 Oct. and 21 Nov. 1634.
[6] S.P.D. Chas. I, CCCCVII, 78 ; Privy Council Register, 3 Feb. 1636. The
fate of Wither would seem to have been as uncertain as that of his predecessor
Leake a generation earlier—*supra*, p. 56.

it was none the less resolved to put an end to their mal-practices and it ordered a further inquiry into them.[1] The merchant adventurers were persistent in pressing for action,[2] and various schemes for the regulation of clothmaking continued to circulate in London.[3] At length, in September 1638, a great commission of inquiry into the whole woollen industry of the kingdom was issued, granting full powers of investigation to the commissioners ; the commission was renewed in the following February, the names of Anthony Wither and three others being added.[4] The eventual report of the commissioners was a long and sweeping document. The abuses of the market spinner they declared to be in-tolerable and they advocated the suppression of all dealers in wool and yarn save in Devon and Yorkshire. Their elaborate scheme for the reorganization of the woollen in-dustry hinged upon the erection of industrial corporations in all centres of manufacture—for Wiltshire they enumerated Salisbury, Warminster, Devizes, Chippenham, and Calne. These local bodies were to exercise general powers of search and regulation and were themselves to be supervised by a permanent commission sitting in London. The commis-sioners in fact wished to return to the centralized adminis-tration characteristic of the medieval aulnage system, and had their proposals been carried into effect all responsibility for the control of the woollen industry would have been re-moved from the hands of the justices of the peace. The report was completed in June 1640 ; it was signed by fifteen persons—including Wither, who must have set his signature with delight to such a document.[5] But by then the govern-ment was up to its neck in political difficulties ; the long parliament was shortly to meet, and the monarchy had entered upon its twilight.

Thus ended the direct efforts of the government to set the broadcloth industry in order. In Wiltshire the tradition

[1] Privy Council Register, 22 July 1634. The result of this does not appear.
[2] S.P.D. Chas. I, CCCXLI, 101, and CCCXCV, 11.
[3] S.P.D. Chas. I, CCCXLI, 100 and 103, CCCLXXVII, 43, and DXXXVII, 60.
[4] S.P.D. Chas. I, CCCXCVIII, 118 and 119, and CCCCIX, 210.
[5] I have published the text of this report in *English Historical Review*, lvii (1942), 482. My thanks are due to Mr. Francis Needham, the librarian at Wel-beck Abbey, for enabling me conveniently to consult the original.

of apprenticeship had been maintained, and although the market spinners had not been suppressed nevertheless the inspection of cloth by the searchers had been wrought to a reasonable pitch of efficiency. The prolonged insistence of the London merchants upon the need for effective local searching and the universal ascription of the continued depression of the sixteen-twenties partly to the failure of the local officials to do their duty help to illustrate how industrial regulation was for the maker of broadcloth regarded as little short of a necessity. He was not in the position of the contemporary Lancashire clothier, who was experimenting with new materials and seeking fresh outlets for his goods,[1] or even of his own neighbour who made Spanish cloth. He was the traditional manufacturer of a standard article for whom an exacting market already existed; as long as it remained his object to cater for that market so long was external pressure necessary to maintain him in the statutory grooves, since otherwise the market would vanish. The shrinkage of this market made action all the more imperative. Wither was able to point out plausibly to his employers that his efforts for the amelioration of broadcloth had saved them some ten thousand pounds annually,[2] a sum which they would otherwise have lost upon faulty cloth which the Dutch or German authorities would have confiscated or which would have been left on their hands as unsaleable. Only when in his turn the Wiltshire clothier was driven to desert the traditional broadcloth manufacture and to experiment with new types of cloth did the system of regulation become economically superfluous.

In their larger issues it is tempting to compare the impacts of the great trade crises of the middle sixteenth century and of the early seventeenth century upon the woollen industry. It may be presumed that the period of boom which covered most of the first half of the sixteenth century was marked by the incursion of inexperienced persons into the clothmaking business and the resultant manufacture of much fraudulent cloth[3]; it is at least tempting to assume

[1] Cf. the account of industrial regulation in industrial Lancashire in Wadsworth and Mann, *The Cotton Trade and Industrial Lancashire*, 59–70.

[2] S.P.D. Chas. I, ccccvii, 78.

[3] Cf. Tawney and Power, *Tudor Econ. Docs.* i, 184.

H

that the clothing statutes from 1536 onwards formed the climax of a long series of fumblings on the part of the London merchants for the purpose of securing a more effective regulation of the woollen industry. Parliament was invoked to pass the acts which they desired, and as a further check the government connived at the *coup de main* on the part of the city of London by which an office for the effective searching of country cloths was established at Blackwell Hall.[1] But whether this interpretation be accepted or not it remains certain that when the woollen industry was caught in similar difficulties two or three generations later the course of events took a different path. There could in the early seventeenth century be little or no fresh legislative action since the bickering of king and commons had virtually brought the parliamentary machine to a standstill; nor were the relations of the crown and the city of London of the happiest. The interference of the government was therefore circumscribed by the narrow limits within which king and privy council alone could operate. The power of the government to interfere with the conduct of industry had thus sensibly declined; and a measure of this decline may be found by comparing the whilom efficacy of the work of Leake and his colleagues at the London aulnage office with the blundering sterility of Wither's investigation. The direct explanation of this discrepancy must chiefly be sought outside the purely economic sphere. The escape of the Wiltshire woollen industry from official administrative control and indeed the triumph of *laissez-faire* in the English textile manufacture as a whole was due in the first instance very largely to the operation of political and constitutional factors during the first four decades of the seventeenth century; but any consideration of these must lie outside the range of the local historian.

[1] The clothing statutes have been regarded as instruments for a deliberate restriction of production after the shrinkage of the market; they have also been envisaged as a reply to the natural response of the clothier to the collapse of his market in cheapening his costs by putting less wool into his cloths and then by overstretching them to the statutory lengths—cf. Fisher, *Commercial Trends and Policy*, 109–14, *et passim*.

VII

THE DEVELOPMENT OF NEW PRODUCTS AND MARKETS DURING THE SEVENTEENTH CENTURY

THE efforts of the government to lift the clouds of the depression which overhung the west country woollen industry for a generation after the Cockayne experiment had little success. The traditional broadcloth manufacture continued to languish and its ancient market in central Europe proved impossible fully to recover. The Wiltshire woollen industry was ultimately rescued from its persistent depression only by the independent development of new products within its confines—a long and sometimes slow process which may plausibly in part be traced to changes operating in the manufacture of broadcloth itself. For these new varieties of Wiltshire cloth fresh markets were sought and eventually found; but the struggles for the discovery of the latter were intimately bound up with the development of English commercial and foreign policy during the century and necessarily therefore lie almost entirely outside the field of the merely local historian.

It must not be supposed that the making of broadcloth ever remained technically static. There were the recognized varieties of broad and narrow, plain and stop-listed cloth, and the official measurements of these were altered from time to time by statute.[1] In the later sixteenth century there was a tendency for broadcloth to be made finer in texture,[2] and the value of every cloth for the London merchant varied greatly according to the quality of its fabric. Richard Sheppard, who may be taken as a representative merchant adventurer of the late sixteenth century, usually paid between forty and sixty pounds for each pack of ten broadcloths—but he gave eight pounds apiece for some fine cloths to Richard Bennett of Harnick and ten pounds to John Grant of Bradford for one particularly fine specimen.[3] Comparatively few coarse cloths were made in

[1] The last of the regulating statutes was enacted in 1623—21 Jac. I, c. 18. Cf. *supra*, p. 4.
[2] *Supra*, p. 5. [3] Cranfield papers, ledger-book of William Sheppard.

Wiltshire by the early seventeenth century.[1] The improvement in the art of spinning noted by John Aubrey at the restoration[2] may thus be viewed as a part of a continuous process going back to the reign of Elizabeth and possibly much further.[3] The advent of the 'new draperies', which already before the end of the sixteenth century were being made in and near Wiltshire, though outside the regular broadcloth area of the county, may have afforded some stimulus.[4] It is conceivable that as early as the sixteenthirties there were in Wiltshire experiments in the crossing of linen and woollen yarn.[5] It is therefore clear that despite the statutory tutelage of the west country broadcloth industry scope for technical enterprise and variety was not lacking in industrial Wiltshire during the early decades of the seventeenth century.

The beginnings of the revolution which was to end the exclusive manufacture of undyed and undressed broadcloth in Wiltshire may directly be traced to the import of fine Spanish wool—an ancient trade with its origins in the high middle ages.[6] By the middle of the sixteenth century the staplers had taken alarm at the supersession of English by Spanish wool in clothmaking districts,[7] though the chief consumers of Spanish wool were probably the feltmakers, of whom a number were to be found in Wiltshire.[8] It is very possible that the finest broadcloth may have contained Spanish wool, but of this there is no definite evidence. It

[1] At least, not many were exported—Friis, *Alderman Cockayne's Project*, 129–30; cf. also S.P.D. Jas. I, xx, 10.

[2] Bodl. MS. Aubrey 2, quot. Clark, *Science and Social Welfare in the Age of Newton* (1938), 44.

[3] Cf. S.P.D. Add. Eliz. xxxiii, 71. There was a parallel technical advance in the Yorkshire woollen industry—Heaton, *Yorkshire Woollen and Worsted Industries*, 198.

[4] Ex. Bills and Answers, 16/178—my attention was drawn to this document by Dr. W. B. Willcox. It is improbable that the making of 'new draperies' in Highworth and Cricklade was ever pursued on more than a very small scale.

[5] In 1632 John Smith of Melksham was described as a 'Lynnen and Woollen Weaver'—Devizes, county muniment room, quarter sessions great rolls, Easter 1632, petition in favour of John Smith dated 26 Feb. 1632. Mere was a centre of the linen manufacture and there were linen weavers here and there in other parts of the county.

[6] Klein, *The Mesta* (1920), 34.

[7] S.P.D. Eliz. xiii, 81. Cf. B.M. Lansd. MS. 48, f. 152.

[8] Ex. K. R. Mem. East. 20 Eliz. 70, 73, 88, &c.

was, however, in the first decade of the seventeenth century that there began the import from Spain of a dyed wool which it was found could be manufactured into a specially fine and very marketable medley 'Spanish' cloth.[1] Later, Spanish wool was being dyed in England by the makers of this Spanish cloth; complaints of a familiar type were soon being made against them—that they were using inferior dyestuffs, that they were overstretching the fabrics after fulling, and so forth.[2] One of the first exponents of this new industry was Benedict Webb a clothier of Kingswood, and another was John Ash of Freshford[3]; its main seat lay along the borders of Somerset and Wiltshire from Frome to Bradford.[4] Webb was a man of resource who ran a large business; he was on one occasion employed by the king on a mission to France, he was held in esteem by the country gentry, and he had in 1624 been so enterprising as to take out a patent for the manufacture in the French fashion from rapeseed of the oil used in scouring cloth; this oil was said to be both cheaper and more reliable than the Spanish oil previously in use.[5] No doubt the difficulties which beset the orthodox makers of broadcloth in the years of depression following the failure of the Cockayne project helped to consolidate the position of the new industry, and it is abundantly certain that by the thirties it had firmly established itself in Wiltshire—so much so, that the wages paid for spinning coloured yarn for medley cloth were higher than those which the broadcloth makers could afford to pay.[6] It is not surprising that despite the trade depression which prevailed during those years Jeremy Potticary of Stockton, another important manufacturer of coloured

---

[1] S.P.D. Add. Jas. I, XXXIX, 34.

[2] S.P.D. Jas. I, LXXV, 84.

[3] Aubrey, Natural History of Wilts., Bodl. MS. Aubrey 2, f. 144. Aubrey's information was derived from the Ash family and he noted Webb as being of Somersetshire.

[4] The Kingswood to which Webb belonged was not the hamlet in Bradford parish but the detached village to the north-west of the county.

[5] Gloucester Public Library, MS. 16,531, 102—for this reference I am indebted to the kindness of Dr. W. B. Willcox. See in addition *supra*, p. 76 and also patent no. 30, 16 Dec. 1624, printed in *Wilts. Notes and Queries*, i (1893–5), 4. Also Steele, *Catalogue of Tudor and Stuart Proclamations*, i, no. 1390.

[6] *Supra*, p. 97.

cloths, was able to maintain his employees at work and even to purchase large amounts of real property.[1]

Imitations speedily began to testify to the success of the Spanish-cloth makers. Although the increased import of Spanish wool brought the fine-wool growers of Herefordshire into low water, it may be suspected that 'Spanish' cloths were often woven wholly or in part from English wool so that there was really no clear line of demarcation between Spanish and ordinary medley cloth made from dyed home-grown wool. Such a suspicion is fortified by the fact that the expanding market for coloured cloths soon tempted some makers of white cloth to dye their fabrics immediately before they were sent to the fulling mill.[2] The failure of the Cockayne and of earlier more modest experiments had demonstrated the inability of English dyers and cloth-dressers to work satisfactorily upon the west country broadcloths after they had been fulled and so had left the hands of the clothier[3]; but better fortune now awaited the manufacturers who ventured to dye their cloths in the say —i.e. after they had left the loom but before they had been fulled.

As early as 1630 there were complaints to the privy council from the makers of Spanish cloths to the effect that their wares had been counterfeited by clothiers who dyed their cloths in the say and after attaching false marks and lists sold them as the genuine article; these facts were corroborated by some London merchants, probably merchant adventurers, who professed to share the fears of the complainants that Spanish cloth would lose its reputation and market if the false manufacturers were not suppressed.[4] But the government hardly possessed sufficient legal authority to suppress the making of say-dyed cloths as such; in the event, it did nothing, and four years later the makers of Spanish cloth sent another protest against the deceptions of the say-dyed clothiers.[5] On this occasion

---

[1] Ex. Bills and Answers, 255/100; *supra*, p. 79.

[2] S.P.D. Chas. I, cccxlvi, 6.

[3] S.P.D. Jas. I, lxxii, 70, quot. Friis, *Alderman Cockayne's Project*, 250–1. Cf. however, the export of dyed Wiltshire cloths to Scandinavia in the late sixteenth century—*supra*, p. 28.

[4] S.P.D. Chas. I, clviii, 42.   [5] S.P.D. Chas. I, cclxviii, 5.

the privy council actually summoned before itself the chief offenders, of whom the ringleaders were William Brewer of Lullington and Christopher Brewer of Beckington—both thus operating in Somerset but close to the Wiltshire border.[1]

It was not, however, until 1639 that the council gave way to the merchant adventurers and the Spanish clothiers so far as to forbid the attachment to say-dyed cloths of ornamental lists which might be confused with those affixed to Spanish cloths[2]; in March 1640 it further investigated the purchase by several London merchants of say-dyed cloths, some of which had been bought direct from the two Brewers without having been sent to Blackwell Hall.[3] There ensued in turn a petition from the say-dyed clothiers of the four counties of Somerset, Gloucester, Worcester, and Wiltshire, led by the Brewers; the eight Wiltshire signatures were headed by that of the enterprising Christopher Potticary of Stockton. The petitioners pointed out that unlike the Spanish clothiers they used home-grown wool and that they had established a flourishing industry which would be killed if the order were enforced; they accordingly asked for a list of distinctive pattern to be assigned to say-dyed cloths so that they might retain their characteristic decoration while no longer giving cause to be considered mere imitations of Spanish cloth.[4] The council referred the matter to an *ad hoc* committee which reported, though with some dissentients, emphatically in favour of the makers of say-dyed cloths; the quality of some of their colours was, it was stated, as good as if not better than the work of Dutch dyers.[5] In June 1640 it was finally ordered that the manufacture of say-dyed cloths might continue for the present but only as an experiment; and each cloth upon pain of forfeiture was to bear its distinctive marking as having been dyed in the say. Further, say-dyed cloths were not in future to be exported to the markets of the merchant adventurers

[1] Privy Council Register, 24 Oct. and 14 Nov. 1634.
[2] Privy Council Register, 19 April 1639.
[3] Privy Council Register, 18 and 20 March 1640.
[4] S.P.D. Chas. I, CCCCLIV, 29.
[5] S.P.D. Chas. I, CCCCLIV, 84. The ubiquitous Wither was one of the signatories.

in Holland and Germany but only to the Baltic and Mediterranean.[1] To these decrees the Brewer brothers formally
submitted after some grumbling[2]; but how far the orders
of the council were in fact obeyed must remain highly
dubious.

While the exports of broadcloth remained low,[3] the
merchant adventurers found that there was a fair and growing
market for the new coloured cloths made in the west country,
at their mart towns of Delft and Hamburg. As early as
1630 Spanish cloth was said to have become one of the
most sought-after English cloths abroad,[4] and despite
repeated laments at its deceitful manufacture[5] its reputation
stood no lower in 1639.[6] The Dutch authorities took alarm
at the increased import of coloured cloths into Holland by
the merchant adventurers, and the ensuing friction was
partly the cause of the removal of their mart town by the
latter from Delft to the more complaisant city of Rotterdam
in 1635.[7] A contributory factor to the success of Spanish
cloths was no doubt the smaller export duty which had to
be paid upon them; as it was levied on each cloth irrespec-
tive of value and as Spanish cloths were finer and therefore
more costly than broadcloth, the merchant stood to gain by
exporting the former rather than the latter.[8] But other reasons
were doubtless stronger—the fineness of the fabric itself,
the improved technique of English dyers, and above all
the inscrutable changes of taste on the continent.

Merchant adventurers were, however, not the only shippers
of the new coloured cloths made in the west country. For
some ten years the export of coloured cloths to the Nether-

---

[1] Privy Council Register, 20 June 1640.
[2] Privy Council Register, 26 June 1640.
[3] In 1629 the merchant adventurers exported to their mart town Delft only
some 30,000 white broadcloths, about half the quantity which they had been wont
to ship to Middelburg twenty years or so earlier—Te Lintum, *De Merchant
Adventurers in de Nederlanden*, 93.   [4] S.P.D. Chas. I, CLVIII, 42.
[5] S.P.D. Chas. I, CCXXV, 64, CCXL, 23, and CCCXLI, 101.
[6] Privy Council Register, 19 April 1639.
[7] Te Lintum, *De Merchant Adventurers in de Nederlanden*, 126–43. The
merchant adventurers already possessed the right to sell cloths dyed and dressed
in England at their other mart town Hamburg—Lingelbach, *The Merchant Adventurers at Hamburg, American Historical Review*, ix (1903–4), 271.
[8] S.P.D. Chas. I, CCCCLXXV, 64.

lands and Germany remained open to all, and a number of interlopers drove a flourishing trade, chiefly at Amsterdam. Most of these were doubtless London merchants. Their presence was a constant source of irritation to the merchant adventurers, who accused them of all sorts of dishonesty,[1] but it was not until 1634 that the government extended the monoply of the merchant adventurers to coloured cloths.[2] The interlopers did not, however, give way without a struggle, and they continued to maintain themselves at Amsterdam despite the royal order.[3] No less alarming for the merchant adventurers was the competition of merchants from the ports of the south-west, above all Exeter, who in the thirties began to ship allegedly large quantities of Spanish cloth and who audaciously asserted in 1638 that the output of the latter had trebled under their patronage during the previous three years. But on the other side it was also complained that the merchants of the south-west outports had begun to visit the industrial areas in their hinterland and that they bought on the spot the cloths of the most popular colours —thus denuding the Blackwell Hall market.[4] It is not impossible that merchants from Exeter during the thirties may have fared as far as the Wiltshire industrial area, though actually the number of Spanish cloths shipped from Exeter to Rotterdam in 1636 was less than four hundred[5]; but ultimately by the terms of a compromise with the merchant adventurers which they reached in January 1638 they bound themselves not to ship cloths made outside Devonshire in future.[6] The Wiltshire clothiers a year or so later, when they were forced to complain of their cloths lying unsold in Blackwell Hall,[7] may have lamented this agreement, even though it was not long observed; in 1647 the merchant adventurers were again complaining and in vain of the

---

[1] S.P.D. Chas. I, CCLXXVII, 124.

[2] Privy Council Register, 15 July 1634; Steele, *Catalogue of Tudor and Stuart Proclamations*, i, no. 1685.

[3] Te Lintum, *De Merchant Adventurers in de Nederlanden*, 146–55.

[4] Privy Council Register, 20 Dec. 1637, 17 and 24 Jan. 1638; S.P.D. Chas. I, CCCLXXVIII, 97, CCCLXXIX, 32, and CCCLXXX, 85 and 86.

[5] Ex. K.R. Port Books, 949/9; Rotterdam was apparently the only Dutch or German port to which the Exeter merchants traded in 1636. *Vide* appendix II.

[6] Privy Council Register, 24 Jan. 1638.

[7] S.P.D. Chas. I, CCCCVII, 98.

competition of the western merchants at Rotterdam.[1] The
matter was still in dispute eleven years later[2] and the
bickering continued after the Restoration; but the trade of
the port of Exeter continued to grow.[3]

The exploits of the merchants of the south-west in the
sixteen-thirties are of particular interest as illustrating a
small early phase of the process by which in these years
the west country woollen industry was very gradually beginning to free itself from its complete bondage to the central
European market. For the Wiltshire clothier the exclusive
importance of Blackwell Hall had hinged originally upon
the ultimate sale of his wares in those parts of the continent
most easily accessible from London, and although no real
alternative marketing centre in England was ever to be
found it remains true that the economic hegemony of
London had now reached its zenith and with the widening
of the horizon of trade had already begun to enter upon its
very slow decline. But the commercial supremacy of London
was strongly entrenched and was never seriously shaken by
the extension beyond central Europe of the market for west
country cloths alone. The prolonged maintenance of the
almost exclusive monopoly of Blackwell Hall was no doubt
due largely to the force of sheer 'geographical inertia';
when during the civil war the western clothing districts
were momentarily cut off from London it was found pain-
fully that no alternative market could be established at
either Exeter or Bristol.[4]

Earlier deviations from the mart towns of the merchant
adventurers had in no way affected the monopoly of the
London merchants; the interlopers had doubtless bought
their cloths at Blackwell Hall as had the handful of authorized adventurers—among whom Anthony Wither was
numbered—who engaged in an uncertain and difficult trade
with the Spanish Netherlands.[5] To members of this latter
group Christopher Potticary of Stockton usually sold his

---

[1] Te Lintum, *De Merchant Adventurers in de Nederlanden*, 176.

[2] *C.S.P.D. 1658-9*, 100.

[3] S.P.D. Chas. II, LI, 64, &c.; Hoskins, *Industry, Trade and People in Exeter
1688-1800* (1935), 66-9.

[4] Privy Council Register, 4 May 1644.

[5] Cf. S.P.D. Jas. I, *passim*.

whole output of cloths, numbering annually probably some hundreds.[1] But the nearest outlet geographically for Wiltshire cloths lay in France; the French textile market, however, remained in the early seventeenth century the more or less exclusive preserve of the north country and Devonshire manufacturers. The reversion, probably intensified after the onset of the great crisis, of a number of Salisbury clothiers to the making of white kersey-like fabrics—'Salisbury plains'—did not win them a large market in France.[2] A few of these 'Salisbury plains' were indeed being shipped across the Channel from the decayed port of Southampton in the middle years of the reign of James I[3] and in the thirties they were still being exported to Rouen and St. Malo—a couple were even sent to the Canaries.[4] But a larger market for these fabrics lay in the Mediterranean. The great majority of those not consumed by the home market were probably sent to Blackwell Hall, and in 1640 all the Salisbury plains shipped from the port of London— not far short of two hundred in number—were destined without exception for the city of Leghorn.[5]

In any case, the trade with France was hardly an easy one and the merchants engaged in it often had reason to complain of the obstacles put in their way by the French authorities. On one occasion the government employed the famous Wiltshire clothier, Benedict Webb of Kingswood, as an envoy to France, possibly in an effort to reach some sort of agreement for the import of English cloth.[6] A few stray Wiltshire broadcloths found their way to Exeter and thence to ports on the other side of the Channel in the twenties and thirties; they were accompanied by larger but still very insignificant numbers of Spanish cloths and

---

[1] S.P.D. Chas. I, CLXXXIV, 65 and 76, and CXCI, 41.

[2] Salisbury kerseys were described in Ex. K.R. Port Book 824/7 as 'olim vocata plaines'. Cf. the description of Roger Wayt in *The Genealogist*, xxvi (1909-10), 233.

[3] Ex. K.R. Port Books, 820/3, quot. Friis, *Alderman Cockayne's Project*, 65; Anderson, *Book of Examinations and Depositions*, i, 46 (*Southampton Rec. Soc. Publ.* xxix, 1929).

[4] Ex. K.R. Port Books, 824/7. The figures for 1637 were—St. Malo 44, Canaries 2½.

[5] Ex. K.R. Port Books, 43/4.

[6] S.P.D. Jas. I, XCVIII, 81; *supra*, p. 103.

coloured broadcloths, of which a fair proportion may have been of Wiltshire manufacture.[1] One or two of these were occasionally shipped even from Barnstaple.[2] There were even larger but still comparatively unimportant exports of these cloths to France in the thirties from London, though Spain and the Mediterranean provided better markets for the London merchants. Nevertheless as late as 1640 the preponderant dependence of the makers of Spanish and similar coloured cloths upon the ancient and unsatisfactory broadcloth market in Germany and the Low Countries was striking.[3]

The making of coloured cloths was not the only nor the most striking innovation in the Wiltshire woollen industry of the seventeenth century. The manufacture of serges presupposed a far greater break with the ancient traditions of the Wiltshire clothier. The wool used by the serge-maker was long-haired, and it was combed and not carded before being spun; finally the woven fabric was not necessarily fulled, so that the pattern of the yarn was thus left visible.[4] Fairly early in the seventeenth century there were wool-combers at Tetbury just over the north-west county boundary,[5] and already serges had for some time been made in Southampton.[6] Certainly before the civil war there were serge-weavers in Wiltshire,[7] but serge-making only took root in the county during the second half of the seventeenth century. Devizes was a chief centre of the industry, but serge was also made at Calne, Slaughterford, and elsewhere.[8] In all probability Wiltshire never seriously rivalled Devon-

---

[1] Ex. K.R. Port Books, 945/8, quot. Friis, *Alderman Cockayne's Project*, 66–7; Ex. K.R. Port Books, 949/9—appendix II.

[2] Ex. K.R. Port Books, 949/11—appendix II.

[3] Ex. K.R. Port Books, 43/4—appendix II; *infra*, p. 118.

[4] Cf. the convenient description of woollen and worsted yarn in Heaton, *Yorkshire Woollen and Worsted Industries*, 259–63.

[5] *Gloucestershire Notes and Queries*, iii (1885–7), 406. The making of the new draperies had begun in Gloucestershire before the end of the seventeenth century —Ex. Bills and Answers, 16/169—this reference has been furnished by Dr. W. B. Willcox. On the new draperies in Wiltshire *vide supra*, p. 102.

[6] *H.M.C. Southampton Corporation*, 95.

[7] *Genealogist*, xxviii (1911–12), 56, and xxx (1913–14), 126.

[8] This may be deduced from the lists of Salisbury diocese marriage licences printed in the *Genealogist*, new series, *passim* and from the lists of Salisbury wills at Somerset House.

shire or even Suffolk in its manufacture of serges; however, some at least of the Wiltshire serge-makers of the later seventeenth century lived in a modest prosperity.[1] Other new types of cloth were also made in Wiltshire in the same period, though the full spate of innovation and experiment was reserved for the eighteenth century.[2]

The development of even the coloured cloth and serge manufacture in Wiltshire was probably impeded considerably by the civil strife which undoubtedly intensified the already long prevalent depression in the manufacture of cloth. The wars affected the woollen industry in various ways. There were interruptions to the routine of county administration when the justices failed to meet at their quarter sessions. There was the dislocation doubtless caused by the departure, whether voluntary or forced, of the industrial workers to the wars and still more by their return. There were military depredations, notably the exactions levied by garrison commanders on the surrounding countryside—the commander of the Malmesbury garrison imposed in 1642 a fine of two hundred pounds upon the town of Chippenham.[3] At Calne the borough expenses in the troubled year 1644 were more than quadrupled in comparison with the average figures for the previous decade.[4] But most serious of all must have been the uncertainty of access for the clothiers to their market at Blackwell Hall. At best they had to pay heavy tolls en route to the garrisons for disobeying the royal proclamation forbidding trade with

---

[1] The inventories of the goods of two working serge-weavers, John Beere of Lacock (1684) and Henry Painter of Devizes (1692), suggest that they lived in greater affluence than most ordinary weavers. Cf. also the serge-makers' wills printed in the *Genealogist*, xxxvii (1921), 78–9. There is a surprising remark made by Hoskins, *Industry, Trade and People in Exeter*, 67, that serges by 1700 were being made only in Devonshire and Suffolk.

[2] Fustian was made in north Wiltshire in the seventeenth century—*Genealogist*, xxvii (1910–11), 237 and xxxiii (1916–17), 126. Wiltshire bays were mentioned in 1661 in the list of cloths on which hallage was due at Blackwell Hall—Guildhall, City of London Journals, 46 f. 74b. Cf. the effort to introduce the making of bays into Bristol in 1610—Latimer, *Annals of Bristol in the Seventeenth Century* (1900), 41.

[3] Goldney, *Records of Chippenham*, 209. Cf. Pafford, *Accounts of the Parliamentary Garrisons of Great Chalfield and Malmesbury 1645–6* (1940), *passim*.

[4] Calne, corporation minute book 1565–1814, f. 64b. Press money accounted for much of this rise.

rebellious London,[1] and it was small comfort that the privy council with the king showed itself willing to encourage an alternative traffic westwards. Efforts to establish cloth markets at Bristol and Exeter proved abortive, since no merchants could be conjured thither to buy.[2] To make matters worse, some merchant adventurers, owing to this severance from the clothiers who normally supplied them, actually set up clothmaking businesses on their own account at Rotterdam and perhaps elsewhere; they employed for the time being Dutch weavers and spinners there to manufacture cloth out of English wool.[3] And even after the civil strife had subsided, the Dutch war helped to throw trade out of gear; so that the merchant adventurers remained in low water despite some improvement during the fifties.[4] It may, however, be suspected that the economic crises of the interregnum affected the making of white broadcloth rather than the manufacture of the new fabrics and that the medley clothiers were indeed comparatively little interrupted in the progress of their industry as soon as the actual fighting was at an end.

Meanwhile, the woollen industry in Wiltshire as a whole continued to languish throughout the years of disturbance. During the wars the sales of wool and yarn in Devizes market again diminished greatly[5] and particularly in the later forties there were many symptoms of industrial distress. In 1646–7 there was a marked shortage of corn; there were riots at Melksham and the inhabitants of Warminister petitioned the justices to suppress some of the maltsters so as to avert violence.[6] In 1647 a pitiable petition purporting to come from the broadweavers of the central industrial area from Calne and Chippenham to Bromham and Melksham depicted their misery; many were entirely out of employment and others working only at half pressure.[7]

---

[1] Cf. the narratives quoted by Waylen, *A History Military and Municipal of the Town of Marlborough* (1854), 220–2.

[2] Privy Council Register, 28 Feb. and 4 May 1644.

[3] Te Lintum, *De Merchant Adventurers in de Nederlanden*, 177–8; cf. S.P.D. Int. I, 34.

[4] S.P.D. Int. IX, 61; XXXII, 101; XXXIV, 64; LXXV, 34, &c.

[5] Cunnington, *Annals of the Borough of Devizes*, I, ii, 112; cf. *supra*, p. 90.

[6] Cunnington, *Records of the County of Wilts.* 183 and 200.

[7] H.M.C. *Wilts.* 115.

In the same year the inhabitants of Westport near Malmesbury pointed out to the justices how the demand for spinners and carders had greatly diminished. The repair of Calne church was held up at this time very understandably for lack of money.[1] At length in March 1649 the speaker Lenthall formally admonished the Wiltshire justices in the name of the parliament to see that the poor laws were at once put into execution.[2] A couple of months previously the corporation of Salisbury had resolved to establish a workhouse to relieve the poor of the city; throughout the middle and later part of the century, indeed, Salisbury was burdened with a heavy pauper problem.[3]

It is therefore not surprising that it is difficult to discern any eager partisanship among the industrial classes of Wiltshire during the civil wars. Possibly a good majority of the gentry may have sided with the king. Even Sir Edward Baynton—the erstwhile foe of the luckless Wither—was a cavalier; his exactions while commander of the Devizes garrison were said to have turned the townspeople against the king's cause.[4] There were royalist clothiers; a composition of thirty pounds was laid on one of them, Henry Hawkins of Chippenham, by the victorious parliament.[5] But it may be suspected that most clothiers would have sympathized with the Wiltshiremen—whoever they were— who before the civil wars were over had together resolved to petition impartially king and parliament and to oppose by all means the rule of violence.[6] On the other hand it is certain that in the epoch of comparative religious freedom ushered in by the rule of the long parliament quakers, baptists, and other sectaries propagated their views widely among the industrial population of the county.[7] In the years

[1] Assize Order Book, Western Circuit 1641–52, entry dated 5 Mar. 22 Car. I; Cunnington, *Records of the County of Wilts.* 200.

[2] Cunnington, *Records of the County of Wilts.* 326.

[3] Benson and Hatcher, *History of Salisbury*, 384, 414, 422–3, &c.

[4] Bull, *A History Military and Municipal of the Ancient Borough of the Devizes* (1859), 202–3. The four chief Wiltshire enemies of the king's cause are listed in Steele, *Catalogue of Tudor and Stuart Proclamations*, i, no. 2288.

[5] Waylen, *The Wiltshire Compounders, Wilts. Arch. Mag.* xxii (1885–6), 81–2.

[6] This anonymous agreement of the Wiltshire clubmen is to be found in B.M. Add. MS. 24862, f. 48.

[7] A census of dissenters in the diocese of Salisbury for the year 1676 has been printed in *Wilts. Notes and Queries*, iii (1899–1901), 535–7.

immediately following the restoration the government was
troubled by fears of a rising in Wiltshire of the 'saints'[1], and
a little later the conforming Aubrey sourly noted the
fanaticism in his county[2]; but how far social discontent
found an outlet in religious enthusiasm it is impossible to
say. Clothiers as well as their employees were numbered
among the dissenters; Anthony Druce, a Bradford clothier
who flourished under the later Stuarts, was, for instance,
a quaker.[3] In the early eighteenth century there were
numerous wealthy dissenters in Wiltshire.[4]

Before then, however, the economic horizon had bright-
ened, for the clouds of depression which had overhung the
Wiltshire woollen industry as a whole since the days of the
Cockayne experiment nearly two generations earlier had
after the restoration at last begun to lift. The makers of the
traditional white broadcloths—who were still numerous[5]—
had presumably adapted themselves to the circumstances
of their shrunken but perhaps momentarily static market,
while the districts in which Spanish and other types of
coloured cloths were made enjoyed a fairly though not
entirely constant prosperity; the population of Bradford,
notwithstanding the operation of the law of settlement,
began to rise more and more rapidly in the seventies and
eighties,[6] and industry actually invaded a village hitherto
so completely agricultural as Corsley.[7] In Bradford and in
Trowbridge the clothiers were building for themselves fine
mansions in the English version of baroque.[8] It is worth
emphasis that the pioneers of this revival from the days of
Benedict Webb onwards did not necessarily belong to the
old families established from generation to generation in the

[1] There is plenty of evidence as to this in the state papers domestic.
[2] Aubrey, *Natural History of Wiltshire*, 11, &c. Cf. the lists of licensed non-
conformist meeting places in *C.S.P.D. 1672, passim*.
[3] Jones, *Bradford-on-Avon*, 62; cf. Knubley, *Abstracts of Deeds relating to the
Family of Methuen, Wilts. Arch. Mag.* xliii (1925–7), 401.
[4] Bebb, *Nonconformity and Social and Economic Life, 1660–1800* (1935), 180.
[5] S.P.D. Chas. II, CCCLI, 150. The industrial population engaged in making
these in Wiltshire was estimated in this memorandum (1673) at thirty thousand;
possibly this was an exaggeration. Cf. *infra*, p. 117.
[6] Jones, *Bradford-on-Avon*, 63–4.
[7] Davies, *Life in an English Village*, 24–7; *supra*, pp. 3–4.
[8] The remains of these buildings, after the lapse of two and a half centuries,
still impress the visitor to the Bradford and Trowbridge district.

clothmaking business in Wiltshire. Original talent was as
necessary as steady application and traditional knowledge
to encourage industrial recovery. The Goldneys of Chippenham and the Yerburys of Trowbridge and Bradford indeed
continued as clothiers, but with the decline of the ancient
broadcloth manufacture there disappeared some familiar
names from Wiltshire industrial life. Some, including the
Hortons, the Wallises, the Middlecots, and the Chiverses
enrolled themselves among the gentry; others were probably
less fortunate.[1]

The most famous Wiltshire clothier of the reign of
Charles II was Paul Methuen, who had settled as a new-
comer at Bradford and who built up his business there. A
notable contemporary of his was William Brewer of Trowbridge, bearer of a name equally unfamiliar in the Wiltshire
woollen industry, who was reported to John Aubrey in the
reign of James II as driving the greatest trade in England
for medley cloths.[2] It is characteristic that both Methuen
and Brewer should have been responsible for the immigration
of foreign workmen into Wiltshire; the former established
in Bradford a spinner with his wife and children from
Amsterdam and the latter transported three Germans or
Poles thither as his employees.[3] There was indeed no lack

[1] Cf. *supra*, p. 42.

[2] Methuen married the daughter of John Ash, the Somersetshire clothier whose
business he inherited—Aubrey, Natural History of Wiltshire, Bodl. MS. Aubrey
2, f. 144. A grandiose pedigree was later invented for the Methuen family—
Britton, *Beauties of Wiltshire*, ii (1801), 293; cf. *The Genealogist*, new series, iv
(1887), 59–61. There is no evidence at hand to prove any relationship between
this Brewer and the Brewers who were making say-dyed cloths in Somersetshire
before the outbreak of civil war, though it is tempting to assume some connexion.
On Methuen and Brewer see also *infra*, p. 127; Paul Methuen is noticed in the *D.N.B.*

[3] Jones, *Bradford-on-Avon*, 54–5. Apart from the appearance in 1658 of a
'Dutchman' at Salisbury, where he was employed in teaching the workhouse
children to spin—Benson and Hatcher, *History of Salisbury*, 441—these are the
only authenticated instances of the arrival in Wiltshire during the sixteenth and
seventeenth centuries of foreigners skilled in the technical processes of the textile
industry. An examination of the subsidy rolls for the sixteenth century has failed
to substantiate Aubrey's gossip about the settlement of Flemish or Walloon weavers
in Wiltshire by Henry VII—*Natural History of Wiltshire*, 112, and *Wiltshire
Topographical Collections*, 304. Cf. Marsh, *A History of the Borough and Town of
Calne* (1903), 118 and *Wilts. Notes and Queries*, iii (1899–1901), 380. There
were Dutch refugees at Southampton in 1567—S.P.D. Add. Eliz. XIII, 80—and
Huguenot weavers arrived at Bristol in 1682—Latimer, *Annals of Bristol in the
Seventeenth Century* (1900), 411.

I

of technical or inventive skill in Wiltshire[1]; but it was nevertheless by such acts of initiative that the woollen industry of the county was enabled to adapt itself to the new conditions. It profited little in the long run to the clothiers of Salisbury that their white cloths had the reputation of being the best in England[2]; the demand was for medley and other new fabrics, and since they were too conservative to change their methods their industry inevitably declined.[3] A similar phenomenon might be observed elsewhere: the ancient and celebrated cloth manufacture of Worcester began to dwindle away in the later seventeenth century for the same reason.[4]

The market for which the Wiltshire clothier catered in the restoration period was no longer exclusively in central Europe. Much of it was no doubt at home: the increasing wealth and population of the kingdom undoubtedly enabled it to absorb a larger proportion of its own woollen manufactures than had previously been the case. An artificial stimulus to the consumption of the coarser woollen cloths was doubtless supplied by the enactment in 1668 of a statute ordering the burial of every corpse in a woollen shroud,[5] while a larger sale for the finer sorts may have been obtained when it was observed that Charles II deliberately wore English cloth upon his own royal person.[6] In proportion to the diminution in the cost of Spanish wool the price of Spanish cloth fell, and it became a fashionable garb among all classes.[7] As to the relative importance of the home and the foreign markets for woollen cloth in the later seventeenth century it is impossible to be definite, but it may be guessed that the former was at least as great as the latter.[8]

[1] Aubrey, Natural History of Wiltshire, Bodl. MS. Aubrey 2, ff. 66–7.

[2] Aubrey, *Natural History of Wiltshire*, 95 and 112.

[3] Yarranton in 1677 noticed that Salisbury as a textile centre was 'much decayed of late years'—*England's Improvement* (1677), 100. Wilton also declined, probably for the same reason—*C.S.P.D. 1666–7*, 218.

[4] *V.C.H. Worcestershire*, ii, 293–7.

[5] 18 & 19 Car. II, c. 4; cf. Ogg, *England in the Reign of Charles II*, i (1934), 70.   [6] S.P.D. Chas. II, cccxcii, 151.

[7] *A Treatise of Wool, and the Manufacture of it* (1685), 22–4. Cf. *H.M.C. House of Lords*, new ser. V, 70.

[8] Two contemporary estimates of the proportion of home-manufactured cloth habitually exported in the later seventeenth century may be noted here: according

The widening of the market both at home and abroad for Wiltshire cloths was all the more necessary since the sales of the traditional white broadcloth in the former central European market finally dwindled to vanishing point in the last decade of the seventeenth century. As late as the sixties and seventies the consignments of west country undyed broadcloth which were still being shipped across to Hamburg and the Netherlands were sufficiently large to evoke protests from the London dyers and cloth finishers in a style reminiscent of the days before the Cockayne experiment[1]; it was even estimated at this time that the production of these merely semi-manufactured goods gave employment to thirty thousand people in Wiltshire.[2] But this ancient trade was soon to sink further and further and into extinction, in part perhaps because of the repeated wars waged by Louis XIV in western Germany and the Netherlands but probably even more because of the competition of fabrics of newer style. During the five years 1697–1702 the annual exports of broadcloth were never near reaching so much as four figures and sometimes barely attained three.[3] It may thus be assumed that by the end of the seventeenth century the special trade which in the later middle ages had raised Wiltshire to a prominent place among the industrial counties of England was nearing the point of death; the period of transition ushered in by the Cockayne experiment had therefore come to an end and the Wiltshire woollen industry had fully entered upon a new phase of its history—a phase which was to be closed only with the advent of an even greater industrial revolution in the nineteenth century.

to one—S.P.D. Will. III, XIII, 149—less than half was exported in peace time and less than a quarter during war, and according to the other—which professed to be founded upon the calculations of aulnage officials and is to be found in *An Answer to the most Material Objections against the Bill for Restraining the East-India Wrought Silks, &c.*, s.l., n.d. (Bodl. fol. θ 658, 54)—not more than a third was sent abroad. Cf. also the estimates of King and Davenant, quot. Hoskins, *Industry, Trade and People in Exeter*, 43.

[1] S.P.D. Chas. II, LXVI, 108, CCCLXI, 152, CCCLXIII, 24, &c.
[2] S.P.D. Chas. II, CCCXLI, 132 and 150; cf. *supra*, p. 114.
[3] Figures for the year 1697–8 are to be found in *Commons' Journals*, xiii, 152–4 and for the years 1698–1702 in *Commons' Journals*, xvii, 366–7. Information as to the availability of such figures is to be found in Clark, *Guide to English Commercial Statistics* (1938), 153 *et seq.*

The process by which the necessary fresh markets had meanwhile been found for the new substitute types of woollen cloth may be traced most illuminatingly in the case of Spanish cloth, the making of which had formed the first serious departure in Wiltshire from the conventional broadcloth manufacture. Before the civil war Spanish cloths were not sold in any considerable quantity outside the territories served by the merchant adventurers; their sale was thus in a sense parasitic upon that of the undyed broadcloths and depended upon the more intensive exploitation of the same dwindling market.[1] It is not surprising therefore to find that the annual quantity of Spanish cloths exported in the generation after 1640 actually diminished. But the shrunken foreign market of the post-restoration years possessed a less precarious foundation in that it was geographically more widely extended. In 1664 the Dutch had indeed almost ceased to buy Spanish cloths, and the most important outlets were provided by Hamburg and Ostend; but over a thousand Spanish cloths were sold in Portugal and not far short of that number in France. The French market, despite the unfavourable commercial policy of Colbert, actually continued to expand; within five years it had more than doubled and by 1685 it had almost doubled again. In the latter year nearly a third of the total number of Spanish cloths shipped abroad from London by English merchants were destined for France, while the next most important market lay in Scandinavia and the Baltic; although there had been some revival of the Dutch market,[2] nevertheless the combined exports to Hamburg and the Netherlands both southern and northern totalled less than a third of the whole.

This liberation from dependence upon the central European market may be further illustrated with reference to the cloths designated by the customs officials as 'long' or 'short westerns', of which a fair proportion were probably

[1] *Supra*, p. 106. The figures upon which the argument of this and the succeeding paragraphs are based will be found in Appendix II. References will only be given to sources not mentioned there.

[2] The Dutch market in the nineties and in the early eighteenth century came to be dominated by Devonshire serges—Hoskins, *Industry, Trade and People in Exeter*, 70.

made in Wiltshire and may plausibly be identified with the medley cloths which were manufactured by Methuen, Brewer, and their contemporaries. These were sold in all quarters of the world, but already in 1664 over four-fifths were being shipped to the two Levantine ports of Smyrna and Scanderoon, while most of the remainder were sent to India.[1] The situation had hardly altered twenty years later in 1685, save that the predominance of the Mediterranean market was somewhat less accentuated. Ordinary 'long cloths' and 'short cloths', of which an unknown proportion was of Wiltshire origin, also went chiefly to the Levant, though some were sold in the Baltic and elsewhere. Serges found a market to some extent in France and Portugal, though by the end of the century their greatest sale was in central Europe; it may, however, be mentioned that they were exported not only from London but also from the out-ports, including Bristol.[2] It is tempting to believe that with the reawakening of Bristol in the later seventeenth century there came a revival of the traffic in Wiltshire cloths west-ward; it may at least be surmised that some of the serges and 'short cloths' exported from Bristol in the last decades of the seventeenth century to the West Indies and to Por-tugal were of Wiltshire manufacture.[3]

Thus already before the end of the reign of Charles II the Wiltshire woollen industry had expanded its former market in Germany and the Netherlands to include not only western Europe but also the near and middle east and even the new world. The repercussions of these together with kindred and no less momentous economic conquests can be traced in the foreign policy of Cromwell and his successors,[4] in the appearance of English war fleets in the Mediterranean and the Baltic no less than in the heightened tempo of the struggle for colonial expansion; the Wiltshire clothier was

[1] On the importance of the Mediterranean market in 1665 some light is shed by S.P.D. Chas. II, cvii, 51, and cxii, 10.

[2] *Commons' Journals*, xvii, 366, 394-5, 397-8.

[3] A number of the cloths exported from Bristol in 1685 were designated 'Norwich stuffs'—Ex. K.R. Port Book 1147/2.

[4] The student of the Wiltshire woollen industry cannot but be impressed by the activity of Cromwell in helping to open up future markets for its products—cf. Ashley, *Financial and Commercial Policy under the Cromwellian Protectorate* (1934), 112-28, 138-49.

now perhaps less directly affected by the troubles of central
Europe, but his fortunes were for the future to be bound
up with the progress of English commerce in all parts of
the world. The industrial depression of the nineties reached
a very low point in the months following the naval battle
off Beachy Head, when for a brief interval the French fleet
commanded the seas.[1] The heyday of the Levantine trade
had already drawn to a close in the eighties of the seventeenth century.[2] The traffic in cloths to Portugal suffered
a setback in 1679 when king Pedro II enjoined upon his
subjects the wearing of native manufactures;[3] however,
with the signature of the Methuen treaty a generation later,
the export of English woollen cloths to Portugal was said
to have quadrupled.[4] Indeed, so close did the dependence
of the makers of Spanish cloths upon the Portuguese market
become that after the end of the war of the Spanish suc-
cession the clothiers of the Trowbridge and Bradford district petitioned the house of commons against the conclusion
of any commercial treaty with France which might prejudice
the import of Portuguese wines and oils into England and
so provoke the Portuguese government into taxing English
cloths.[5]

The Wiltshire woollen manufacture had indeed been
restored and maintained by the enterprise of innovating
clothiers from Benedict Webb and Christopher Potticary
to Paul Methuen and William Brewer, and upon the basis
provided by the exploitation of a world market its life as a
great industry was thus prolonged for another couple of
centuries. But it had won no more freedom from periods
of depressed trade than it had enjoyed in the old days when
it had catered for a geographically limited outlet. There
is no evidence to suggest that the lot of the manual worker
in the Wiltshire woollen industry ceased to worsen in the

---

[1] Cf. the S.P.D. for the period, *passim.*

[2] Wood, *A History of the Levant Company* (1935), 102–12.

[3] Lodge, *The English Factory at Lisbon, Tr. R.H.S.*, 4th ser., xvi (1933), 217.
No doubt the issue of this decree accounts for the smallness of the Portuguese
market in 1685—*vide* Appendix II.

[4] Wallis-Chapman, *The Commercial Relations of England and Portugal, 1487–
1807, Tr. R.H.S.*, 3rd ser., I (1907), 171. Cf. Hoskins, *Industry, Trade and
People in Exeter*, 73.

[5] *Commons' Journals*, xvii, 391–2.

eighteenth century as a whole or that the cleavage between his class and that of the capitalist clothier ceased to widen —rather the reverse. And although there lay periods of thriving activity in the future, particularly in the later eighteenth century, nevertheless it may be observed that in at least one other way there were seeds of future trouble inherent in the more ecumenical character which the Wiltshire woollen industry assumed in the later seventeenth and eighteenth centuries; for the increased variety of its products brought it into a more direct competition with the manufactures of the north country—a competition which was ultimately to be largely responsible for its major disasters in the nineteenth century.

VIII

CHANGES IN THE ORGANIZATION OF THE WILTSHIRE WOOLLEN INDUSTRY DURING THE SEVENTEENTH CENTURY

IN the course of the seventeenth century the structure of the Wiltshire woollen industry changed with an increasing momentum, so that the business of the clothier who lived under the early Stuarts resembled far more that of his ancestor who had made broadcloth in the days of Henry VII than that of his grandson who carried on the trade in the post-restoration epoch. These changes were engendered chiefly by the industrial depression which was ushered in by the failure of the Cockayne experiment but which was maintained primarily by the continuance of the thirty years' war in central Europe. They were made possible because the woollen industry was not in the grip of any watertight administrative system which forbade change or discouraged experiment; the clothing laws had been indeed all-embracing in scope, but in so far as they could be effective in seventeenth-century Wiltshire they concerned chiefly the making of white broadcloth alone and so to a large extent simply ceased to be applicable as soon as the clothier turned his attention to the manufacture of other fabrics.

If the restrictive legislation by which the technique of clothmaking was regulated was to remain effective it would have had to undergo frequent adaptation so as to bring the new varieties of cloth within its purview. There was no restriction upon the size or texture of Spanish and the other new cloths; their making was therefore exempt from the attentions of the cloth searchers. There was indeed little beyond the custom of apprenticeship which applied to their manufacture. It is therefore hardly surprising that from the very beginning there should have been complaints of the deceits alleged to be prevalent in the making of Spanish cloth[1] and that the merchant adventurers should have wished to put it under the yoke of the broadcloth legislation—a measure strongly urged by the anxious Wither in 1633.[2]

[1] S.P.D. Jas. I, LXXV, 84.   [2] S.P.D. Chas. I, CCXL, 23.

Three years later the merchant adventurers were still vainly grumbling about the false manufacture of Spanish cloth[1]; their complaints about the making of say-dyed cloths received a tardy and doubtful satisfaction.[2] The city of London authorities indeed saw meanwhile to the enforcement of the monopoly of Blackwell Hall as the metropolitan market for Spanish cloth and were supported in this by the action of the privy council[3]; but no new legislative shackles could be forged until a parliament was summoned which should have leisure to devote itself to economic questions. Political strife, however, filled the air, so that this never happened; and thus to a considerable extent the new manufacture of coloured cloths in Somerset and Wiltshire developed in an atmosphere of comparative freedom not unlike that which enveloped the contemporary cotton industry in Lancashire.[4]

The development of that industrial *laissez-faire* which was to become an increasingly prominent characteristic of the Wiltshire woollen industry in the seventeenth century is therefore to be associated with the failure of the legislative machine to work as long as king and parliament were at loggerheads. But even when executive and legislature again dwelt in harmony there was no return to the former system of regulation.[5] The reasons for this were many; but though it would be irrelevant for the historian of a local industry to discuss most of them, one at least may be mentioned here —the decline in wealth and influence of the merchant adventurers. It was they who for the best part of a century had supplied the driving force behind the whole series of efforts to impose a fixed order upon the woollen industry; their hand was to be discerned in the mid-sixteenth century and later clothing statutes, in the momentarily successful attempt by the city of London authorities to institute a municipal inspection of country cloths in Blackwell Hall,

[1] S.P.D. Chas. I, CCXLI, 101.
[2] *Supra*, pp. 104–6.
[3] Guildhall, City of London Repertories, 46, f. 221 ; Privy Council Register, 30 Mar. and April 1638.
[4] Cf. Wadsworth and Mann, *The Cotton Trade and Industrial Lancashire*, 59–70.
[5] There are to be found in plenty traces of efforts to secure parliamentary authority for a refurbishing of the clothing laws during the middle and even later seventeenth century—*C.S.P.D. 1649–50*, 277 and 297 ; *1651–2*, 211 ; *1655–6*, 112, &c. Cf. *The Clothiers' Complaint* (1692), 2 and 8–9.

and finally in the hazardous incursion of Wither into the west country during the eleven years' tyranny. But subsequent governments were less sympathetic to the claims of a monopoly company; and, perhaps more important, the steady expansion of English trade beyond the limited stretch of Dutch and German coast within which their activities were confined lessened more and more their proportionate importance in the maintenance of English commerce. In the years after the restoration the merchant adventurers were but a shadow of their former selves and finally in 1689 their trade was thrown open by statute.[1] Their formal organization indeed persisted until the nineteenth century, but already before the revolution of 1688 it may thus be said that with them there had declined a most powerful force hitherto striving for governmental interference with the processes of the woollen industry.

The decay of the merchant adventurers was in this respect almost certainly more significant than any damage which the civil war may momentarily have inflicted upon the structure of local government in Wiltshire. During the four years 1643–6 the Wiltshire justices did not sit more than twice a year at quarter sessions and in 1645 they did not meet at all.[2] It is very likely that in this disturbed period the system of cloth searching finally ceased to function. But as in any case it only applied to the manufacture of the white cloths which formed now a probably steadily diminishing proportion of the output of the woollen industry in the county the importance of this breakdown does not deserve heavy emphasis; in the absence of further legislation it would in any case have transpired in the course of time. Other traces of a drift towards *laissez-faire* during the interregnum as distinct from earlier or later periods are difficult to discern. A new schedule of wage rates was drawn

---

[1] Lipson, *Economic History of England*, ii (1931), 265–8. Cf. Te Lintum, *De Merchant Adventurers in de Nederlanden*, 204, 214, and 219. This latter study, of which use has been made in this and preceding chapters and to which the last reference has now been made, is somewhat of a great work *manqué*. It throws much light on the export of English cloth in the seventeenth century, but its author was unhappily restricted to Dutch sources of information only, so that the picture he presents is somewhat lacking in proportion.

[2] Cunnington, *Records of the County of Wilts.* 1–2.

up by the justices in 1655 and subsequently proclaimed each year; it was slightly amended in 1685.[1] Unlike the earlier scale of 1602 this revised table frankly fixed maximum rates only—it not improbably thus reflected the actual practice of the first half of the century.

The custom of apprenticeship was undoubtedly infringed by the return from the armies of soldiers who—sometimes at an unripe age—forthwith launched into business as weavers or the like without having served a master for the statutory seven years, though it must be remembered that their privilege was one which had sometimes previously been enjoyed by veterans who had served in the wars abroad. It is not surprising that in the specially hard year 1647 there should have been sharp protests from the weavers of Devizes and Westbury against the competition of such newcomers.[2] But not all ex-soldiers evaded their term of apprenticeship,[3] nor is there evidence to suggest that others followed in the wake of the privileged few. Apprentices continued to be indentured throughout the century[4] and on the very morrow of the first civil war the justices of assize enforced the binding of apprentices by parish officials in conformity with the law.[5] In 1658 it was necessary for the inhabitants of Westbury to petition the justices of the peace so that the burlers of the town might continue their work undisturbed by the charge that they had not been apprenticed—burling, it was claimed, had never been a 'prentice trade'.[6] It may well be that the apprenticeship law was less honoured in the later seventeenth than it had been in the sixteenth century, though

---

[1] The 1655 assessment is to be found in *H.M.C. Wilts.* 170–3 and in Cunnington, *Records of the County of Wilts.* 290–6—the two lists do not entirely agree. It may be observed that whereas the earlier rate was published allegedly after agreement between clothiers and weavers the later was promulgated 'with respect to . . . the cheapness of all sort of provision'. As far as any comparison is possible the later rates for spinning and weaving seem to be slightly higher than the earlier.

[2] Cunnington, *Records of the County of Wilts.* 189–90; *H.M.C. Wilts.* 114.

[3] Cunnington, *Records of the County of Wilts.* 157.

[4] So at Chippenham—Goldney, *Records of Chippenham*, 193–202.

[5] Assize Order Book, Western Circuit 1641–52, f. 121.

[6] *H.M.C. Wilts.* 153. Burling was a simple process well suited, as the petitioners remarked, for child labour—it consisted chiefly of picking the knots and other roughnesses out of the cloth.

the Wiltshire justices continued to enforce it at quarter sessions during the reign of Charles II and later.[1] But on *a priori* grounds alone it might be urged that the prosperous years of the restoration period and the spirit they engendered were more responsible for the very gradual whittling away of the tradition of apprenticeship than the momentary infringements of the law during the years of acute depression which marked so much of the interregnum.

Meanwhile the clothier was slowly adapting himself to the new conditions. There are indications that in this period his business was sometimes apt to be a much more tentative and miscellaneous affair than it had been a few generations earlier. William Gaby of Netherstreet near Devizes, who traded as a clothier from the fifties to the eighties, was occupied by activities somewhat more varied than those of his counterpart even half a century earlier. He bought and sold both wool and yarn, each of assorted grades of fineness; he paid not only for the dyeing of his wool but also for the fulling and burling of his cloths by presumably independent craftsmen—though it is not suggested that at this time there subsisted in Wiltshire a class of independent fullers. And apart from the complicated transactions resulting from these processes he had other irons in the economic fire: he operated as contractor and farmer as well as clothier.[2] It may be surmised that it was the need for technical adjustment to the novel demand for coloured fabrics which gave an opportunity for the new men—Methuen, Brewer, and the others—to rise to the fore and that despite the persistence of depressed conditions until the sixties there existed in industrial Wiltshire during the middle decades of the seventeenth century a *carrière ouverte* for anybody with the requisite capital and ability and in a fashion unparalleled in the years both immediately preceding and succeeding.[3]

[1] Devizes, county muniment room, quarter sessions minute books, *passim*.

[2] An account-book of Gaby's has survived owing to the accident that it was later used as a register for family births, marriages, and deaths. It is in private hands, but a complete transcript is in the library of the Wiltshire Archaeological Society at Devizes. All the passages, however, of any interest to the student of the woollen industry have been printed by Mr. E. Coward in an article entitled *William Gaby, His Booke*, in the *Wilts. Arch. Mag.* xlvi (1932–4), 50–7.

[3] *Supra*, ch. VII, *passim*.

It is not improbable that this type of small entrepreneur represented by Gaby became less important after the restoration, for with the expansion of trade the day of the big clothier was returning. The market spinners sank once more into insignificance. Methuen and Brewer were but the greatest of a whole group of large industrialists who flourished in the Avon valley in this period. Only the Methuens indeed rose to more than local importance, and that within two generations—an almost unprecedented achievement which recalls the days of William Stumpe of Malmesbury. Less meteoric in their social ascent were the Houltons of Bradford; for though they were already established there before the end of the sixteenth century it would seem that the main architects of their family fortunes were Robert and Joseph, father and son, who flourished as clothiers under the later Stuarts; before the middle of the eighteenth century the Houltons too had established themselves among the county gentry.[1] They were connected by marriage with the Goldneys, who dwelt in an ancient mansion at Chippenham[2]; Henry Goldney, who died in 1684, owned in the neighbourhood of Chippenham much property, both freehold and leasehold, which he had himself purchased, and his legacies to his family totalled over two thousand pounds.[3] His brother Gabriel, who had died a little earlier, had lived in a large house with no less than three butteries and possessed in ready money or owing in debts over five hundred pounds; his personal apparel was valued at ten pounds.[4] Although the Goldneys had for a couple of centuries been engaged in the woollen industry, nevertheless it is clear that much of the family wealth had been very recently acquired; an earlier Gabriel Goldney, father of the brothers Henry and Gabriel and who had died in 1670, though he had indeed been a man of some property, had nevertheless been in a much smaller

[1] *Wilts. Notes and Queries*, vi (1908–10), 83–4 and 272–3.
[2] Aubrey, *Wiltshire Topographical Collections*, 67.
[3] Will of Henry Goldney, P.C.C. 125 Hare (1684), pr. in *Wilts. Notes and Queries*, vi (1908–10), 211. It is curious to observe that in 1674 this Henry Goldney was numbered among the makers of the traditional white broadcloth—S.P.D. Chas. II, CCCLXI, 132. Perhaps it may be assumed that he also manufactured coloured cloths—if it be the same man.
[4] Wilts. Archdeaconry Court, will and inventory of Gabriel Goldney, 1684.

way.[1] Related as well to the Goldneys were the Scotts of Chippenham, also large clothiers.[2]

Other notable industrial families were the Awdrys of Seend, the Paradices of Devizes, and the Selfes of Melksham; the last intermarried later with the Methuens.[3] The social status of such families cannot have been less than that of their prototypes in the sixteenth century. Like them they built up landed estates, like them they had the chance of rising in a few generations to take their place among the county gentry, and like them they often sent off their younger sons to make their way in the great world. A Houlton throve in London as a mercer,[4] and other clothiers' sons entered the church. Robert Child, a clothier of Heddington, trained up his eldest son and namesake in his own business but apprenticed in 1656 to a London goldsmith another son, Francis[5]; the latter as Sir Francis Child became one of the magnates of the banking and financial world. No less famous was John Methuen, a son of the Bradford clothier. He was educated at St. Edmund Hall, Oxford, which at this period had a strong Wiltshire connexion; he was later called to the bar and subsequently he carved out for himself a successful career as a politician and diplomat. The most dignified office he held was the lord chancellorship of Ireland, but he later acquired fame more particularly with the signature of the celebrated treaty with Portugal which bears his name.[6]

There is nothing to suggest that the employee of the prospering Wiltshire clothier benefited particularly from the industrial renaissance of the later seventeenth century. Spinners remained in Wiltshire as elsewhere 'an unorganized mass of sweated labour'[7]; Aubrey observed that on

[1] Wilts. Archdeaconry Court, will and inventory of Gabriel Goldney, 1670.

[2] Monuments to the Scotts and Goldneys of these years exist in Chippenham parish church.

[3] Aubrey, *Wiltshire Topographical Collections*, 295 and 302; *The Genealogist*, xxxvii (1920–1), 151–4.

[4] *Wilts. Notes and Queries*, vi (1908–10), 272.

[5] *Wilts. Notes and Queries*, vi (1908–10), 266–70; Aubrey, *Wiltshire Topographical Collections*, 45.

[6] There are notices of Sir Francis Child and John Methuen as well as of the latter's father in the *D.N.B.*

[7] This apt description is borrowed from Wadsworth and Mann, *The Cotton Trade and Industrial Lancashire*, 90.

their meagre wages they were kept just alive and reflected that their way of life therefore nourished theft, sedition, and rebellion.[1] Nor is it to be believed that the condition of the weavers was substantially better, although they were not always without organization. There were doubtless philanthropic clothiers other than Henry and Gabriel Goldney of Chippenham, who each bequeathed twenty pounds to the weavers who worked for them.[2] But apart from such rare largesse most weavers had probably little more than sufficed to keep body and soul together; and credit difficulties were sometimes wont to compel the clothier to resort to paying them in truck.[3] The onset of bad times was as ever liable to provoke them to riot; it often threw them upon the charity of the poor law, so that the clothier had to give security if he wished to settle his employees in a parish.[4] A naïve effort made at Trowbridge in 1677 to raise wages by combination was speedily nipped in the bud by the action of the clothier William Brewer—who now sat on the bench of justices.[5]

There were more artificers concerned in the manufacture of each Wiltshire cloth in the seventeenth than in the sixteenth century. The expansion of the coloured cloth industry from the twenties onwards entailed a certain development of the art of dyeing in Wiltshire. As a knowledgeable merchant of the Eastland company pointed out in 1613, there were comparatively few dyers and cloth-finishers to be found in the west country in proportion to the great numbers of spinners, weavers, fullers, and clothiers to be found there[6]; and this observation would have applied with particular force to Wiltshire, where no counterparts to

---

[1] Aubrey, *Natural History of Wiltshire*, 110. From the context it may be suspected that Aubrey meant by 'spinners' all the employees of the clothier.

[2] Wills of Henry and Gabriel Goldney (1684), quoted *supra*, p. 127.

[3] Cf. *The Interest of England Considered* (1694), 25–6 and *The Clothier's Complaint*, 7–8.

[4] Cunnington, *Records of the County of Wilts.* 282–3; Jones, *Bradford-on-Avon*, 54–5.

[5] Cunnington, *Records of the County of Wilts.* 259–60. An eloquent Latin epitaph upon this Brewer is to be found in Trowbridge parish church. Cf. Mrs. Gilboy's remarks upon the industrial worker of the west country in the eighteenth century—*Wages in Eighteenth Century England* (1934), 241.

[6] S.P.D. Jas. I, LXXII, 70.

Stroudwater scarlets or to the azures and plunkets of
Somersetshire were made. As the same merchant further
remarked, it would be long before a sufficient number of
dyers and cloth-dressers could be trained up in the west
country to deal with the immense quantities of white cloths
which were made there; and the Cockayne scheme some
four years later hinged upon the transformation of the white
broadcloths by the dyers and cloth-finishers of London.
In the period following the onset of the great depression,
however, dyers became more numerous.[1] A few continued
as in the Tudor period to own their own furnaces, vats, and
other implements,[2] and there remained throughout the
seventeenth century in Wiltshire such independent craftsmen who worked on commission,[3] no doubt chiefly for
clothiers and perhaps market spinners. Since the demand
for their services must have been growing fairly quickly it
is not surprising to find that some at least lived in modest
comfort; in the thirties Tobyas Moncke of Bradford rented
a field in which he kept cattle and Edward Halliday of
Bishop's Cannings owned an orchard.[4] Others were mere
employees and classed as such with weavers and spinners
in the county wage assessments. The fabrics were finished
by the clothworker, whose labours were equally specialized
but whose status was probably more variable. Some dyers
concerned themselves with the clothworking business also.[5]
Clothworkers increased likewise in number in Wiltshire as
the seventeenth century advanced.[6] But it may be believed
that throughout the period a number of Wiltshire cloths

[1] At least, incidental references to dyers in the quarter sessions great rolls become more frequent.

[2] Wilts. Archdeaconry Court, inventories of the goods of William Day of
Dauntsey (1670) and of Thomas Colborne of Lacock (1699).

[3] Devizes, county muniment room, quarter sessions great rolls, Trinity 1626,
information of Thomas Derrington of Lacock, dyer, 24 June 1626. Derrington
dyed yarn and cloth into various colours.

[4] Devizes, county muniment room, quarter sessions great rolls, Easter 1627,
examination of Tobyas Moncke of Bradford, dyer, 31 Mar. 1627; and Michaelmas 1635, information of Dorothy, wife of Edward Halliday of Bishop's Cannings,
dyer, 20 Aug. 1635.

[5] William Day, *soi-disant* dyer of Dauntsey, owned four pairs of tucking and
five of burling shears as well as a gig-mill—*vide* inventory already cited.

[6] This is very noticeable in the lists of wills proved in the Salisbury diocesan
courts.

continued to be dyed and dressed in London in the fashion, for instance, of Devonshire serges.[1]

As in the Tudor period, the metropolitan market for Wiltshire textiles remained throughout the days of the Stuarts at Blackwell Hall, the premises of which were yet further extended, notably in 1631 and after the restoration.[2] Like the very character of the cloths which the Wiltshire clothier brought or sent by carrier to this market in the seventeenth century, the nature of the market itself was being simultaneously and deeply altered. The merchant adventurers and even the drapers became less and less important as buyers; but their place was taken not so much by other merchants as by a new class of middlemen, the factors of Blackwell Hall, who took into their own hands the organization of the market and long before the end of the century succeeded in cutting off the clothier from all direct contact with the draper and the exporting merchant. The process by which this separation took place can be traced far back.

During the sixteenth century clothiers were led in time of emergency to pawn their cloths,[3] and Wiltshire manufacturers were no doubt driven more particularly to this desperate expedient during the lean years following the Cockayne experiment.[4] In 1622 it was asserted that there existed a number of middlemen who made their living exclusively by purchasing cloths when the clothier could find neither draper nor merchant to buy them[5]; possibly these may in part be identified with the usurers and moneyed men whom the privy council as a last resort ordered to buy up the cloths in Blackwell Hall the same year.[6] How much earlier such a class had existed it is impossible to ascertain, but its utility must have been increased by the abandonment by the merchant adventurers about this period of their ancient and corporate practice of shipping cloth only

[1] Hoskins, *Industry, Trade and People in Exeter*, 16.
[2] Guildhall, City of London Repertories, 45, f. 541b and Journals, 45, f. 161.
[3] *A Discourse of Corporations*, pr. in Tawney and Power, *Tudor Econ. Docs.* iii, 272; *supra*, p. 28.
[4] S.P.D. Jas. I, cxxviii, 50, and Add. Jas. I, xl, 128.
[5] S.P.D. Jas. I, cxxxiii, 36.
[6] S.P.D. Jas. I, cxxvii, 88.

K

twice a year[1] and still more by the increasing variety of the fabrics offered for sale in Blackwell Hall. There were other more insignificant traffickers in cloth too; early in the reign of Charles I there was a complaint from the London drapers of the sale of defective cloths by clothiers to a class of forestallers who catered for the home market and who were alleged to haunt the clothmakers' own houses.[2] But even for his good cloth the manufacturer had his difficulties; especially in times of stress, but not merely then, the clothier of the early seventeeth century had to wait longer to find a customer for his particular type of cloth than his forerunner a generation or two earlier, when there was less specialization.

The more important middlemen may at least in part be identified as London clothworkers, who had long been wont to purchase country cloth for finishing[3] and a small but probably wealthy minority of whom undoubtedly trafficked in cloths in the sixteen-thirties if not earlier. Their activities stung the drapers in 1634 to protest to the government at what they conceived to be an infringement of their monopoly, and the resulting inquiries revealed that both merchant adventurers and clothiers believed the maintenance of a class of dealers in cloths—including clothworkers and others—who were neither exporters nor drapers to be necessary for the smooth working of the cloth trade.[4] Humbler clothworkers were at this time employed by merchant adventurers to examine and pack the white cloths which they had bought from the clothiers. This was a comparative innovation[5]; after their hopes had been dashed by the failure of the Cockayne experiment the London clothworkers and dyers had besought such employment from the merchant adventurers,[6] and how soon success had attended their petitions is unknown.

---

[1] S.P.D. Chas. I, DXXXV, 32.   [2] S.P.D. Chas. I, CLXXX, 75.
[3] They bought much Suffolk cloth throughout the sixteenth century—Unwin, *Studies in Economic History*, 273.
[4] S.P.D. Chas. I, CCLXXVIII, 104, CCLXXXII, 130 and CCLXXXIII, 39; Privy Council Register, 26 Nov. 1634, 30 Jan. and 13 Feb. 1635. The commercial activities of the London clothworkers in the early seventeenth century might repay investigation: cf. the extracts from the court books of the clothworkers' company pr. in Unwin, *Ind. Org.* 233–4.
[5] S.P.D. Chas. I, CCCXLI, 101, and CCCLXXX, 85. Cf. Misselden, *Circle of Commerce*, 61.   [6] S.P.D. Jas. I, XC, 148, and XCVII, 128.

Even more important than the clothworkers in the evolution of a class of middlemen dealers in cloth in London were the administrative hirelings of Blackwell Hall, whose work took on a new significance when the necessity for habitually storing cloths arose. After the erection in 1588 of the new Blackwell Hall[1] various annexes were from time to time added; in 1638 the lords of the council sanctioned the use of Leadenhall as an addition to the cloth market and after the restoration the premises were yet further augmented.[2] The responsibility and importance of the keeper of Blackwell Hall and the various concurrent factors and porters in the running of this complex of storerooms and market halls must have grown ever greater, and it is not surprising that the discharge of their offices should have attracted more and more the attention of the city authorities. In the sixteenth century only the exceptionally wealthy west country clothier had usually maintained his agent in London; the rest had no doubt managed to arrange things between themselves.[3] But when the sale of cloth became more complicated and uncertain and when the clothier had to resign himself frequently to leaving his goods in store while he himself returned home it is easy to understand how the factors and porters in Blackwell Hall came to play a more important part in his life.[4] It was they who protected his cloth against theft and mishandling in his absence, a protection whose necessity was well demonstrated in 1607 when the goods of three clothiers were stolen from Blackwell Hall.[5] This dependence was all the more close since the city as far as possible continued to enforce the monopoly of the Hall as the London cloth market.[6]

But the activities of the accustomed denizens of Blackwell Hall might well have seemed to the clothier more dangerous than the depredations of a common thief. In 1611 it was discovered that a Blackwell Hall factor in conjunction with certain confederates had secured such a grip on the London

[1] *Supra*, p. 25.
[2] Privy Council Register, 30 Mar. and 13 April 1638; Guildhall, City of London Journals, 45, f. 161.
[3] *Supra*, p. 25.   [4] Cf. *The Clothiers' Complaint*, 13.
[5] Guildhall, City of London Repertories, 28, ff. 140b and 254.
[6] There is plenty of evidence as to this in the City of London Repertories.

K*

trade in north country cloths that the merchants who dealt in them had been largely ousted from their business, and the common council of the city at once bestirred itself with the matter.[1] In 1616 the common council again set up a committee to report upon the complaints which had been made against the clerks and porters of Blackwell Hall,[2] and three years later another committee was appointed similarly to hear certain charges against the leidgers and factors of Blackwell Hall.[3] In 1620 there were fresh complaints against factors and brokers who bought and sold cloths there; these were once again referred to committee.[4] There was later a further outcry from the clothiers of Worcester and Reading,[5] and accordingly it was found necessary in 1623 to pass an act of common council forbidding for the future any traffic by middlemen in Worcester or Reading cloths.[6] It is thus abundantly clear that in the early decades of the seventeeth century the activities of the Blackwell Hall factors were already an object of suspicion and even sometimes of resentment to clothiers, to merchants, and to the authorities of the city of London.[7]

The luckless clothier may possibly have suffered as much from the practices of the merchant adventurers who, it was asserted towards the end of the reign of James I, regulated the market for the wares both of the individual and of an industrial area at their whim; it was they who by acting in collusion were able to fix the purchaser, the price, and the

[1] Guildhall, City of London Repertories, 30, ff. 80–2. The committee which examined the doings of the delinquent factor Robert Key reported that 'the dealinges & devises practized by the said Key in his tradinge (which is chiefly (though not only) in Cloth) are so many so subtile so assisted with stocke & Creditt, and so compacted as wee could not have suspected in a person seeminge otherwise plaine and of no great shewe'—ib. f. 80.

[2] Ib. 32, f. 353.

[3] Ib. 34, f. 132b.

[4] Guildhall, City of London Journals, 31, f. 122 ; the delinquents were described as 'divers Packing Clothworkers Factors Lidgers Straingers and foreiners'.

[5] Guildhall, City of London Repertories, 36, f. 158b.

[6] The text of the act is to be found in the City of London Letter Books, HH, f. 178b.

[7] On the whole subject of the origin of the Blackwell Hall factors it must be recognized that Professor Heckscher was justified in his criticism of the view of Dr. Arup and Dr. Friis—Alderman Cockayne's Project, 22—that they did not appear until the middle of the seventeenth century—Vierteljahrschrift für Sozial- und Wirtschaftsgeschichte, xxi (1928–9), 463.

time of purchase of the cloths in which they dealt.[1] But they were still a powerful and wealthy corporation, well entrenched behind their traditional privileges, while the factors were more easily assailable. Complaints continued to be made about the latter in the twenties and later.[2] After the restoration of the monarchy the city of London authorities made a serious attempt to put the cloth market in order— their heavy hand indeed provoked a dispute with the clothiers which dragged on for some years and which at one point led the latter to invoke the intervention of privy council and parliament.[3] It was *inter alia* ordered in 1661 by act of common council that in future all Blackwell Hall factors, brokers and leidgers should be formally approved and admitted by the court of the lord mayor and aldermen and should enter into recognizances before they might ply their trade ; from time to time afterwards various individuals were accordingly licensed as middlemen for the sale of cloth.[4]

This official regulation of the Blackwell Hall factors may plausibly be interpreted as an indication of their ever increasing importance in the organization of the woollen industry. When in 1656 William Gaby came up from Wiltshire to London to sell his cloths he left them neither in store at Blackwell Hall nor in the hands of the merchant who had bought them but in the keeping of a Blackwell Hall factor who subsequently saw to their disposal.[5] Thus even before the restoration the factors were probably frequent and serviceable intermediaries between the country clothier and his customers and it was but a small step further for the factors finally to oust the drapers and merchants from all contact with the clothier. This was accomplished before the end of the century ; the crucial point was reached

[1] B.M. Add. MS. 34,217, f. 14.
[2] Guildhall, City of London Repertories, 42, f. 110b and 59, f. 19.
[3] Guildhall, City of London Journals, 41, ff. 195–9, 45, ff. 152–7, and 46, ff. 68 and 77b; Repertories, 68, ff. 47b and 58b, 69, ff. 56b, 86b, 93, 101b, 185b and 187b; Privy Council Register, 14 Jan. and 18 Feb. 1663; S.P.D. Chas. II, xcv, 82–6, and xcviii, 35, &c.
[4] Guildhall, City of London Repertories, 68, ff. 66b and 173b; in 1675 one William Walrond was admitted to deal specifically in Spanish cloths—*ib.* 80, f. 275b.
[5] Coward, *William Gaby, His Booke, Wilts. Arch. Mag.* xlvi (1932–4), 53.

in the period of the fire and of the great plague, during which the factors managed to secure for themselves the possession of the stalls in Blackwell Hall. Thus within two or three generations they had developed from being the occasional servants and agents of the country clothier to a position of pivotal importance in the whole woollen industry.

Since even in the early part of the century their activities had met with suspicion and rancour it was only to be expected that their rise to eminence should make them a target for abuse. The economist Yarranton attacked them in the seventies, pointing out how they had brought the poor cloth manufacturers into a helpless dependence upon themselves,[1] and there can be little doubt that the simple country clothier resented not only their upstart and town-bred magnificence but still more their allegedly frequent failure to pay promptly for his cloths. Nevertheless the greatest grievances of the former were not social nor even directly concerned with the factors' monopoly of the cloth market but were in the last quarter of the century rather connected with the extension of the latters' trade from the simple buying and selling of cloths to a traffic in the raw materials of the woollen industry. The factors came actually to deal in wool itself, particularly Spanish wool, and it was alleged that they forced their client clothiers to buy their own wool, oil and dyestuffs. Indeed they went further, and by granting or withholding credit controlled the output of cloths in each county; they went even to the length of setting up men of straw to act as clothiers for them in the country. Such practices on the part of the factors were denounced by the Somersetshire grand jury even before the death of Charles II and subsequently the publication of a number of pamphlets testified to the anger they had aroused among the clothiers.[2] In 1697 the latter secured the passage

---

[1] Yarranton, *England's Improvement*, 97–9.

[2] The information in this and the preceding and succeeding paragraphs is chiefly drawn from these pamphlets, admittedly a not entirely satisfactory source. The most useful is *The Clothiers' Complaint: or, Reasons for Passing the Bill, Against the Blackwell-Hall Factors, &c.* (1692); others are *The Interest of England considered in an Essay upon Wooll, Our Woollen-Manufactures, and the Improvement of Trade* (1694), *Reasons of the Decay of the Clothing-Trade* (1691), *A Treatise of*

of an act of parliament with the object of regulating the market and curbing the abuse of credit by the factors at the expense of the clothier,[1] but this statutory limitation proved only momentarily effective and the clothier soon slipped back into his former dependence upon the good-will of the factor.[2] It is difficult to see how indeed things could have been otherwise, for the market for cloths was now so complex that the services of the factors were necessary to organize it if the requirements of merchants and clothiers were to receive mutual satisfaction; and as indispensable intermediaries they were naturally in a position to exact substantial compliance from the clothier. In the eighteenth century the power exercised by the Blackwell Hall factors over the woollen industry was to be greater even than that of the merchant adventurers in the days of Elizabeth.

The market at Blackwell Hall for which the Wiltshire clothier catered in the late seventeenth century was thus very different in its ways from that which his counterpart a hundred years earlier had known. The Hall itself was now little more than a storehouse and a place where cloth brought to London was entered according to the municipal regulations; the fixed two and a half days on which it was open, from Thursday morning to midday on Saturday, were hardly different from the rest of the working week save that on Thursday mornings drapers were wont to inquire whether any new sorts of cloth had come up from the country. The real business was done in the factors' warehouses. Here were kept patterns of every sort of cloth likely to tempt the draper or merchant, and the factor was ready to ply him with these any day in the week. The clothier meanwhile after delivering his cloths to the factor had little further business to keep him in town save to plead with the latter for a quick sale and early payment—arrangements which, it was alleged, were all too seldom forthcoming, for there was little forthright chaffering in the ancient style, or at least in the style which passed as ancient in the

Wool, and the Manufacture of it (1685). These pamphlets were much used by Westerfield in his account of the rise of the Blackwell Hall factors—*Middlemen in English Business* (1915), 296–304.
[1] 8 & 9 Will. III, c. 9.
[2] *Gentleman's Magazine*, ix (1739), 89–90.

later seventeenth century. Whether the factors were much less prompt in payment than the Hansards or merchant adventurers of the earlier time may remain a matter of doubt.

The clothier, however, remained a perennially dissatisfied creature—or at least throughout the period covered by this study he seldom raised his voice save when he had a grievance to air. It was he who organized what Defoe in the first half of the eighteenth century claimed to be 'the greatest single Manufacture' and which 'occasions the greatest Trade both Abroad and at Home, of any Manufacture that is to be found in any particular Nation in the World'[1]; yet he remained individually a remote and insignificant figure. Not one of the clothiers whose activities lay at the base of the Wiltshire woollen industry during the sixteenth and seventeenth centuries could be considered worthy of mention in any text-book of English history during the period. Yet collectively their importance was no less than that of—for instance—the Howard or the Villiers family under the Tudors and Stuarts; in some ways it was materially greater. Though the clothier might amass a fortune and though with its backing his family might in time enter the ranks of the squirearchy there yet remained insurmountable barriers, social and political, to his own advancement to a position of more than local and transitory authority; the career of William Stumpe was even more exceptional than that of Paul Methuen. The strength of the Wiltshire clothier remained based upon his power over the happiness and misery—chiefly the latter—of the anonymous generations of working folk who in the sixteenth and seventeenth centuries toiled in their cottages, from Castle Combe and Malmesbury on the edge of the Cotswold country across the industrial towns on the Avon to Westbury, Edington and the other villages 'under the plain'.

[1] Defoe, *A Plan of the English Commerce* (1728), 134.

APPENDIX I

THE BLACKBORROW PROSECUTIONS

ALTHOUGH his prosecutions of the country clothiers were thus foiled—*vide supra*, p. 59—Peter Blackborrow subsequently laid other informations against a number of west-country broadcloth makers for various infringements of the industrial code. Edward Horton of Westwood, the most prominent Wiltshire object of his prosecutions, was indicted in the court of exchequer in 1577 on no less than four charges simultaneously—Ex. K.R. Mem. Mich. 19 Eliz. 88–92 ; Horton was probably a man of considerable standing in the county and may possibly have taken a prominent part in securing the protective act of the previous year, so that a personal motive of vengeance might conceivably be suspected to have lain behind these attacks. It may have been the example or the instigation of Blackborrow which impelled other prosecutions of certain clothiers during these years, the chief informant being Richard Howse of Westbury, yeoman *alias* weaver, and the others Thomas Hawkins of Bradford, weaver, and Lodowick More of Salisbury, yeoman—Ex. K.R. Mem. Mich. 18 Eliz. 74 ; Mich. 19 Eliz. 82 ; Hil. 20 Eliz. 64, &c. There was doubtless much local resentment in the industrial districts against Blackborrow's proceedings, and it is not surprising that the privy council found it very difficult to enforce the collection of money in Wiltshire and the adjoining counties during 1577 and 1578 to relieve his poverty—cf. *Acts of the Privy Council*, 1575–7, 121, 204–5, 220, 263 ; 1577–8, 238.

Blackborrow had also in December 1576 written for the benefit of the council a paper—B.M. Lansdowne MS. 22, f. 36, pr. in Tawney and Power, *Tudor Econ. Docs.* i, 190–1—pointing out that the aulnagers in Gloucester, Somerset, and Wiltshire were in the habit of selling their seals to the clothiers without first inspecting the cloth—a fact which can hardly have been news to the government. Nevertheless, Blackborrow's views were apparently believed to be not without value, since in September 1577 and in the following February letters were sent to certain justices in the three shires ordering them to make an inquiry into the abuses prevalent in the cloth industry and how they might be reformed—with special reference to the opinions of Peter Blackborrow—*Acts of the Privy Council*, 1577–8, 28–9, 157–8.

The object of Blackborrow in reporting the negligence of the aulnagers was frankly confessed—he wanted their lucrative offices for himself, and he was prepared to pay an extra rent of twenty pounds per annum for each county—Tawney and Power, *Tudor Econ. Docs.* i, 191 ; cf. Unwin, *Studies in Economic History*, 188–9. Far less certain is the motive which had impelled him in the first place to lay the series of informations against so many broadcloth clothiers of the west country. It is tempting to believe that he was acting on behalf of merchant adventurers or of drapers, but there is at present no evidence whatsoever available to support such a suspicion. He certainly cannot be considered as in any sense the representative of the urban as against the rural clothiers—cf. Gay, *Aspects of Elizabethan Apprenticeship*, 149—for the protagonists of industrial strife were not divided geographically but rather upon the more or less horizontal social lines of large clothier against independent or quasi-independent craftsmen—*supra*, ch. II, *passim*. It is not improbable that Blackborrow was a mere adventurer prepared to blackmail rich clothiers with the threat of legal proceedings but whose bluff was called by his prospective victims. Further information probably awaits the historian of the Somersetshire woollen industry.

APPENDIX II

THE MARKET ABROAD FOR WILTSHIRE CLOTHS IN THE SEVENTEENTH CENTURY

SOME idea of the geographical extent and perhaps even of the size of the foreign market for Wiltshire cloths during the seventeenth century may be gathered from an analysis of the relevant entries in the series of Exchequer K.R. Port Books, a short account of which is to be found in Clark, *Guide to English Commercial Statistics, 1696–1782*, 52–6. Unhappily there are difficulties in the utilization of the resulting figures to illustrate the development of the Wiltshire woollen industry, since for the later two-thirds of the century the customs officials did not usually—there were exceptions—mention the county in which the cloth whose export they were chronicling had been manufactured. All therefore that can be done is to select the types of cloth which were being made in Wiltshire during this period and make tacit allowance for their production in other counties. In the following pages figures are given for the export of 'Spanish cloths', 'long western cloths', and ordinary 'long cloths' and 'short cloths' during certain years in the seventeenth century: they relate necessarily to the total export of these fabrics, regardless of their county of origin.

There are other difficulties. Hundreds if not thousands of cloths were no doubt systematically smuggled away every year in order to avoid payment of the export duty: some reference to this illicit commerce during the sixteen-thirties is to be found in the case of Gouge *v.* Southwood in C.R. Chas. I, 1488. It may be further observed, for instance, that Ex. K.R. Port Book 43/4, quoted below, contains no entries whatsoever concerning the persistent trade of the interlopers at Amsterdam—cf. Te Lintum, *De Merchant Adventurers in de Nederlanden*, 146–9. Yet another defect lies in the fact that e.g. under the general designation of 'Spanish cloths' the customs officials almost certainly at first lumped together fabrics manufactured wholly or partly of Spanish wool and the various imitations made from the native product and dyed in the say—cf. *supra*, pp. 104–6. But within certain limits the results yielded by an analysis of the port books are of value; they do at least give a picture—albeit one which errs on the side of modesty—of the geographical extent of the market for which the Wiltshire clothier catered, and they do enable certain changes in its area to be detected.

An examination of Ex. K.R. Port Book·43/4 reveals that during the year 1640, Jan.–Dec., the Spanish cloths shipped from the port of London by native merchants were sent to various destinations which can conveniently be divided into eleven groups, as follows:

1	Ireland			9
2	Mart towns of the merchant adventurers			6,725
	Hamburg	2,794	Rotterdam	3,931
3	Spanish Netherlands			3,210
	Dunkirk	3,085	'Flanders'	77
	Ostend	48		
4	France			71
	Dieppe	18	Rouen	21
	St. Valéry	18	Bordeaux	14
5	Spain and Spanish possessions in the Atlantic			429
	Bilbao	7	Cadiz	15
	'Galizia'	15	Canaries	392
6	Portugal			17
	Lisbon	13	Oporto	4
7	Mediterranean			386
	Genoa	9	Naples	58
	Leghorn	261	Venice	18
	Mallorca	40		
8	Scandinavia			65
	Greenland	7	Sweden	8
	Norway	50		
9	Danzig[1]			42
10	New England			28
11	Destination unidentified: probably most of these may be assigned to group 2			1,453
			Total	12,435

These figures may be supplemented by an account of the quantities of Spanish cloths shipped abroad from Exeter during the year 1636; these can be calculated from the entries in Ex. K.R. Port Book 949/9. The numbers are:

Rotterdam		691
Morlaix 22 St. Malo 127 } Brittany . . . . St. Michel 18		167
	Total	858

To this should be added the following minute quantities shipped from Barnstaple in the same year—Ex. K.R. Port Book 949/11—

Cork	1
La Rochelle.	8

[1] The Sound customs register reveals that in 1635 some 26 Spanish cloths passed into the Baltic—Bang, *Tabeller over Skibsfart og Varetransport gennen Øresund,* ii (1922), 437.

The evidence of other Port Books suggests that neither Bristol nor Southampton was utilized for the export of Spanish cloths during the thirties; practically no cloths at all were exported from Bristol, while from Southampton came the merest trickle of Salisbury plains, Hampshire kerseys, Welsh cottons, and the like, directed towards northern French ports.

The Exeter figures are almost certainly below the mark. The years 1634–7 were notable for an invasion of the territory of the merchant adventurers by the Exeter merchants; the former took alarm at the purchase of Spanish cloths in large quantities by the latter and invoked the aid of the government to limit severely the sphere of activity of the Exeter merchants from 1638 onwards—*supra*, pp. 106–8. Probably rather less Spanish cloths were therefore exported by the latter to the Low Countries in 1640—if the orders of the privy council carried any weight in Devonshire.

A generation later the market had perceptibly altered. From Ex. K.R. Port Book 50/1 figures giving the quantities of Spanish cloths exported from London by native merchants during the year 1664, Jan.–Dec., have been extracted—a few 'half Spanish cloths' are included. Here is the resultant table:

1 Ireland				18
	Dublin	6	'Ireland' 12	
2 Hamburg				2,335
3 United Provinces				331
	Amsterdam	6	Rotterdam 102	
	Dordrecht	81	Middelburg 2	
	Haarlem	5	Flushing 135	
4 Spanish Netherlands				2,499
	Bruges	174	Ostend 2,325	
5 France				919
	Dunkirk	303	Caen 6	
	Calais	11	St. Malo 1	
	Boulogne	57	Bordeaux 23	
	St. Valéry	49	Bayonne 3	
	Dieppe	262	'France' 108	
	Rouen	96		
6 Portugal				1,154
	Oporto	285	'Portugal' 26	
	Lisbon	843		
7 Spain and Spanish possessions in the Atlantic				248
	'Gallatia'	3	Canaries 73	
	Cadiz	171	Madeira 1	
8 Mediterranean				395
	Malaga	3	Venice 18	
	Figueras	37	Smyrna 33	
	Leghorn	304		
9 Scandinavia and the Baltic				522
	Elsinore	9	'Russia' 105	
	'The Sound'	64	Stockholm 15	
	Danzig	121	'Norway' 208	

| 10 'Guinea' | . | . | . | . | . | . | . | . | . | 27 |

| 11 'East India' or 'India' | . | . | . | . | . | . | . | 8 |

| 12 America | . | . | . | . | . | . | . | . | . | 236 |

| | Newport | 56 | | Virginia | 19 | |
| | 'New England' | 107 | | Barbados | 54 | |

| 13 Destination unidentified | . | . | . | , | . | . | . | 110 |

Total 8,802

With this may be compared the figures for the year 1685—Christmas 1684 to Christmas 1685—yielded by Ex. K.R. Port Book 126/1. Here is a table to illustrate the export of Spanish cloths—again including a few half Spanish cloths—from London by English merchants during the year 1685:

| 1 Ireland | . | . | . | . | . | . | . | . | . | 11 |
| | Dublin | 7 | | 'Ireland' | 4 | |

| 2 Germany | . | . | . | . | . | . | . | . | 2,113 |
| | Bremen | 1 | | Hamburg | 2,112 | |

3 United Provinces	.	.	.	.	.	.	.	1,588
	Amsterdam	169		Middelburg	10	
	Dordrecht	15		'Holland'	10	
	Rotterdam	1,376		'Zealand'	8	

4 Spanish Netherlands	.	.	.	.	.	.	946
	Bruges	512		'Flanders'	416	
	Ostend	18				

5 France	.	.	.	.	.	.	.	.	$4,600\frac{1}{2}$[1]
	Dunkirk	1,092		St. Malo	19	
	Calais	$199\frac{1}{2}$		Bordeaux	26	
	St. Valéry	1,973		Bayonne	15	
	Rouen	79		'France'	1,135	
	Caen	62				

6 Portugal	.	.	.	.	.	.	.	.	366
	Oporto	115		'Portugal'	205	
	Lisbon	46				

7 Spain and Spanish possessions in the Atlantic	.	.	.	$679\frac{1}{2}$
	Bilbao	345		Canaries	2	
	Cadiz	$215\frac{1}{2}$		'Spain'	117	

8 Mediterranean	.	.	.	.	.	.	.	602
	Figueras	9		Smyrna	159	
	Leghorn	100		Scanderoon	109	
	Lipari	126		'Barbary'	16	
	Constantinople	83				

9 Scandinavia and the Baltic	.	.	.	.	.	.	3,423
	'The Sound'	969		'Neva'	4	
	Elsinore	93		'Russia'	181	
	Danzig	1,274		Stockholm	605	
	Königsberg	61		Gothenburg	16	
	Riga	102		Bergen	18	
	Reval	6		'Norway'	94	

| 10 India | . | . | . | . | . | . | . | . | . | 8 |

[1] In the year Christmas 1688 to Christmas 1689, the number of Spanish cloths exported to France was $2,349\frac{1}{2}$—*Commons' Journals*, xvii, 366.

11 America   143
    'New England' 67   'Virginia' 5½
    'East Jersey' 2   Jamaica 26
    New York 33½   Barbados 9
12 Destination unidentified   6
                       Total 14,486

The figures for long western cloths exported from London by English merchants during the year 1664 have also been calculated from the entries in Ex. K.R. Port Book 50/1. Here they are:

1 Hamburg   9
2 United Provinces   124
    Amsterdam 4   Rotterdam 20
    Dordrecht 81   Flushing 19
3 Spanish Netherlands   262
    Bruges 256   Ostend 6
4 France   39
    Dunkirk 6   Bordeaux 13
    Rouen 20
5 Portugal   44
    Oporto 11   Lisbon 33
6 Spain and Spanish possessions in the Atlantic   .   .   .   15
    San Lucar 9   Canaries 1
    Cadiz 5
7 Mediterranean   8,308
    Leghorn 390   Scanderoon 5,068
    Smyrna 2,850
8 America   38
    'New England' 28   Newport 10
9 'East India' or 'India'   693
10 'Guinea'   28
                      Total 9,560

With these may again be compared the analogous figures for the year 1685, as taken from Ex. K.R. Port Book 126/1; they are given in the following table:

1 'Scotland'   15
2 Hamburg   315
3 United Provinces   445
    Amsterdam 46   'Holland' 81
    Dordrecht 18   'Zealand' 9
    Rotterdam 291
4 Spanish Netherlands   219
    Bruges 102   'Flanders' 117
5 France 266½
    Dunkirk 37   Bordeaux 13
    Calais 22½   Bayonne 9
    St. Valéry 154   'France' 29
    Dieppe 2
6 Portugal   73
    Oporto 30   'Portugal' 33
    Lisbon 10

7 Spain and Spanish possessions in the Atlantic		· · ·	295½
Bilbao	61	Cadiz	178½
San Sebastian	7	'Spain'	45
'Biscay'	4		

8 Mediterranean		· · · ·	· 7,524
'The Straits'	544½	Constantinople	371
Figueras	5	Smyrna	3,860½
Leghorn	117	Scanderoon	2,388
Lipari	67	'Barbary'	171

9 Scandinavia and the Baltic		· · ·	· 839½
'The Sound'	255½	Stockholm	130½
Danzig	64	Bergen	1
'Neva'	5	'Norway'	68½
'Russia'	312½	Faroes	2½

10 'Guinea'	· · · · · · · ·	25

11 'India'	· · · · · · · ·	·2,664½

12 America		· · ·	147
'Hudson Bay'	27	'Virginia'	4
'New England'	19	Jamaica	2
New York	82	Barbados	10
'Pennsylvania'	3		

13 Destination unidentified	· · · · ·	72
	Total	12,901

'Short western cloths' were sent abroad in 1664, though in small quantities; in 1685 they had apparently ceased to be exported. The figures for 1664, from Ex. K.R. Port Book 50/1, are as follows:

1 Bruges	· · · · · · · · · · ·	9
2 Bordeaux	· · · · · · · · · ·	6
3 Oporto	· · · · · · · · · ·	31
4 Canaries	· · · · · · · · · ·	1

5 Leghorn	22		
Smyrna	894	} Mediterranean · · · · · ·	· 1,091
Scanderoon	175		
		Total	1,138

On the other hand, plain 'long cloths' and 'short cloths' were exported in 1685 in larger quantities than before. Here are the figures for 'long cloths', culled from Ex. K.R. Port Book 126/1—a few 'half long cloths' are included:

1 Hamburg	· · · · · · · · ·	35
2 Rotterdam	· · · · · · · · ·	88

3 Spanish Netherlands		· · · · · ·	10
Bruges	4	'Flanders'	6

4 France		· · · · ·	33½
Dunkirk	7½	St. Valéry	17
Calais	8	'France'	1

5 Portugal		· · · · ·	90½
Oporto	40	'Portugal'	50½

6 Spain and Spanish possessions in the Atlantic . . . 346½
        Bilbao   30½   Cadiz   313
        'Galicia'   3

7 Mediterranean . . . . ·4,959½
        'The Straits' 341   Smyrna   2,046
        Leghorn   54   Scanderoon 2,107½ -
        Lipari   68   Cyprus   1
        Constantinople 292   'Barbary'   50

8 Scandinavia and the Baltic 914½
        'The Sound' 60   'Russia'   816½
        Elsinore   ½   Stockholm 1
        Danzig   29   Gothenburg 5
        Riga   2½

9 'Guinea' 1½
10 America 11½
        'New England' 9   New York   2½

                                         Total 6,490½

And the figures for 'short cloths', including a few 'half short cloths' and some 'short white cloths', from the same source :

1 Ireland 9
        Cork   1   'Ireland'   8

2 Hamburg 675
3 United Provinces 203
        Amsterdam 63   Rotterdam 113
        Dordrecht 27

4 Spanish Netherlands 129
        Bruges   46   'Flanders' 83

5 France 214
        Dunkirk   38   St. Malo   9
        Calais   76   Bordeaux 54
        St. Valéry 32   'France'   5

6 Portugal 42
        Oporto   18   'Portugal' 24

7 Spain and Spanish possessions in the Atlantic . . . 305
        Cadiz   299   Canaries   6

8 Mediterranean 912¼
        'The Straits' 252   Constantinople 9½
        Figueras   4   Smyrna   198
        Leghorn   24   Scanderoon 14
        Lipari   36   'Barbary' 375

9 Scandinavia and the Baltic 333
        'The Sound' 36   'Russia'   5
        Danzig   187½   'Norway' 95
        Riga   9½

10 America 69¼
        'New England' 38½   'Pennsylvania' 5½
        New York   24   Nevis   1¼

11 Destination unidentified 9

                                         Total 2,901

REPORT OF THE CLOTHING COMMITTEE OF THE PRIVY COUNCIL, 22 JUNE, 1622

May it please your Lordships

Havinge receiued direccions by your honorable Lettres dated the xxiiijth daye of Aprill last, to take into our Consideracions, what are the true groundes and motives of the great decaye of the sale and vent of our Englishe Cloth in Forreine partes and what are likelie to be the fittest Remidyes for the same, and thereof to make report to your Lordships in writinge, Wee haue with the best of our Endeavours applied ourselves to observe your Lordships Commandementes; and upon manie Conferences had with the Merchants Adventurers, and the Merchants of other Societyes and Companies, with the Gentlemen of quallitye of seuerall Countyes of this Realme, with the Clothiers of the seuerall clothinge Shires, with the officers of his Majeste Customehowse in the port of London, and the drapers and dyers of London, and after manie daies spent in this weightie service; For those twoe principall pointes which were recomended by your Lordships to our Care we humblie offer these thinges followinge in answere.

The Causes of thes decaie of the vent of our Cloth

1. The makinge of Cloth and other draperyes in Foreigne partes in more abonndance then in former tymes: beinge thereunto cheifelie inhabled by the Woolles and other materialles transported from the kingdomes of England Scotland and Ireland: Wee Conceaue to be the Cheife Cause that lesse quantitye of ours are vented there.

2. The false and deceitfull makinge, dyinge and dressinge of our Cloth and stuffes which disgraceth and discreditteth it in forreigne partes.

3. The heavy burden upon our clothe, wherebie it is made so deare to the buyer, that those whoe were wont to furnishe themselues therewith in Forreine partes, either buy Cloth of other Conntreys, or cloth themselues otherwise in cheaper manner then our Cloth can be Afforded. And the Clothiers apprehend that the Staplers Jobbers and Broggers of Wooll are alsoe a Cause of the endearinge of Wool by deceitfull minglinge and often sellinge yt from hande to hande before it come to the Clothier.

4. The present state of the tymes, by reason of the Warres in Germanye is Conceaved by manie to be some present impediment to the Vent of our Clothe, partely by reason of the interrupcion of the passages, partlie by want of money occasioned by Forrageinge of the Countries.

5. The pollicyes of the Merchant Adventurers, which drawe upon them a suspicion of Combinacion in tradinge; and the Smalenes of their Nomber, which nowe doe usuallie buye and vent Clothe, and the like pollicyes of other Merchantes whoe are not able or willinge to extend themselues in this tyme of extremitye to take of the Clothe from the hande of the Clothier.

6. The Scarsitie of Coyne at home, and the Baseness of Foraine Coynes Compared with ours.

7. The want of meanes of retournes for our merchauntes especiallie out of the Eastland Conntries; which discourageth them to carry out Clothe thether, because they can neither sell for readie money, nor in Barter for vendible Commodities.

8. The too Little use and wearinge of Cloth at home, and the too much of silkes and foreine Stuffes which ouerballance our Trade.

The Remidyes humblie propounded

1. That for preventinge of the makinge of Cloth beyond the Seas; there be a strict Course taken under the seuerest penaltyes both against the Transporters, and against all Officers belonginge to the Custome house which shall Connive thereat, to prohibite the exportacion of Woolls, Woolfells, Yearne, Cornish hayre; Fullers Earth, and Woodashes out of England at all, and out of Scotland and Ireland to be carryed out of the kinges dominions. For it is generally Conceaved; that in those partes where Cloth is nowe made beyond the Seas, they Cannot possiblie furnishe themselues otherwise soe comodiously and soe Cheape to undersell us.

Also to prohibite the bringinge of anie woolls in to the Lowe Countryes or Germany, from Spayne Turky &c in anie Englishe bottomes or by any Englishemen in anie Forreigne Bottomes.

And that all Licences alreadie granted for transportacion of wooll be revoked (so much excepted as is fitt for Jersey and Gernesey, for their owne imployment onlie in point of Manuffacture) And for a present helpe herein (as farr as it maie) That his Matie by his Royall proclamacion may forthwith prohibite these thinges.

2. That for the preventinge of the false and deceitfull makeinge and dyeinge of Clothes and Stuffes, theis thinges may be observed. That whereas the Lawes nowe in force concerninge the makinge and dressinge of Cloth, are so manie, and by the Multitude of them soe intricate That it is very hard to resolve, what the Lawe is herein: That those former Lawes (when oportunity shall serve) might be repealed, and one Clere Lawe made for a direccion herein. And in the meane tyme, till these can be donn, That some Committee may be chosen to peruse the Lawes nowe in force, that those which are fitt for the present tymes maie be quickned, and those which are lesse fitt, maye bee tollerated.

That where there is yet noe Lawe made concerninge the newe draperyes, that some plaine rules, and easye to be observed, may be prescribed, for the true makinge, dyinge, dressinge and pressinge of those Stuffes which beinge observed may bringe them into request againe.

That a Corporacion in euerie County be made of the most able and sufficiente men of the same, Whereby they maie be Authorized to looke Carefullie to the true makinge dyenge and dressinge of Cloth and Stuffe in euerie Shire, and not to trust to Meane and Mercenary men by whose Connivencie too manie Faults are committed to the great disgrace of our drapery. And the Committee to be appointed, maye also take into their consideracion the manner of puttinge this into Execucion.

That the Alneagors Seale may not be sett to anie Cloth or Stuffe untill it
haue bene searched tryed and approved by such as shalbe thereunto appointed
and that none whoe for that tyme doth themselves use Clothinge be made
deputy Alneager.

That the use of all false dyinge Stuffe be strictly Forbidden for Cloth and
the new draperyes.

3. That for the ease of the heavy Burthen upon Cloth, his Matie is
humblie desired by the aforesaid gentlemen, Merchantes Clothyers and others
to interpose his power with the Archdutchesse and States to take of their
Consumpcion and Licence money. And it is also by them desired That the
Merchant Adventurers would take of their private Imposicions which they
terme Imprest Money (Care being had) for the Repayment of such moneys
as bona Fide they haue disbursed for his ma^{tes} service, and which they haue
not yet reimbursed againe.

And that neither that, nor anie other Company of Merchantes be hereafter
suffered to impose upon their owne members to the endearinge of the Cloth
exported without the Allowance of the State.

And it is the generall opinion of the gentlemen Merchant Officers of the
Custome-howse and Clothiers with whome wee have had conference, that the
pretermitted Customes, and the Earle of Cumberlandes Licence are so great
a Burthen upon Cloth, that it much hindereth the vente.

And although they hope that the Encrease of trade will recompence these
Losses to the kinge in his Customes; Yet because this is soe weighty a pointe
to the kinges Revennew, We will not presume to giue our opinion therein,
because wee cannot secure the evente.

That dyinge Stuffes be not made deare, by Pattentes of Privyledge, as that
of the sole importacion of Gynnywood, or by ingrossinge of dyeinge Comodityes at home, before it Come to the dyer or Clothier; else the dyed Clothes
will Continewe deere, although woolls be over Cheape.

And the Clothiers desire that the wooll Jobbers, which are but Ingrossers
and Forestallers of their markettes may be forbidden except in Yorkshire and
Devonshire, where the manner of Clothinge differinge from other Countryes
maketh them usefull; but in those places where they shalbe allowed, it wilbe
Fitt to tye them to these Condicions:

That they sell imediatelie to the Converter and not to Come to him at
the Second or Third hande.

That they mingle not their woolls deceiptfully before they sell.

That they sell not againe in the same Markett they buye.

And the Clothiers also Complaine that the woollgrower doth not Clippe off
his Pitchmarke before he winde his Fleece, which wee thinke fitt were
reformed.

4. For the warrs in Germany, wee can onlie praie to god to staie the
effusion of Christian blood. But wee Conceave, That the wastinge of seuerall
partes of theis Countries by the warrs, the Consumpcion of their Flockes, the
disturbance of their Trade in makinge, are probable meanes to open the waie
for our better vent, when it shall please god to send peace, or but to settle the

warres soe, as that their may be a Free and safe inter Course for the Merchantes, and that they dare trust their wares for reasonable tyme.

5. For the pollicyes of the Companie of Merchant Adventurers and other Societyes of Merchauntes spoken against by many Wee Conceaue that such Ordinances as tende to gouerment of Trade must necessarily be Continued, But such as drawe with them a suspicion of Combinacion, either in buyinge at home or sellinge abroad, should be forbidden.

And to encrease and incourage the number of Merchauntes, and so enlarge trade which is said to be imprisoned as it is nowe carryed Wee humblie propounde

That into the merchant Adventurers company, and all other Companyes of Merchantes such others as shalbe desirous of it may be received for the Fyne of Five markes and noe more, thereby to encrease the Number of buyers and Adventurers.

And that none maie be discouraged to come into their companies, for feare of private impositions or unequall Charges to be putt upon them; Wee thinke it fitt that the Orders and Constitucions of the Companyes of Merchauntes (in whome the publique hath so greate an Interest) either alreadye or hereafter to be made, be surveyed and approved by a Committee to be appointed by his Matie for that purpose To the Ende they may putt noe such Ordinances in Execucion, which shall tende more to their private then to the publique good.

That because the Merchaunt Adventurers have disbursed great sommes of money which they affirme come to the kinges purse, it wilbe but iust (that they layinge downe their impositions) those moneys be repaied unto them by such a way as Your Lordships in your wisdomes shall thinke Fittest.

That in noe Societye of Merchauntes there be a Joynt Stocke (excepte in the East Indye Compannye as Longe as it shall Continewe which cannot be avoyded) for in that Course it is as if one man alone were the Adventurer and Buyer.

That such be not admitted to trade as Merchauntes, whoe shall not submitt them selues to gouerment in some Company or other. Nor that any beinge admitted as Merchauntes to trade, shall sell by Retayle the same comodityes they retorne.

6. For the scarcity of money at home, Wee conceave this rather to be a generall hinderance of all sortes of trade then of Cloth in perticuler.

Some remedyes whereof wee conceave may be theis.

That a Cairefull Eye be had that our Coyne be not stollen or Carryed awaye and that it be seuerally punished in the offendors.

That some Course may be taken, that money (which is *Communis mensura rerum*) may beare some equallitie with us and with our neighbour Nations, with whome wee trade; or else if ours hould still soe greate a disproporcion of value, as nowe it doth to that it is esteemed abroad, gredines of gayne will intice the stealinge over of our money though the kingdome smart for it.

But the most important remedye as wee Conceaue is to provide against the overballaunce of trade; for if the vanitie and superfluitye of our importacion be a greater then the exportacion of our home commodityes will beare, the stocke of this kingdome must neede be wasted, for money must necessarilie turne the Scale.

The helpe of this Consisteth in these two thinges.

To improue our native Comodityes in their use and vent, as tyme will give Leaue, whereunto our Manufactures doe cheifelie Conduce; and of these aboue others our newe draperies. And amongst theis improvements of our kingedome wee heartilie wishe, that the Fishinge upon our Coastes as a matter of great and important Consequence maie not onlie be cherished, but that the Subjectes of this kingdome in all the seuerall Countyes Cittyes and Port townes be drawn to undertake the building furnishinge and maynteyninge of fishing Busses at their publique Charge, and for their publique benefitt, whereas nowe that trade is in a manner wholy possessed by Straungers. This beinge well managed would enhable the kinge to mainteine his absolute right to the Narrowe Seas; by Maynteyninge a fitt Number of able Shipps there, aswell for defence as offence upon all Occasions; And that without extraordinary Charge or noyse: It would encrease Navigacion in generall, Sett many people on worke, Begett money: and revive the Outportes: Whoe nowe doe and longe have languished, and hardly will fynde anie other meanes then this to restore them to trade.

And generallie Wee wishe that such Comodityes of our kingdomes as our Neighbour Nations cannot well spare as Corne Tynn, Seacoles, &c. might retorne a proporcion of Bullion: And out of this Consideracion Wee humbly recomende to your Lordships wisedomes that a Staple for Seacoles might be appointed; whence all straungers should fetch their Coales for ready money brought from foreigne partes. And our owne shippinge onlie to be imployed in carryinge of Coales to the Staple: or if your Lordships shall thinke fitt that the Seacole be still fetcht from New Castle, Yet wee wishe that the Stranger should paie ready money for them there and not Barter for Comodities: or if the Englishe shall merchandise them beyond the seas, that they maie be bound to retorne at the Least the one halfe of their value in Bullyon or money.

That whereas the East Indye Companye stand accused by manie for carryinge awaie of money to furnishe their trade, and retorne onlie Comodityes againe, We humbly offer this to redeeme them from this complainte.

1. That according to their Couenant with his Matie it be Looked unto, that they doe trulie and really bringe in that money from forreigne partes, wherewith to furnishe themselves, and not to expende our owne money or bullyon, or buy their forraigne money from other merchauntes that els would haue brought the same hether to the kinges Minte.

2. That, when they haue retorned hether their East Indian wares, Care be had that a reasonable proporcion beinge taken for the use of the kingdome, the surplusage be exported from hence as a Merchandise of our kingedome, and of the proceed of that Retorne, at Least so much in Bullyon or money be retorned to the Minte as shall equall that somme they first carryed out to furnishe their trade withall. And that like Care be taken for the Turkey Trade and other trades, that they use the best husbandrie they maie in buyinge as Little of Foraigne Comodityes with money as they Canne.

L

The other Helpe is, to restreyne our over much vanitie in importinge Forreigne Commodityes, especiallie those which are superfluous and needeles, and which Cost readie money. And whereas a Masse of money is Yearlie bestowed upon Lawnes, Camebrickes Hollandes Slesia and other Lynnen Cloth brought from beyonde the Seas; Wee wishe that to ease that expence, and to sett our poore on worke Flaxe and Hempe might be enioyned (accordinge to the Lawes) to be sowen and Converted into Lynnen Cloth; And that the vanitie of Ruffes and Laces brought from beyond the Seas be restrayned.

That Merchaunt Strangers and denizens whoe drive a greate trade with us: as alsoe the Masters of Shippes of Forreigne Bottomes for their Fraight may be held to observe the Statutes of Imployments in some good measure.

That strangers naturalized take their oathes in their owne persons in the Custome-howse that they carrye out and bringe in their owne proper Commodities and Merchandise onlie, and Coullor not the goodes of straungers.

That noe Englishe assure or underwrite anie pollicye of Assuraunce for anie shippe or goodes for anie straunger or denizen fraught from or for anie port beyond the seas.

7. To helpe the Retourne of our Merchauntes, that some Course bee taken accordinge to the Lawes for bringinge in our Merchandises in Englishe and not in Straungers Buttomes, which are not of the proper growth of that Country.

That the Eastlande Merchantes may have allowance to make their Retournes in Corne; and haue free Libertie to transporte againe that Corne into Forreigne partes with this restriccion:

> That what Corne they bringe in, shall not be vented in our kingedome to the hindrance of our Husbandry at Home, when Corne is under such Rates, as the Corne of the growth of our Country may by the same be exported.

8. To helpe the expence of Cloth within our kingdome, that there may be the Lesse left to vent abroade, and the Lesse vanitie in the Expence of Silkes and Forraigne Stuffes. That the Nobilitie and gentrye of the kingdome might be perswaded to the wearinge of Cloth in the Winter season by example rather then Commaundement.

That the meaner sort of people as apprentices, Servantes and Mechanickes be enioyned by proclamacion to the Weare of Cloth and Stuffe of Wooll made in this kingdome, which would be more durable and lesse Chargeable.

That when blackes are given at Funeralls, that they be of Cloth or woollen Stuffe made in this kingedome.

And yet that Huswifes maie not make Cloth to sell againe but for the provision of themselues and their Families, that the Clothiers and drapers be not discouraged.

And lastlie because manie questions may arise from tyme to time betwene the Woolgrower Clothyer and Merchantes Wee humblie propound to your

Lordships, That a Comission may be granted by his Ma^{ty} to some selected persons whoe may thereby have Authoritie

      To heare and determine all such differences

      To looke unto the Statutes of imploymentes by Strangers and denizens

      The Licences and previledges for Wooll and dying Wood

      And generallie for all other thinges which may conduce to those endes before propounded, whereby Trade may be orderlie governed and duly ballanced.

And although matters of greater difficultye maie be ever brought to this honorable Board; by your Lordships to be determined or directed. Yet thus may your Lordships be eased of much trouble and Losse of tyme, Which theis kindes of Grieveaunces haue often caused heretofore. And the Suitors be dispatched more speedelie which shall have occasion to attend thereabout.

	Jo: Suckling	
22th June 1622	Thomas Coventrye	
	R. Heath	
	Paul Pinder	Geo: Paule
	Ri: Sutton	Heneage Finche
	Wm Richardson	William Turnor
	Thomas Man	H. Stafford
		Abraham Dawes

APPENDIX IV
A NOTE ON SOURCES

For the titles of the printed works which have been used for the present study reference may be made to the footnotes and to the following:

Dahlmann-Waitz, *Quellenkunde der deutschen Geschichte* (1931);
Davies, *Bibliography of British History, Stuart Period* (1928)·
Goddard, *Wiltshire Bibliography* (1929);
Pirenne, *Bibliographie de l'histoire de Belgique* (1902);
Read, *Bibliography of British History, Tudor Period* (1933).

Despite the labours of generations of Wiltshire local historians and antiquarians, from John Aubrey and John Britton to J. E. Jackson and E. H. Goddard, comparatively few documents from archives in the county have been printed. A report for the Historical Manuscripts Commission on the contents of the county muniment room at Devizes was made by W. D. Macray (16th rep. 1901), and in 1932 a further though unhappily overlapping selection of documents from the same source was published by B. H. Cunnington in his *Records of the County of Wilts*. Municipal archives have so far fared no better. A selection of Chippenham town documents was printed by Sir F. H. Goldney in his *Records of Chippenham* (1889) and the Devizes municipal muniments have been explored by B. H. Cunnington, in *Annals of the Borough of Devizes* (two vols., 1925–6). There is also a Hist. MSS. Commission report on the Salisbury city archives (17th rep. 1901).

The most useful histories are the following:

Benson and Hatcher, *History of Salisbury* (1843);
Jones, *Bradford-on-Avon: a History and Description* (ed. Beddoe, 1907);
Marsh, *A History of the Borough and Town of Calne* (1903).

The most valuable periodical was, during its unhappily short life, *Wilts. Notes and Queries* (1893–1916).

The unprinted material awaiting the historian of the Wiltshire woollen industry is of gigantic bulk, and the present writer can make no claim to completeness in his search for evidence. This is particularly so with regard to the seventeenth century; although the mass of documents bearing upon this period in existence is far greater than for the sixteenth century yet much less of it is for all practical purposes accessible—so that paradoxically it is considerably easier to work upon sixteenth- than upon seventeenth-century local history. It may be hazarded that few completely satisfactory accounts of the various branches of English industrial organization during the seventeenth century will be written until all the legal records for the period have in some measure been calendared or indexed. It may perhaps not unfairly be claimed that the authorities at the Public Record Office have tended to give a disproportionate share of their attention to making the medieval rather than the later documents under their charge accessible to the student.

This, however, is admittedly a matter open to controversy. Far more unhappy is the reluctance of other guardians of public muniments to allow the free access of the searcher to the documents in their care. Access to the Wiltshire county records was only obtained after much delay and difficulty, for the Wiltshire standing joint committee has made practically no provision for their perusal by local historians. A heavy fee was charged at the Salisbury Diocesan Registry for permission to consult the documents there. Even the national archives are not freely open to the *bona fide* historical student; at Somerset House only the register-books of wills may be perused without payment. For the production of inventories—which are generally more likely to interest the student of economic history than wills—and of all original wills—for by no means all wills were registered—a fee is charged per search. No satisfactory distinction is made between the inquirer after sixteenth- or seventeenth-century documents and the citizen curious to discover how much property has been left, and to whom, by his recently deceased neighbour.

A list of the chief manuscript sources used by the present writer is appended. Classes of documents of which only very small use has been made have not been included. Exact references are given in the footnotes.

I. NATIONAL ARCHIVES

(*a*) *Public Record Office.* (i) *Administrative papers.*

Privy Council Registers—for the years after 1627 when the printed series ends.

State Papers, Domestic Series, from the reign of Edward VI to that of Anne. The indexes to the printed calendars are generally though not always satisfactory.

Letters and Papers for the reign of Henry VIII.

Ex. K.R. Port Books. The most helpful books have been analysed in Appendix II, *supra*.

Ex. K.R. Subsidy Rolls. These have been used mainly for checking names in the middle sixteenth century. I have not found any Wiltshire roll which indicated the occupations of the taxpayers.

Inquisitions Post Mortem.

(ii) *Legal records.*

Assize Order Books, Western Circuit. A few of these exist for the middle seventeenth century.

Early Chancery Proceedings. The printed lists of these are now complete; they are particularly valuable for the first third of the sixteenth century.

Chancery Proceedings. The bulk of these is immense, and to a large extent there are indexes either printed or manuscript to them. But as the jurisdiction of chancery from the reign of Elizabeth onwards did not generally cover the cases of greatest interest to the social or economic historian, they are disappointing in content and for the later seventeenth century I have disregarded them.

Proceedings in the Court of Star Chamber. These have been searched as far as possible, though for the reign of Elizabeth there exists only a very imperfect manuscript index of names.

Proceedings of the Court of Requests. These have proved a valuable mine of information, though unhappily there is no calendar or index to them after the death of Elizabeth. Much light may be thrown upon the social and economic life of the country during the early seventeenth century as soon as these proceedings are made accessible for the reigns of the first two Stuarts.

Ex. K.R. Memoranda Rolls—a rough calendar for these is provided by the Agenda Books. Owing to the use of the exchequer for quasi-administrative purposes these provide valuable information—e.g. the lists of clothiers which begin in Ex. K.R. Mem. Hil. 7 Eliz. 329-32—*supra*, p. 55.

Other classes of exchequer records also yield information; for the four following there are indexes printed or manuscript in existence:

Ex. Depositions by Commission. Ex. Bills and Answers.
Ex. Barons' Depositions. Ex. Books of Orders and Decrees.

(*b*) *Somerset House.*

Registers of wills proved in the Prerogative Court of the archbishop of Canterbury.

Wills and inventories and registers of wills proved in the various courts of the diocese of Salisbury.

(*c*) *British Museum.*

There is a wealth of references to Wiltshire scattered throughout the miscellaneous accumulations of the Additional Manuscripts, but for the purposes of the present work little of value is to be found save in the Cecil papers which have found their way into the Lansdowne Manuscripts.

2. Local Public Archives

(*a*) *In Wiltshire.* (i) *Calne, office of the town clerk.*
Corporation Minute Book 1565-1814 ('Burgus Book').

(ii) *Devizes, county muniment room.*
Quarter sessions great rolls. Quarter sessions minute books.

(iii) *Salisbury, diocesan registry office.*
Inventories of the goods of persons domiciled within the diocese.

(*b*) *Outside Wiltshire.* (i) *London, Guildhall.*
Letter-Books of the city of London.
Journals of the court of aldermen.
Repertories of the common council.
For all these there are full manuscript indexes.

(ii) *Southampton, Civic Centre.*
Brokage Books. In these were recorded the goods imported and exported from Southampton and which paid port charges. I have examined the books for years 1492-3, 1493-4, 1528-9, 1543-4 and 1558-9.

3. Private Archives

(*a*) *Oxford, Bodleian Library.*
Aubrey MSS. From the printed version of the *Natural History of Wiltshire*, edited by John Britton (1847), much of interest to the economic historian was omitted.

(*b*) *Knole House, Sevenoaks, Kent.*
Papers of Lionel Cranfield, especially the ledger book of Richard Sheppard.

(*c*) *Welbeck Abbey, Nottinghamshire.*
Report of the clothing commissioners, 1640.

INDEX

Abingdon, 24.
Abyn, John, 20.
Act of Parliament. *See* legislation.
Adlam, John, 45n.
Adventurers, merchant. *See* merchant adventurers.
Agent. *See* factor.
Alwaye, John, 15n.
America, 143–146.
Amsterdam, 107, 115, 140, 142–144.
Antwerp, 28, 29, 67.
Apprentices, apprenticeship, 60–62, 64n., 85, 99, 122, 125, 126.
Archard, Adam, 43n., 44.
Archard, Nicholas, 71, 73n., 83.
Arms, college of, 46n.
Ash, John, 103, 115n.
Assize, justices of. *See* justices of assize.
Aston Magna, 7.
Atlantic, 141–146.
Attorney general, 94, 96.
Aubrey, John, 102, 115.
Augmentations, court of, 32, 34.
Aulnage, aulnager, 47, 52, 53, 55–58, 87, 98, 100, 139.
Avon, Bristol Avon, 2, 3, 23, 71, 86, 92, 127, 138.
Awdry, family of, 128.
Aynell, William, 15n.

Badgers, of yarn, yarnmaker, yarnman, 14, 30, 89–91.
Bailey, family of, 41.
Baltic, 72, 106, 118, 119, 141n.–143, 146.
Banking, 126.
Bankrupt, bankruptcy, 21, 75.
Baptists, 113.
Barbados, 143–145.
Barbary, 143, 145, 146.
Barkesdale, family of, 41.
Barley, 12.
Barnard, John, 24n.
Barnstaple, 110, 141.
Barter, 23.
Bartholemew Fair, 54.
Bartilmewe, Richard, 29.
Basinghall St., London, 25.
Bath, 22n.

Batt, family of, 41
Batt, Richard, 16, 48.
Batt, Robert, 71n.
Bayly, John, 22n.
Baynton, Sir Edward, 37, 92, 113.
Bayonne, 142–144.
Bays. *See* cloths.
Beachy Head, 120.
Beckington, 22n., 87n., 105.
Beere, John, 111n.
Bennett, Richard, 101.
Bergen, 143.
Berill, Sir William, 37n.
Berkeley, house of, 36.
Berkshire, 2, 37, 41.
Bilbao, 141, 143, 146.
Bills, 27.
Bishop's Cannings, 130.
Bishopstrow, 12, 19, 27n., 59n.
Biss, river, 4.
Blackborough, Robert, 59n.
Blackborrow, Peter, 59, 60n., 139.
Blackwell Hall, London, 12, 20n., 24n.–27, 30, 36n., 38, 40n., 50, 54–56, 67n., 68, 70, 74, 76–79, 86, 100, 105, 107–109, 111, 123, 131–137.
Blagden, family of, 41.
Bolton, Ralph, 38, 39.
Bordeaux, 141–145.
Boulogne, 142.
Bradford, Bradford-on-Avon, 3, 6, 20n., 40, 41, 43, 44, 57, 61, 71, 85, 87n., 92, 93, 101, 103, 114, 115, 120, 128, 130, 139.
Bremhill, 37, 70n., 75, 87n.
Brewer, Christopher, 105.
Brewer, William, 105, 115, 119, 120, 126, 127, 129.
Brewer, brothers, 106.
Brewhouse, 80.
Briant, John, 10.
Bridge, William, 70n.
Bristol, 23, 108, 111n., 112, 115n., 119, 142.
Bristol Avon. *See* Avon.
Broadcloth. *See* cloths.
Broggers of wool, brokers, dealers, woolmen, 7–10, 30, 31, 33, 89, 90.
Brokers, of cloth. *See* factors.
Bromham, 59, 61, 76, 77, 92, 112.

INDEX

Pennsylvania, 145, 146.
Philip, king, 20.
Philipp, Walter, 15n.
Pigs, 13.
Plague, 79, 136.
Plunket. *See* cloths.
Poland, Poles, 29, 115.
Poor, poor law, 35, 80, 85, 113, 129.
Porters. *See* factors.
Portugal, Portuguese government, Portuguese market, 118–120, 128, 141–143, 145.
Potterne, 12, 17, 28, 90n.
Potticary, Christopher, 82, 93, 105, 108, 120.
Potticary, Jeremy, Jherome, 61, 103.
Potticary, Richard, 12, 25, 67.
Privy council, council, lords of the council, 10, 39, 47, 50, 53, 57, 59, 68, 73, 79, 81, 85–89, 92, 93, 95–97, 100, 104, 105, 112, 123, 133, 139, 142.
Proclamations, 64, 85, 94, 96, 111.
Profits, 69.

Quakers, 113, 114.

Rack, 'racke close', 19.
Ramsbury, 2.
Randle, Thomas, 82.
Rapeseed, 103.
Ray, Robert, 5.
Ray, Thomas, 70.
Rays. *See* cloths.
Reading, 19n., 24, 134.
Reval, 143.
Rhine, river, 29, 67.
Rich, lord, 37n.
Rich, Richard, 37n.
Riga, 143, 146.
Riot, rising, 3, 12, 16, 72, 77, 78, 81, 112, 129.
Rotterdam, 106–108, 112, 141–145.
Rouen, 109, 141–144.
Rowde, 2, 78.
Rutland, earl of, 37.
Russia, 142, 143, 146.

St. Edmund Hall, Oxford, 128.
St. Malo, 109, 141–143.

St. Michel, 141.
St. Valery, 141–145.
Salisbury, 1–3, 13, 18–22, 24n., 25, 27, 30, 43, 44, 51, 60n., 64, 70, 80, 85, 87n., 97, 98, 113, 115n., 116, 139.
San Lucar, 144.
Satin, 42.
Scanderoon, 119, 143–146.
Scandinavia, 118, 141–143, 146.
Schröder, Jacob, 29.
Scotland, 144.
Scott, John, 47.
Scott, family of, 128.
Scouring, of cloths, 19, 24.
Scrope, Richard, 34n.
Seals, searchers', 93.
Searchers, inspection, searching, of cloth, 12, 22n., 25n., 38, 39, 43, 55–58, 63, 64, 75, 76, 78, 86, 92–95, 98–100, 122–124.
Sectaries, 113.
Seend, 43, 72, 82, 128.
Self, Isaac, 61.
Selfe, family of, 128.
Semington, 59.
Sergeant's Inn, London, 55.
Serges. *See* cloths.
Servants, 42.
Seymour, Sir Francis, 96, 97.
Shears, 130n.
Sheppard, Richard, 42, 50, 51, 101.
Shepton Mallet, 1.
Sheriff, 34.
Shipton Moyne, 39.
Shroud, woollen, 116.
Silks, 42.
Silver, 42.
Singer *alias* Smithe, Thomas, 24n.
Slaughterford, 15, 93, 110.
Smith, John, 30n., 102n.
Smith, William, 72n.
Smyrna, 119, 142–146.
Somerset, Somersetshire, 1, 4, 22, 30, 40, 41, 45, 59, 87, 97, 103, 105, 115n., 123, 130, 136, 139, 140.
Somerset, duke of, protector Somerset, 85.
Sound, the, 142, 143, 146.
Southampton, 21, 22, 109, 110, 115n., 142.
Spain, 21, 23, 103, 110, 141–6.
Spanish Netherlands. *See* Netherlands, Spanish.
Spencer, Walter, 55n.
Spinners, spinning, 13–15, 22, 76, 78, 80,

Printed in the United Kingdom
by Lightning Source UK Ltd.
108223UKS00003B/2

9 780714 613550